BILINGUAL EDUCATION: POLITICS, PRACTICE, AND RESEARCH

BILINGUAL EDUCATION: POLITICS, PRACTICE, AND RESEARCH

Ninety-second Yearbook of the National Society for the Study of Education

PART II

Edited by

M. BEATRIZ ARIAS AND URSULA CASANOVA

Editor for the Society

KENNETH J. REHAGE

Distributed by THE UNIVERSITY OF CHICAGO PRESS ● CHICAGO, ILLINOIS

The National Society for the Study of Education

Founded in 1901 as successor to the National Herbart Society, the National Society for the Study of Education has provided a means by which the results of serious study of educational issues could become a basis for informed discussion of those issues. The Society's two-volume yearbooks, now in their ninety-second year of publication, reflect the thoughtful attention given to a wide range of educational problems during those years. In 1971 the Society inaugurated a series of substantial publications on Contemporary Educational Issues to supplement the yearbooks. Each year the Society's publications contain contributions to the literature of education from more than a hundred scholars and practitioners who are doing significant work in their respective fields.

An elected Board of Directors selects the subjects with which volumes in the yearbook series are to deal and appoints committees to oversee the preparation of manuscripts. A special committee created by the Board performs similar functions for the series on Contemporary Educational Issues.

The Society's publications are distributed each year without charge to members in the United States, Canada, and elsewhere throughout the world. The Society welcomes as members all individuals who desire to receive its publications. Information about current dues may be found in the back pages of this volume.

This volume, *Bilingual Education: Politics, Practice, and Research*, is Part II of the Ninety-second Yearbook of the Society. Part I, which is published at the same time, is entitled *Gender and Education*.

A listing of the Society's publications still available for purchase may be found in the back pages of this volume.

Library of Congress Catalog Number: 92-063306
ISSN: 0077-5762

Published 1993 by
THE NATIONAL SOCIETY FOR THE STUDY OF EDUCATION

5835 Kimbark Avenue, Chicago, Illinois 60637
© 1993 by the National Society for the Study of Education

First Printing, 4,500 Copies

Printed in the United States of America

v

Acknowledgments

The National Society for the Study of Education is indebted to Professor M. Beatriz Arias and Professor Ursula Casanova for planning this volume on bilingual education, an exceedingly complex topic that is of increasingly great concern to educators. They and other distinguished contributors have provided a collection of essays that give an excellent overview of many dimensions of the problem of attending effectively to the needs of language minority students. The Society deeply appreciates the work of the authors and editors that has enabled us to bring out this important yearbook.

Professor Margaret J. Early of the University of Florida has again volunteered to assist with the editing. Her perceptive comments and excellent suggestions reflect not only her own high standards but also her strong feeling that NSSE Yearbooks should be the best they can be.

KENNETH J. REHAGE
Editor for the Society

Editors' Preface

We wish to thank the National Society for the Study of Education, and particularly its Board of Directors, for the opportunity to include this volume in its series of Yearbooks. Their support has allowed us to gather in one volume many of the different aspects that contribute to the concept of bilingual education—the social, psychological, linguistic, legal, political dimensions of this broad field. In doing so, we have had to make difficult decisions about what to include in an area that involves all age levels, thousands of different languages in hundreds of different countries, and all the varieties of educational endeavor. Several volumes would be needed if we were to do justice to the field.

Given the restrictions of space, we had to establish criteria for what was to be included. First, the chapters in this volume discuss bilingual education only as it affects the Hispanic population of the United States. Although Hispanics are not the only or the most important group benefitting from bilingual education, they do constitute the largest segment of the country's population involved in these programs. It is also the case that, in the mind of the general public, Hispanics are most closely associated with this topic. However, most of the principles, theories, and pedagogy that underlie bilingual education have universal qualities. Scholars and educators interested in bilingual education for other minority language groups should not feel excluded. The examples and the literature in this book are drawn from the Hispanic experience but many aspects of that experience are very similar to that of other linguistic minorities.

Second, it is also necessary to clarify that the term "Hispanic" is a political artifact invented by the government as a collective noun to include all persons in the United States who trace their cultural history to Spain or to Spanish colonization. It includes immigrants from Spain as well as from Central and South America and the Caribbean. It also includes long-term inhabitants of the United States, many of whom are descendants of the Spanish explorers who preceded the *Mayflower* by a century. Others were Mexicans long before the United States appropriated large parts of the southwest, and still others were made U.S. citizens as a result of the Spanish-American War. Variations in these groups' historical association with the United States are exceeded by variations in their physical characteristics. Their appearance may reflect genetic connections to the Celts, the Arabs, or the Jews, to natives of Africa, to American Indians, or any combination thereof. There is only one thing all Hispanics have in common: an association, sometimes rather tenuous, with Spain and its language. This connection to a common language is evidence of the powerful influence of the vernacular on social and ethnic identity. Language has been the glue that has joined together all these disparate groups in support of bilingual education.

Third, the content of the book is also limited to the age levels which constitute the bulk of the school population and which are also the ones most highly affected by bilingual programs—students in kindergarten through twelfth grade. Most of the research in bilingual education has also been directed at the age groups these grade levels encompass, and most of it at the elementary school level.

Last, we have chosen to subtitle the book "Politics, Practice, and Research" because we believe these categories define the field well. Bilingual education is above all political. It was initiated not only for pedagogical reasons but also as a response to a social problem. We have chosen to address politics rather than policy because the implementation of bilingual education programs has been buffeted by the uneven funding and interpretations provided by different political administrations. In particular, the federal role in the evaluation of the effectiveness of bilingual education for the Hispanic populations has been directed by political rather than by instructional concerns and, as a result, has focused on a very narrow issue: whether or not bilingual education helps language minority students to learn English faster. For this reason it is important to highlight for our readers the significant role politics has played in this area.

Politics gave birth to bilingual education, and practice has shaped its development. Programs labeled "bilingual education" were set in place long before a knowledge base existed to support the strategy. Much of the early effort under the Bilingual Education Act was directed at developing materials and training teachers who could invent the new pedagogical configurations needed to carry out instruction in two languages. Many of these teachers went on to become administrators in charge of bilingual education at different government levels, while others pursued advanced academic training and have gone on to become leading scholars in the field. Many of them are represented in this volume or are cited by our authors. Thus, in a very real way, practice has led research in the field of bilingual education.

Research has been used through the years to alternatively support and attack bilingual education programs. From the negative findings of Baker and DeKanter in 1973 to the increasingly positive findings of Willig in 1985 and Ramírez, Yuen, Ramey, and Pasta in 1991, the thoroughness and frequency of federally commissioned research has been unprecedented. It is interesting that assiduous attention has been bestowed on bilingual education while similarly funded programs for the gifted and talented have remained largely unquestioned. The research reported throughout this volume shows how investigations with bilingual populations during the last thirty years have enhanced our understanding of language and cognitive development and of the cognitive and social implications of the pedagogical strategies used in bilingual instruction.

We have assumed our audience to be at least partly comprised of scholars who may be recognized experts in their fields and yet have little knowledge of bilingual education. For this reason, we have tried to provide enough background to contextualize the issues in bilingual education for our readers while also recognizing the extensive disciplinary knowledge they are likely to have. But we also expect some of our readers, whether practitioners or researchers, to be knowledgeable about bilingual education. We hope they will find in this volume some original thinking about issues with which they are already familiar.

In our attempt to reach a wide audience with unequal background knowledge of the topic, we have tried to avoid the jargon internal to the field. We have also supplemented this effort with a glossary of acronyms and specialized terms for the uninitiated. Additionally, we have avoided the popular label "Limited English Proficient" ("LEP"), which is applied by the federal government to language minority students and which we find offensive. We find this label misleading in that it suggests a limitation rather than a language difference, and we find the acronym "LEP" to be particularly unpleasant as it is reminiscent of a label applied to another historically marginalized group. After much serious discussion, and an unwillingness to submit to the use of any labels, we have agreed to limit ourselves, when a label is unavoidable, to "language minority students (LMS)." Although still a label, LMS is more descriptive and neutral than the alternative. In this volume, the official "LEP" label (and any other officially assigned labels) will only appear in quotation marks.

Finally, we want to acknowledge the expert contributions of our advisory committee: Carol Edelsky, Wallace Lambert, Luis Moll, and Richard Tucker. They provided guidance and constructive criticism to keep us accurate and honest. This volume is better because of their contribution. We know they are all extremely busy people and we appreciate the time they devoted to this effort. We also want to thank our patient, knowledgeable, and thorough editor, Kenneth J. Rehage. He was supportive throughout, even when family and professional crises made us doubt we would ever finish. We were very fortunate to have such a kind and understanding editor. We want also to acknowledge the stamina, competence, and good humor of Marisue Garganta, who has been much more than a secretary or even an administrative assistant throughout this process. She has been in constant touch with our authors and editor and has managed to maintain a positive attitude even during our most difficult days. We were lucky to have her by our side.

M. BEATRIZ ARIAS
URSULA CASANOVA

Table of Contents

PAGE

THE NATIONAL SOCIETY FOR THE STUDY OF EDUCATION iv

BOARD OF DIRECTORS OF THE SOCIETY, 1992-93; CONTRIBUTORS TO THE
YEARBOOK v

ACKNOWLEDGMENTS vii

EDITORS' PREFACE ix

Section One
Politics

CHAPTER
I. CONTEXTUALIZING BILINGUAL EDUCATION, *Ursula Casanova* and
M. Beatriz Arias 1

II. SYMBOLS AND THE POLITICAL CONTEXT OF BILINGUAL EDUCATION
IN THE UNITED STATES, *Walter G. Secada* and *Theodora Lightfoot* . 36

III. THE EVALUATION OF BILINGUAL EDUCATION, *Ann C. Willig* and
J. David Ramírez 65

Section Two
Practice and Research

IV. BILINGUAL EDUCATION AND ENGLISH AS A SECOND LANGUAGE: THE
ELEMENTARY SCHOOL, *Robert D. Milk* 88

V. SECONDARY SCHOOLING FOR STUDENTS BECOMING BILINGUAL,
Tamara Lucas 113

VI. ASSESSMENT OF STUDENTS IN BILINGUAL EDUCATION, *Carmen
Mercado* and *Magdalia Romero* 144

VII. LANGUAGE AND CULTURE IN THE PREPARATION OF BILINGUAL
TEACHERS, *Barbara J. Merino* and *Christian J. Faltis* 171

xiv TABLE OF CONTENTS

CHAPTER   PAGE

VIII. A LOOK AT LANGUAGE AS A RESOURCE: LESSONS FROM LA CLASE
       MAGICA, *Olga A. Vasquez* 199

  IX. THE HOME-SCHOOL CONNECTION IN BILINGUAL EDUCATION, *Claude
       Goldenberg* 225

GLOSSARY 251

NAME INDEX 253

SUBJECT INDEX 259

INFORMATION ABOUT MEMBERSHIP IN THE SOCIETY 263

PUBLICATIONS OF THE SOCIETY 264

Section One
POLITICS

CHAPTER I

Contextualizing Bilingual Education

URSULA CASANOVA AND M. BEATRIZ ARIAS

Introduction

The intimate relationship between individuals and their vernacular languages can be discerned in allusions to language as the "mother tongue"—an expression which has acquired a deeper meaning following the discovery of infants' ability to distinguish, from among many, their mother's voice and language. Unamuno, the great Spanish writer and philosopher, said it more dramatically: "My language," he said, "is the blood of my soul."

This powerful manifestation of human groups has incited the curiosity of scholars through the centuries. In recent years many of these scholars have turned to the classroom as a useful laboratory for the study of language. Classrooms are artificial settings responsive to the particular sociopolitical contexts which affect the use of language. And it is in the classroom where a child's language is first scrutinized and judged by strangers. What the teacher understands or fails to understand, the expressions which are deemed appropriate and those which are not, force the child to confront the social rules governing language.[1] Incompatibilities between the language variety learned at home and the standard deemed acceptable in school create problems for many children, even when they speak a variety of English as do those, for example, who reside in Appalachia or Harlem. But the

Ursula Casanova is Associate Professor in the Department of Educational Leadership and Policy Studies, College of Education, Arizona State University. M. Beatriz Arias is Associate Professor in the College of Education, Arizona State University, where she is also the Director of the Center for Bilingual Education and Research.

1

confrontation can be especially traumatic for children who are not fluent in English, the language of most schools in the United States.

The purpose of this chapter is to provide a background to help the reader understand the context of bilingual education for Hispanics in the United States. We will review briefly some of the history and controversies surrounding this pedagogical program, the demographics that demand it, and lastly provide a brief review of the research and theory that undergird bilingual education.

BILINGUALISM AS AN ECONOMIC ADVANTAGE

The economic importance of foreign languages is recognized by a publisher who recently sent out promotional material carrying an urgent announcement. "Speaking English is no longer enough" states the brochure advertising a video language course for children. "Tomorrow's world," it continues, "belongs to those who are prepared to move beyond the nation's borders in outlook . . . and in language." Who, may we ask, can be better prepared for that tomorrow than the child who bridges two cultures and two languages? But the publishers' promotion is not directed at those children. The accompanying photograph shows a blonde child sitting in front of a large, expensive television in a well-appointed living room. Her well-dressed parents smile approvingly in the background while she attends to the language lessons.

The publisher of the video language course is clearly aware that middle- and upper-class parents value bilingualism. Those parents want their children to be bilingual rather than monolingual in English because they see personal, academic, social, and economic advantages in that accomplishment. However, the same individuals frown on the use of ethnic languages for the instruction of language minority students in the schools, either on a part-time or an equal-time-with-English basis. They easily accept the use of minority languages for social, religious, and familial purposes within the boundaries of the home and community centers but do not accept their use within the schools.[2]

The economic advantages of bilingualism have not escaped the nation's decision makers. Two former Secretaries of Education under President Ronald Reagan, Terrel Bell and William Bennett, also promoted foreign language education. Secretary Bell blamed American education for making us into "a bunch of monolingual bumpkins" and Secretary Bennett included two years of foreign language education among the requirements for graduation at his model Madison High School. Neither of these men seemed to experience any discomfort in promoting their respective positions while also decrying the provision of bilingual education for the country's language minority children, the ones who are most likely to become fluent bilinguals.

It is also ironic that U.S. English, an organization that has been a persistent foe of bilingual education, expressed a preference for an individual with bilingual skills in its search for an executive director. This appears to signal their own recognition of the potential career advantages of bilingual competency.[3]

CONTRADICTORY VALUES

The contradiction inherent in the beliefs about bilingual competence expressed by middle-class citizens and political leaders in this country has been addressed by Kjolseth.[4] He questions why we attempt to promote bilingualism where it is most artificial and least likely to succeed, and yet discourage it where it is most natural and likely to be reinforced through daily use. He concludes that bilingualism in the United States is construed in two qualitatively different ways—positively when it is an individual characteristic and negatively when it is a group characteristic. He argues that this bivalent view of bilingualism, which places high value on school-acquired foreign languages but devalues and discourages vernacular languages, is designed to reaffirm the status quo and maintain social stratification by helping the society explain away social injustices. "If a group was seen as advantaged culturally, but disadvantaged economically, by virtue of being bilingual, then the reasons for its subordination would have to be sought elsewhere, namely in the economic and political sphere."[5] This contradiction is discussed more extensively by Secada and Lightfoot in chapter 2 of this volume.

COGNITIVE AND SOCIAL ADVANTAGES

As documented in this chapter and elsewhere in this volume, there are also cognitive advantages to be gained by those who achieve "true bilingualism"[6]—advantages denied to language minority (LM) students who are forced to abandon their first language as they learn a second.[7] And there are social advantages to be considered. The linguistic connection that binds Hispanic families is an intimate code made up of soft, warm words like "mi'jo" (my child), "cariño" (untranslatable but close to "my dear one"), "mamacita" (a term of endearment for mother, also untranslatable and emotionally loaded) and "comadre" or "compadre" (literally "co-mother" or "co-father" but more broadly labels for close supportive relationships central to the Hispanic community). Such connections bind families and communities together. They are the infrastructure of society and, like all infrastructures, they tend to become weaker across the generations unless they are properly maintained.

Loss of the mother tongue has been the norm in the United States, although that is not the case in many other countries. In fact, language recovery has been initiated in many nations in order to preserve languages in danger of extinction.[8] In the United States, in contrast, the migrant's loss of the vernacular has been considered a positive symbol of assimilation. Given the historical and sociopolitical pressures that accompany that assumption, language loss across the generations is perhaps unavoidable in this country. But should the school play an active role in its demise?

Samuel Betances tells a story about his first school experiences in New York City as a newly arrived Spanish-speaking Puerto Rican child:

My teachers thought they knew exactly what they needed to do in order to prepare me for the future, so the first thing they told me . . . was: "Learn English." So I said, "Sí, sí." Then, in the same vein, they came up with, "Forget Spanish." And interestingly enough, before I learned English I forgot Spanish, and soon I was illiterate in two languages.[9]

Betances credits his teachers for insisting he learn English. But, he adds, "when they told me to 'forget Spanish,' they were wrong. . . . You cannot argue in the name of education that it is better to know *less* than *more*."[10] Betances is right. Education should expand a child's horizons, not contract them. To refuse to acknowledge the advantages children can gain from competence in two languages is to refuse to see the potential that LM children have for gaining the social, economic, and cognitive advantages of bilingualism and for occupying positions where their native language can be useful to them. The policy of subtractive bilingualism[11] applied to Betances and it applies as well to most LM children. It stands in contrast to the enrichment bilingualism offered to monolingual English-speakers in elite magnet programs and private schools. This difference in the value attached to the language when it is the child's vernacular rather than a school-learned subject smacks of "linguicism," which Skutnabb-Kangas defines as "ideologies and structures . . . used to legitimate, effectuate, and reproduce an unequal division of power and resources . . . between groups which are defined on the basis of language."[12]

Our belief that the best programs for LM children are those that use dual language instruction does not blind us to the problem of quality. It is true that not all programs in bilingual education are worthy of support, but then neither are all reading or mathematics programs. Yet no one suggests abandoning reading and mathematics programs just because some are ineffective. Rather, we try to improve them. We believe the same stance should be taken relative to bilingual education. Indeed, the authors in this volume devote much space to the achievement of pedagogical quality. Those who seek ways to improve bilingual education will find many new ideas here.

We also do not advocate, nor do we know any who do, Spanish monolingualism for any resident of this country. Supporters of bilingual education have never-denied the need for English competence, but their insistence on first-language maintenance has been consistently distorted and misrepresented by those who oppose bilingual education. We argue that for LM children the ability to become competent users of the English language can be enhanced through the preservation of vernacular skills. Dual language instruction, we believe, also offers the best possibility for achieving the social goals of education as well as for contributing to the linguistic resources of the country.[13] As was succinctly expressed by Hymes,

If one rejects a child's speech, one probably communicates rejection of the child. In rejecting what one wishes to change (or to which one wishes to add), one probably is throwing away the chance for change. In accepting what one wishes to change (or to which one wishes to add) for what it is to the child, one probably is maximizing one's opportunity for change.[14]

The close connection suggested by Hymes between the vernacular language of children and their personal identity unavoidably connects language to politics. Through the years, conquerors in wartime and dominant groups in peacetime have imposed their own languages on other groups. As a result, different languages are accorded different political rights depending on the power relationship between the speakers of those languages.[15] This has sometimes resulted in interethnic conflicts which are then blamed on the group's language, the most obvious symbol of ethnic membership. However, Fishman, who has devoted his life to the sociology of language, has concluded that it is "entirely unwarranted" to assume a relationship between civil strife and linguistic heterogeneity.[16]

BILINGUALISM IN U.S. HISTORY

In the United States, a polyglot land long before the arrival of the Europeans,[17] concerns over language have ebbed and flowed in response to the changing political context. During most of the nineteenth century any immigrant group with sufficient political power, whether Italian, Polish, Czech, French, Dutch, or German, was able to incorporate native language instruction into the schools as separate subjects or as languages of instruction.[18] This part of the nation's educational history is ignored by most citizens who tend to see current programs of bilingual education as an aberration and blame them on recently arrived immigrants from Latin America. The perception that the United States is, and has always been, a monolithic English-speaking nation is a persistent myth belied by the nation's history.

When the first Europeans arrived, the inhabitants of what is now the continental United States spoke over 200 mutually unintelligible languages belonging to about fifteen language families. This tradition of linguistic diversity was continued by settlers who maintained their native tongues in communities all over the country. Through the colonial period and the years of early nationhood, intellectual leaders encouraged the study and maintenance of foreign languages. Thomas Jefferson, for example, considered the study of both French and Spanish to be very important. The enthusiasm for foreign languages was also supported by social and religious organizations, newspapers, and, most specifically, by public and private schools.[19]

According to Leibowitz bilingual education, and even monolingual education in languages other than English, was pervasive throughout the eighteenth century and most of the nineteenth.[20] School instruction in Pennsylvania, Maryland, Virginia, and the Carolinas was given in German, sometimes exclusively. In Wisconsin, a resolution was passed at the 1847 state convention to allow districts with large populations of foreign-born settlers to provide instruction in the mother tongue. As a result German, Norwegian, Dutch, and Swiss became languages of instruction within ethnic enclaves throughout the state. In some of these districts school boards could only hire German-speaking teachers; some others assigned as much as a third of their funds to the purchase of German language textbooks. In the political arena, German received special attention. It just missed becoming a second official language of the new Republic, and it was the only other language chosen to express the Articles of Confederation. And in the state of New Mexico in 1884 a law was passed requiring each county to constitute a school district to teach reading and writing in either Spanish or English, according to the school director's decision.

Heath argues that this openness to foreign languages in the second half of the nineteenth century was motivated by the competition between public schools and private academies where instruction was often given in languages other than English.[21] In the campaign for a common school system immigrants were seen as potential clients to be courted and accommodated, and instruction in languages other than English proliferated. Findings from a historical study of a northeastern community by Montero-Sieburth and Peterson confirm the extent of special programs available at all levels of public education for immigrants without sufficient knowledge of English in that community.[22]

It was not until the late nineteenth and early twentieth century that legal, social, and political forces began to oppose the maintenance of foreign languages. As immigration increased, and public schools filled up their classrooms, the need to make accommodations for immigrant children became less important. Increases in immigration also gave rise to fears of the "foreign element" and the lack of English language and literacy were proposed as reasons for restricting entry into the country.

By the end of the nineteenth century the resurgence of nativism had marked the beginning of a decline in bilingual education. After 1900 the "Americanization" campaign was launched and competency in English became associated with political loyalty. The Nationality Act, passed in 1906, became the first legislation to require aliens to speak English in order to become naturalized.[23] But it was the entrance of the United States into the war in 1917 that brought instruction in two languages to an absolute standstill. Anti-German feeling gave rise to a wave of language restrictions expressed most dramatically by Governor Cox in Ohio, who argued that the German language posed a menace to Americanism.[24] The possibilities for extensive use of dual language instruction did not reappear in the United States until the early 1960s when the Cuban political exiles arrived in Florida.

Experiences with bilingual education in the United States were already forgotten when Dade County (Florida) began its innovative program in Spanish/English bilingual education in 1963. González notes the Cuban exiles' success in instituting a bilingual program and contrasts it to the intransigent monolingualism faced by the country's other linguistic minorities.[25] He attributes their success in establishing a dual language program to the unique characteristics of this immigrant group, such as their middle- and upper-class backgrounds, the high number of professionally trained individuals among them, their condition as victims of a communist state, and the national expectation that they were here only temporarily, thus justifying the need to maintain their mother tongue. These characteristics, added to their unquestioned loyalty to U.S. policies, gained national sympathy for the Cubans. The resulting political support and a generous grant from the Ford Foundation gave rise to a new effort at dual language instruction.

The Movable Legal Landscape

LEGISLATIVE HISTORY OF BILINGUAL EDUCATION

An important aspect of the history of bilingual education in the United States is that prohibitions against the use of languages other than English in the classroom were frequently interpreted as sanctions against the free speech of immigrants and minority group members in schools. In the previous section we described early years of bilingual education as a "permissive" period[26] when languages other than English were tolerated in the schools. This first period, from the late 1800s to the pre-World War I years, was characterized by significant linguistic pluralism in the schools. Joel Perlmann notes that during this time schools were largely controlled by and reflective of their communities, drawing bilingual teachers from the local neighborhood.[27] There was no federal intervention in education at that time and few state education codes specified language of instruction. "In some rural areas where Germans were heavily concentrated, schools— the public schools—were conducted for many years entirely in German." Perlmann concludes that these schools persisted for a long time due to popular will even after English-only legislation.[28]

A cycle of linguistic intolerance and antagonism was ushered in with the changing nature of immigration and the advent of the common school movement, as noted in the preceding section. During this time, schools came to be seen as the focal point of immigrant socialization, and concern for the instillation of American culture coupled with the anti-Germanic feelings prompted by World War I resulted in elimination of any language other than English from schools. While difficult to pinpoint, this phase began about 1917 and continued through the late 1960s. During this period many states established sanctions against the use of languages other than English in schools, and language was used as the rationale for the segregation of Mexican-American and Native-American students in the Southwest. Language minority students were subjected to severe punishment whenever they resorted to a language other than English on the playground or in the classroom. The legacy of that period continues today, as demonstrated by language minority parents whose ambivalence toward bilingual education often reflects fears that their children will be punished for using a non-English language.

With the advent of federal intervention in the schools, heralded by the Great Society programs of the 1960s, attention became focused on the exclusionary practices experienced by linguistic minorities in school, especially linguistic isolation and segregation.[29] The brief period between 1960 and 1980 was a watershed time for the establishment of the rights of language minority students in the schools. State education codes which had previously prohibited the use of languages other than English in the schools were gradually revoked in light of federal legislation and a Supreme Court decision which affirmed equal educational opportunity for LM students. During this time, it appeared that non-English languages would be tolerated and perhaps encouraged in schools. And where LM students were previously punished for using the home language on the playground, schools now recruited translators to assist in parent-teacher conferences and to facilitate interaction with the school community.

In 1974, the U.S. Supreme Court affirmed the right of language minority students in *Lau v. Nichols*,[30] although it did not specifically mandate bilingual education. Nevertheless, some instructional remedy was required. The Court stated: "No specific remedy is urged upon us. Teaching English to the students of Chinese ancestry who do not speak the language is one choice. Giving instruction to this group in Chinese [that is, bilingual education] is another. There may be others."[31] Secada has observed that courts, rather than prescribing bilingual education, prefer to retain flexibility by urging that appropriate actions be taken to assure equal educational opportunity for LM students but leaving open what constitutes such action.[32] This purposeful ambiguity has fueled the debate rather than resolving the role of the native languages in school.

Since the 1980s, the period of linguistic advocacy championed by the courts and federal legislation has been tempered by increasing linguistic chauvinism as exemplified by the emergence of the English Only movement.[33] This movement seeks to prohibit most uses of languages other than English by local, state, and federal government. To many observers, these efforts are a throwback to the post World War I phase of linguistic and ethnic intolerance. Indeed, some of the features of that period, such as hostility toward recent immigrants and racism, are as prevalent today as they were in the 1930s.[34]

Given that the history of languages in the public schools has undergone such cyclical transformations, it is no surprise that the evolution of federal bilingual education policy also reflects political crosscurrents. Bilingual education was first authorized as a discretionary federal program, part of the Elementary and Secondary Education Act (ESEA) of 1968. Rather than being seen as an innovation in language education, the first Bilingual Education Act was largely perceived as a "poverty program" targeted at students who were poor and "educationally disadvantaged," presumably because of their inability to speak English.[35] Title VII resources were allocated to train teachers, develop and disseminate instructional materials, and encourage parental involvement. While the Bilingual Education Act, in spite of its name, did not require schools to use languages other than English, it symbolically allowed children's home language into schools, thus ending a decades-long practice of linguistic exclusion.

Following on the heels of *Lau v. Nichols*, which affirmed the right of language minority students to special instructional approaches, the 1974 amendments to the Bilingual Education Act sought to expand the program. At the reauthorization hearings it was noted that although the Title VII program had funded projects in twenty-six languages, only 6 percent of the eligible students had participated. The 1974 law dropped the requirement for poverty status of children and required schools receiving grants to include instruction in the student's native language and culture "to the extent necessary to allow a child to progress effectively through the educational system." Effective progress could occur in the native language and/or English. Since the amendments did not specify a sole instructional approach, many bilingual educators saw this as the green light for implementing an instructional approach stressing the development of literacy skills in the native language before the acquisition of English.

Subsequent debates over the merits of bilingual education were to turn on just how much of the student's native language should be used in school. On the one hand, advocates of the "maintenance" approach saw the goal of Title VII as the development of students who function well in two languages. Others supported the imperatives of teaching English and assimilating children into the mainstream. Influenced both by a negative national evaluation of bilingual education and by those who wanted the schools to be the basis of the American melting pot, Congress reauthorized "transitional" bilingual education in 1978 mandating that the native language would be used "to the extent necessary to allow a child to achieve competence in the English language." Title VII funds could not be used for maintenance of bilingual education programs, yet student eligibility was expanded to all areas of literacy. That is, the 1978 amendment provided for assistance to all children with "limited proficiency" in speaking, reading, and writing English. Finally, because of concern that Title VII support had been used inadvertently to maintain segregated classrooms, Congress allowed up to 40 percent enrollment of English-speaking students in bilingual programs.

One decade after requiring the use of a student's native language in the bilingual program, Congress reversed its policy by allowing a small percentage of Title VII programs to adopt an "English only" methodology. The 1984 amendments as well as the 1988 amendments have allowed increasing percentages of the total funds to be allocated to "bilingual" programs where the students' first language is not used, in spite of thorough evaluations which support the use of the students' native language as instructionally appropriate, and even preferable.[36]

Although the political debate has not subsided, the importance of the 1968 establishment of a federal bilingual education program cannot be underestimated. The inception of that program allowed states to begin to eliminate their "English Only" instructional policy and recognize the curricular needs of the LM population. According to García and August, in 1990 twelve states and Guam had legislation requiring bilingual instructional services, twelve states permitted bilingual education, and twenty-six states had no relevant legislation.[37] West Virginia was the only state which still prohibited special instructional services in a non-English language. Twenty-two states allowed or required instruction in another language and twenty-eight states required special certification for bilingual education teachers. These policy changes have profound implications for language minority students. At a personal level, students will no longer experience the punishment and sanctions their parents experienced for speaking a language other than English in school. Furthermore, as a result of these changes, bilingual education, as an instructional practice, has been tried and found effective with LM students.[38] Nevertheless, as noted earlier, these successes are now tempered by recent efforts to make English the official language of the United States.

THE ENGLISH ONLY MOVEMENT

The English Only movement, born in the 1980s, spawned a national effort to pass a constitutional amendment making English the official language of the United States. While that seems innocuous enough, it should be noted that the amendment originally proposed in 1981 by Senator Hayakawa, the movement's leader, also forbade the making or enforcement of any law, ordinance, regulation, order, program, or policies requiring the use of any language other than English. Although the proposed amendment did not prohibit instruction in a language other than English as a transitional step for LM students, its proponents also opposed bilingual education.[39] Between 1986 and 1988, U.S. English, an organization promoting English only, supported efforts in forty states to pass legislation making English the official state language; ten of these efforts were successful. It is revealing to look at the states which have passed resolutions for Official English in relation to their numbers of language minority citizens and students.

Of the five states with the largest number of language minority students three (California, Florida, and Illinois) have passed English Only resolutions. These states have a combined population of over 12 million home speakers of non-English languages and they are also the states most highly affected by waves of immigration in the 1980s. Arizona, one of the top ten states in language minority population, passed a constitutional amendment making English the official state language, but it was ruled unconstitutional in 1991. It appears, then, that as the numbers of immigrants increase, anti-immigrant sentiment also increases and so does public opinion against bilingual education.[40] This fact does not augur well for bilingual education or for the population of LM students needing special instructional services.[41]

THE POLITICS OF NUMBERS

Efforts to identify the numbers of "limited English proficient (LEP)" students to be served officially began with the 1974 amendments to the Bilingual Education Act. Defining and accurately counting language minority students in the United States has eluded policymakers since the 1974 amendments were enacted. The amended Act mandated a count by the states of limited-English-speaking children and adults in the United States. However, identifying persons limited solely in speaking ability restricted the eligible population by excluding persons who were also limited in their ability to read, write, or understand English. Consequently, the 1978 amendments to the Bilingual Education Act designated the group to be counted as "limited English proficient." The definition, as found in Title VII, Bilingual Education Programs (P.L. 100-297), Sec. 7003, is as follows:

The terms "limited English proficiency" and "limited English proficient" mean:
  A. individuals who were not born in the United States or whose native language is a language other than English;
  B. individuals who come from environments where a language other than English is dominant, and
  C. individuals who are American Indians and Alaska Natives and who come from environments where a language other than English has had a significant impact on their language proficiency; and who, by reason thereof, have sufficient difficulty speaking, reading, writing, or understanding the English language to deny such individuals the opportunity to learn successfully in classrooms where the language of instruction is English or to participate fully in our society.

A review of the uneven history of identifying language minority students raises speculations as to the extent to which actual identification was problematic or whether it reflected an underlying reluctance to acknowledge the large numbers of children and adults in the United States who are "limited English proficient" and therefore entitled to special services. The initial problems identified by Waggoner were: (1) locating an appropriate survey which could assess individuals as identified in parts A, B and C of the above definition; (2) determining in a statistically unbiased manner how many language minority persons have difficulty with English; and (3) determining the level of English proficiency needed by children to succeed in classrooms. Waggoner concluded that "the resolution of these problems plagues efforts to agree on the numbers of LEP children to this day."[42]

Several national surveys initiated to identify the eligible language minority student population have reported disparate figures. In 1978, the Children's English and Services Study (CESS) identified 3.6 million school-aged children (ages 4 to 18) who were of "limited English proficiency."[43] This assessment was followed by a reanalysis conducted by Barnes and Milne, who reported that the "target

population of children who have serious difficulty in school because of
dependence on a language other than English is in the range of
700,000 to 1.3 million, or about one-third of the 3.6 million figure
estimated by CESS."[44]

Determining the size of the eligible population is critical not only
in order to assess the adequacy of federal civil rights guarantees but,
perhaps equally important, to develop essential information for
funding the annual appropriation of the federal bilingual education
program. In this manner, the political agenda rears its head again: the
fewer "LEP" students identified nationally, the smaller the
appropriations allocated to the federal bilingual education program. In
fact, the federal bilingual program has had a history of underfunding.
In 1982, Secretary Terrel Bell reported that "only about a third of the
children aged 5 to 14 . . . are receiving either bilingual instruction or
instruction in English as a second language. . . . Schools in general are
not meeting the needs of 'LEP' children."[45] This estimate was based
on an undercount of identified students. Consequently even less than
one-third of identified "LEP" students were being served.

It was to be expected that a debate would ensue regarding the
numbers of eligible students in an administration which was
antagonistic to bilingual education. The debate raged on as the figures
reported by Secretary William Bennett in 1986 clashed with the
realities school districts were confronting around the country.
Bennett's *Condition of Bilingual Education in the United States* found that
at least 94 percent of the eligible 1.2 million "LEP" students were
receiving special language programs. Observers argued that this figure
failed to consider the explosive growth in immigration since the 1980
Census. Waggoner maintained that an accurate national estimate of the
"LEP" population would find from 3.5 to 5.3 million students who
could benefit from bilingual services. This number reflected only the
legal immigration figures. Meanwhile, school districts were reporting
an unprecedented increase in identified "LEP" students. California,
for example, showed an increase of 73 percent in the "LEP" student
population from 1980 to 1986. And New York City reported that
44,000 of its 110,000 "LEP" students were not receiving services to
which they were entitled.

Expectations that the 1990 census would provide definitive information on the number of eligible language minority students have yet
to be met. The release of a definitive count has been delayed because
of (1) inconsistencies in the aggregation of the data (states used different criteria for LM students); (2) the questions used (respondents

were asked only about English-speaking ability); (3) sampling errors; and (4) undercounts.

In general, however, the 1990 census reaffirms two facts: the language minority population is growing and a considerable factor in this growth is the increase in immigration. According to the estimates, nearly one in five persons in the United States has a language minority background. Immigration accounted for a large part of this growth; the foreign-born population of over 19 million has increased over 40 percent since 1980.

Conservative estimates indicate that in 1990 there were almost 32 million people in the entire United States aged five and over who spoke a language other than English in their homes. Table 1 shows the estimated number of such individuals (NELS) in each of the twenty-four states where more than 70,000 home speakers of non-English languages were reported. The table also shows the estimated number of NELS aged five and over in each state who have difficulty speaking English, and the percent of the state's population aged five and over represented by that number. In addition, the table shows the number of foreign-born persons in each state (irrespective of language background) in 1990 and the percentage of increase in foreign-born population since 1980.

Table 2 shows that between 1979 and 1989 there was an average increase of 40 percent in the numbers of home speakers of other languages. It displays this increase by language, showing the greatest percentage increase in Cambodian, followed by Creole languages, Asian Indian languages, Korean, and Vietnamese.

Finally, table 3 displays the 1989 language distributions for the over 5 million school-age persons in the United States classified as LM. This table indicates that Spanish language background persons far outnumber any other language group and account for over 65 percent of all persons in that age group.

These tables indicate several factors that need to be considered with regard to bilingual education and attitudes toward bilingual instruction. First, students who may require bilingual services are a significant subpopulation of school-age children. In some states, one out of every five students has a non-English language background. This statistic has important implications for teachers and teacher preparation. Given that these demographic trends are expected to continue, teachers in states with large numbers of LM students need to be knowledgeable about pedagogical approaches for students of

TABLE 1

ESTIMATED NUMBERS OF HOME SPEAKERS OF NON-ENGLISH LANGUAGES (NELS)
AGED 5+, AND ESTIMATED FOREIGN-BORN POPULATION IN 24 STATES (1990)

STATE	TOTAL NUMBER OF NELS AGED 5+	NELS AGED 5+ HAVING DIFFICULTY SPEAKING ENGLISH		FOREIGN-BORN POPULATION 1990	PERCENT INCREASE 1980 TO 1990
		NUMBER	PERCENT OF STATE POPULATION AGED 5+		
Arizona	700,000	276,000	20.8	278,000	42.2
California	8,619,000	4,423,000	31.5	6,459,000	50.4
Colorado	321,000	110,000	10.5	142,000	40.0
Connecticut	466,000	184,000	15.2	279,000	32.0
Florida	2,098,000	961,000	17.3	1,663,000	39.7
Georgia	285,000	109,000	4.8	173,000	52.0
Hawaii	255,000	124,000	24.8	163,000	41.0
Illinois	1,499,000	658,000	14.2	952,000	39.0
Indiana	246,000	87,000	4.8	94,000	32.4
Louisiana	392,000	128,000	10.1	87,000	39.8
Maryland	395,000	148,000	8.9	313,000	47.2
Massachusetts	852,000	349,000	15.2	574,000	38.9
Michigan	570,000	189,000	6.6	355,000	26.3
Minnesota	227,000	79,000	5.6	113,000	45.6
New Jersey	1,406,000	609,000	19.5	967,000	39.8
New Mexico	494,000	160,000	35.5	81,000	38.6
New York	3,909,000	1,766,000	23.3	2,852,000	41.7
N. Carolina	241,000	87,000	3.9	115,000	45.3
Ohio	546,000	190,000	5.4	260,000	27.2
Pennsylvania	807,000	293,000	7.3	369,000	31.5
Texas	3,970,000	1,766,000	25.4	1,524,000	47.1
Virginia	419,000	161,000	7.3	312,000	50.8
Washington	403,000	165,000	9.0	322,000	39.9
Wisconsin	264,000	93,000	5.8	122,000	33.7

Note: This table includes only states reporting over 70,000 persons coming from
non-English language backgrounds.

Source: Adapted with permission from *Numbers and Needs: Ethnic and Linguistic
Minorities in the United States*, vol. 2, no. 2 (July, 1992): 2.

"limited English proficiency." Second, given that the numbers of
students are so significant, there is a window of opportunity for this
generation to become the most multilingual in the history of the
United States. This optimistic perspective is accompanied by a more
pessimistic prospect. The continuation of current policies which discourage and devalue languages other than English may perpetuate LM
students' disaffection with and alienation from their schools. Since we
prefer to remain optimistic, our focus in this volume is on bilingual
education as enrichment.

TABLE 2

HOME SPEAKERS OF LANGUAGES OTHER THAN ENGLISH (AGED 5+) IN 1979 AND
1989 AND PERCENTAGE CHANGE, BY LANGUAGE

(NUMBERS IN 1,000s)

LANGUAGE	1979	1989	% CHANGE
Total	17,632	24,837	+40.9
American Indian/Alaska Native languages	185	240	+29.7
Arabic	177	357	+101.7
Armenian	74	113	+52.7
Asian Indian languages	98	284	+189.8
Cambodian	7	145	+1,971.4
Chinese languages	514	834	+62.3
Creole languages	20	186	+830.0
Farsi	91	156	+71.4
Filipino languages	419	638	+52.3
French	987	1,082	+9.5
German	1,261	849	−32.7
Greek	366	284	−22.2
Hungarian	106	124	+17.0
Italian	1,354	906	−33.1
Japanese	265	370	+39.6
Korean	191	503	+163.4
Lao	NA	181	NA
Polish	731	454	−37.9
Portuguese	245	395	+61.2
Russian	65	116	+78.5
Spanish	8,768	14,489	+65.2
Vietnamese	157	398	+153.5
Yiddish	234	161	−31.2
Other languages	1,316	1,572	+19.5

Source: *Numbers and Needs*, vol. 2, no. 1 (January, 1992): 2.

Bilingual education, then, is not just a pedagogical intervention; it is also a political issue. Indeed, the value of the term as a label for an instructional strategy is questionable since it has become so confounded as to be pedagogically meaningless. The lack of precision of this term is, in fact, one of the problems faced by researchers in the field. (See chapter 3, this volume.) Programs labeled "bilingual education" hardly ever consist of instruction in two languages equally distributed across the school day.[46] Children in these programs may actually receive instruction in their native language for only a small portion of the school day; sometimes the vernacular may not be used

TABLE 3

SPEAKERS OF LANGUAGES OTHER THAN ENGLISH (AGED 5-17)

(NUMBERS IN 1,000s)

LANGUAGES	TOTALS
Spanish	3,578.8
Other Languages	317.5
French	228.3
Chinese Languages	136.8
Vietnamese	135.7
Korean	124.7
Filipino Language	105.9
Arabic	84.6
Portuguese	64.0
Lao	63.9
German	61.1
Asian Indian Language	61.1
Cambodian	57.3
American Indian/Alaska Native Languages	47.5
Greek	43.7
Italian	39.9
Yiddish	38.3
Japanese	37.4
Creole Language	37.0
Polish	30.0
Armenian	25.0
Farsi	22.6
Hungarian	12.3
Russian	11.6
Total	5,240,000

Source: Adapted from *Numbers and Needs*, vol. 2, no. 2 (January, 1992): 4.

at all. Thus, the labels attached to programs designed to serve the needs of language minority students are often misleading. These programs may be called "bilingual" although they may consist only of concentrated English language instruction.

In this volume we use "bilingual education" to refer to dual language programs. Programs that differ significantly from that model will be described and labeled according to federal government definitions. (See chapter 4, this volume.)

A Brief Overview of Research in Bilingual Education

CHARACTERISTICS OF THE FIELD

Several idiosyncrasies characterize bilingual education as a field of study: the paucity of researchers who must cover a wide interdisciplinary range, the marginalizing of bilingual education in educational research, and the broad spectrum of languages and age levels encompassed by bilingual education. We discuss these factors in the paragraphs that follow.

Because of the small number of scholars working in the field of bilingual education, a large volume of work has been conducted by a slim band of researchers. These researchers cut across many different disciplines: anthropology, sociology, psychology and linguistics, all of which are represented in this volume. Scholars in bilingual education are thus forced to stay abreast of work in many different disciplines in order to keep up with the field. Then, too, within each of those disciplines, researchers interested in bilingual education remain isolated from their colleagues. Thus, psychologists in general tend to have scant knowledge of bilingualism or bilingual education, although much of the research on these topics has been conducted by psychologists.

The marginalizing of bilingual education from mainstream research in education is a curious phenomenon. It has been noted by Edelsky and by Hakuta[47] and can be inferred through a rough analysis of the content of several prestigious research publications. Between 1976 and 1991, for example, the *Journal of Educational Psychology* published a total of 1414 articles, seven of which were on bilingual education. A similar analysis shows that out of 430 articles published in the American Educational Research Association's flagship journal, *Educational Researcher*, only one was on bilingual education. Another of the association's journals, the *American Educational Research Journal*, included only two articles on bilingual education among the 578 articles published from 1976 to 1991.[48]

The marginalizing of this field in educational research is surprising because bilingual education offers a fertile field for the study of cognition. Some investigators have surmised that the practical issues of bilingual education (for example, language learning and literacy) may be based in important ways on cognitive skills.[49] Following this line of reasoning, many researchers have conducted studies of cognitive development in bilingual children. Since the 1970s this connection has been investigated by Cummins, DeAvila and Duncan, Hakuta, Díaz, and Kessler and Quinn among others.[50] Yet their scholarly work does not often cross over into the general research in cognitive development because students of cognition seldom consider this research in their reviews of the literature and few books on cognitive psychology consider bilingualism. In this respect Segal, Chipman, and Glaser are exceptions.[51] Two of the forty-six chapters in their two-volume publication on thinking and learning discuss bilingual issues.

During the last thirty years research with bilingual populations has enhanced our understanding of language and cognitive development and has also pointed out the positive cognitive and social implications of bilingual instruction.[52] This chapter cannot do full justice to the extent or variety of research produced during that time. Readers desiring an extensive analysis of the literature should examine the many comprehensive reviews available.[53] What follows is a cursory, chronological review of the research which has been most influential in the field and of the direction of current efforts. Readers will find more detail about specific topics within each of the chapters in this volume.

THE EFFECTS OF BILINGUALISM

Early findings from research on bilingualism continue to haunt current perceptions of the effects of bilingual education or bilingual upbringing, even among otherwise knowledgeable educators and scholars. According to Hakuta, the connection between "language handicap" and bilingualism dates from the early part of the century.[54] As the countries of origin of the immigrants arriving at Ellis Island changed, so did their welcome. "New immigrants" from southern Europe were not as happily received as their predecessors. They were thought to compare unfavorably to the "old immigrants" from northern European countries. The latter were considered to be more intelligent and more willing to assimilate. This perception of change in the quality of the immigrant population coincided with the fascination of the country's psychological community with the newly developed intelligence tests.

The "new immigrants" did not perform as well as the "old" ones on IQ tests administered in English. Explanations for their inferior performance varied according to each psychologist's theoretical bent. Those who considered genetic endowment as the predominant influence on IQ theorized that the lower performance of the "new immigrants" was a clear indication of inferior intelligence resulting in a "language handicap." Psychologists who placed more importance on environmental or experiential influences also believed the "new immigrants" suffered from a "language handicap" but for them this was the natural outcome of early exposure to two languages.

Psychologists were thus able to overlook obvious differences between the earlier and later groups of immigrants in length of residence in the United States, and therefore their opportunity to learn English. They had such confidence in the new technology of measurement and quantification that they were unwilling to consider the possibility of limitations in the tests themselves. "In either case, the concept of language handicap . . . came to be a trait of the bilingual individual's mind, whether based on experience or genetic qualities."[55]

The association of bilingualism with intellectual deficiency persisted beyond the first half of the twentieth century. Public attitudes toward bilingualism were based on a set of beliefs which, though unfounded, continue to be deeply held by many influential individuals. These beliefs are (1) that children who receive bilingual instruction will suffer intellectual retardation, (2) that they will be unable to learn content at a high level, (3) that they will never reach an acceptable level of native language competence and thus will always feel alienated from both ethnolinguistic groups.[56]

The first serious challenge to these notions was not made until the early 1960s. Peal and Lambert decided that the negative findings of early studies were due to researchers' failure to distinguish between different levels of bilingualism.[57] They proposed making a distinction between "pseudobilinguals" (who know one language much better than the other and do not use the second language for communication) and "real (or true) bilinguals" (who master both languages during childhood and easily communicate in both). They tested their hypothesis by administering several measures of bilingual competence to ten-year-old children in Canada. Two groups of children were identified and administered intelligence tests. Those who were found to be "balanced (or true) bilinguals" in French and English were compared with a control group of monolingual children. Findings from this study were the first in psychological and educational research to suggest that bilingualism could be an advantage instead of a handicap. Bilingual children were found to perform significantly better than monolingual children in both verbal and nonverbal tests of mental ability when variables in gender, age, and socioeconomic status were controlled. They appeared to be superior to monolinguals in concept formation and in tasks requiring mental or symbolic flexibility.[58]

Many researchers in many different settings have since confirmed Peal and Lambert's 1962 findings. Learning a second language in childhood, either by simultaneous acquisition or in the context of bilingual education, has been consistently associated with positive cognitive gains.[59]

Studies of the effects of bilingualism have rested on two paradigms. One, modeled after Peal and Lambert, compares bilingual to monolingual children and requires careful attention to variables such as language proficiency, socioeconomic status, and any other possibly confounding variables. The other seeks to assess the effects of bilingualism by studying variations in second language proficiency among bilingual children. In this case a child's "degree of bilingualism" becomes the independent variable and different cognitive measures constitute the dependent variables. This model allows researchers to study the relationship between second language proficiency and cognitive ability.[60] However, it leaves open the question of whether bilingualism enhances cognition or whether intellectual giftedness leads to balanced bilingualism.

Hakuta and Díaz used the second model to study bilingual children and they employed multiple regression techniques to separate the effects of bilingualism from those of cognition.[61] The cognitive ability of children in primary level bilingual programs was assessed through their proficiency in their first language. This initial assessment was followed by an assessment of their second language proficiency. The researchers were thus able to identify three groups of children equivalent in their level of first language proficiency but very different in their level of mastery of their second language: (1) proficient bilinguals, (2) partial bilinguals, and (3) limited bilinguals. Their findings indicated a significant contribution of second language proficiency to cognitive abilities, including analogical reasoning, metalinguistic awareness, and visual and spatial skills. The design of the study called for measures of language proficiency and cognitive ability at two points in time and therefore allowed the researchers to suggest cautiously that *if* a causal relationship exists between intelligence and bilingualism, bilingualism is the most likely causal factor.

Although the positive influence of a child's bilingual mastery on concept formation, classification, creativity, analogical reasoning, and visual and spatial skills has been demonstrated through both research models, researchers are still struggling with the reasons why this is so.[62] Díaz offered three explanatory hypotheses: code-switching, objectification, and verbal mediation.[63] Code-switching refers to the capacity of bilinguals to change easily from one language to another. Peal and Lambert suggested that code-switching experience might contribute to more flexibility in the thinking of bilinguals.[64] Objectification refers to a bilingual child's objective awareness of language. Researchers suggest that such an awareness enhances the child's ability to operate at higher levels of abstract and symbolic thinking. The verbal mediation hypothesis is based on Vygotsky's notions of language as a tool.[65] The Russian psychologist posited that the cognitive development of young children is influenced by their reliance on language as a tool of thought. Hakuta and Díaz, among others, have suggested that the bilingual experience and resulting metalinguistic awareness promote a more efficient use of language in the Vygotskyan sense.[66]

All of these explanations will need to remain as hypotheses until further research. It is even possible that none of them (or those which may be developed later) will succeed in untangling the relationship between bilingualism and cognition because bilingualism does not occur in a void. It is embedded within a socio-historical context wherein "every conceivable relationship between bilingualism and intelligence *could* obtain."[67] To disentangle this relationship we turn once again to Lambert and his recognition of two different processes leading to bilingualism—the additive and the subtractive. This theory neatly connects the cognitive and the social dimensions of bilingualism and is well illustrated by the much publicized Canadian immersion studies.

ADDING AND SUBTRACTING

The Canadian immersion program is often cited as a better alternative by opponents of native language maintenance in bilingual education. The program, designed for Anglophone children, was a response to middle-class parents' complaints about the low level of competence achieved by their children in traditional French-as-a-foreign-language classes. In this program the students are instructed in French from the very beginning of their school experience. Immersion was found to be successful in facilitating second language acquisition without detrimental effects on the students' first language or on their social or cognitive development.[68]

The assumption by educators in the United States that a similar approach would be appropriate for linguistic minorities in this country drew a strong reaction from the researchers responsible for the program: "The claim that the results from studies of Canadian immersion programs lead to the conclusion that minority group youngsters in the United States, Canada, or the third world should be immersed or submerged in the target language is false."[69] They pointed to differences in the social context, particularly in the social status accorded the two languages, to explain why their results would not transfer successfully to the United States context.

The Canadian immersion program was initiated by parents who value the language to be learned by their children as a second language but also understand that their first language will continue to be dominant in their children's lives. These conditions appear to make an enormous contribution to the success of that program. The Canadian program, therefore, is additive; children are encouraged to maintain and develop their home language while they add a second language. In contrast, minority parents in the United States are excluded from the decision-making process, and their language, as is evident in the efforts to replace it with English, is devalued in the school. The instructional experience of LM children in U.S. schools, therefore, is subtractive. It was Lambert who suggested that the way in which a second language is developed might have a significant effect on the outcome.[70] His insight helped researchers to understand why findings from studies documenting minority children's progress in second language acquisition could diverge so drastically from the results of studies involving majority children.

Additive bilingualism entails the *maintenance* of all linguistic skills in the vernacular as the child acquires a second language. Subtractive bilingualism seeks to *replace* the child's vernacular with the second language. Foreign language education in the United States follows the additive model while immigrant children in the United States, as well as in other countries, are most often taught in a subtractive mode. They are expected to forget their language (as Betances' teacher demanded) and replace it with the second language. Lambert expected additive bilingualism to affect cognition positively while the opposite would be true of subtractive bilingualism.[71] The Canadian program tends to support this theory.

But "additive" and "subtractive" apply to more than an individual's experience with bilingual education. They also describe the social settings within which individuals develop their language abilities. The situation of additive bilingualism obtains when the society values both languages and perceives the acquisition of the second language as a positive achievement. In Finland, where Finnish and Swedish languages and cultures are both valued, almost everyone is fluent in both languages. However, when two systems are in conflict or in competition with each other, there exists a condition of subtractive bilingualism such as is found in settings where the languages of ethno-linguistic minorities are not valued.[72]

Lambert's theory was endorsed and expanded by Cummins, who argued that a child's level of native language proficiency would mediate the cognitive consequences of bilingualism. That is, a child must reach a "threshold" level of competence in the native language in order to obtain the cognitive advantages of bilingualism. Cummins's threshold theory is based on his hypothesis of a common underlying proficiency which assumes that skills learned in different languages reside in the same part of the brain and reinforce each other. According to this theory, the most cognitively demanding and decontextualized skills, including literacy, are interdependent across languages while the surface aspects of language may differ substantially. This means that a child who masters academic skills in the native language will transfer them to the second language. However, a child who fails to reach a "threshold" level of competence in the native language may remain cognitively retarded in both languages.[73]

Cummins's theory of a common underlying proficiency challenges the assumption that instruction in the native language interferes with the acquisition of a second language. That assumption guides much of the emphasis on early exit from native language instruction and is based on the belief that language skills are not transferable. But according to Cummins, the research evidence is clear: "The results of virtually every bilingual program that has been evaluated during the past fifty years show either no relationship or a negative relationship between amount of school exposure to the majority language and academic achievement in that language."

Cummins has also made a distinction between contextualized and decontextualized language. He has argued that school success depends on a child's development of decontextualized language such as is required in formal instructional settings. LM children who acquire basic interpersonal communication skills may appear to be fluent in English and ready to transition into English-only classrooms. However, these children are often dependent on visual clues that enable them to contextualize the language during interpersonal communication. Those clues tend to be minimal or altogether absent from the decontextualized language of the classroom. The inability to cope with the demands of abstracted language in the classroom environment can be the cause of failure for many of these children.[74]

The claim that academic success for LM children is less dependent on the specific language a child knows than on the ways of using that language is also made by Heath.[75] She notes that children must have the opportunity to use both oral and written language in a variety of situations. They must have the opportunity to use their language not only in interactions based on intimate knowledge or shared backgrounds where expectations are clear, but also in situations where the language is depersonalized, where it stands somewhat autonomous from explicit knowledge. She believes, with Cummins, that it is in interactions with those who do not share their knowledge where children get practice in the kind of decontextualized, impersonal language that the school and other mainstream institutions value.

The connection between children's experiences outside of school and their academic success has been the focus of ethnographers such as Heath. These researchers have extended the study of language learning and language use beyond the individual characteristics emphasized by the traditional psychological perspective. Through the use of various observation techniques borrowed mainly from anthropology, ethnographers seek to describe the culture of a community or a society. The choice of ethnography as the methodological framework for the study of language development has encouraged the documentation of the conditions outside of school under which LM children learn best. This knowledge, in turn, contributes to our understanding of children's responses to the instructional environment of the school.[76]

Comparisons of children's responses across different environments have made researchers aware of the influence of context on learning. Labov was among the first to point to the influence of context in countering the popular cultural deprivation theory used to explain the underachievement of minority students. He demonstrated how the verbal performance of African-American children varied across settings. Youths who seemed inarticulate under the usual formal testing conditions became very articulate when the power relations between adult and child were changed. Researchers have uncovered similar patterns in widely varying communities. In the Warm Springs Indian Reservation, in the Piedmont Carolinas, Alaska, and Hawaii researchers have found consistent evidence that patterns of communication are context specific.[77] These findings have cast doubt on traditional assessments of language proficiency based on a limited perception of language as only an abstract formal system of communication. The context-specific approach requires the description of communicative activities which make up the lesson environment of which language is a part.

Following this model, Díaz, Moll, and Mehan investigated the influence of specific teaching and learning conditions within classrooms on the academic achievement of language minority students.[78] Through their analyses of videotapes documenting reading instruction for the same group of children in English and Spanish in different classrooms, these researchers were able to demonstrate (1) the relationship between teaching reading in different linguistic and pedagogical settings; (2) how current pedagogical practices constrain academic achievement; and (3) how better teaching environments can be created.[79]

These researchers found students who operated at an advanced level of reading and comprehension in Spanish struggling with primer-level material in English. They identified three factors that contributed to the discrepancies observed between the two classrooms: lack of coordination between teachers; the use of language as the basis of ability grouping (based on the misguided but commonly held assumption that productive language skills are indicative of reading ability); and the confounding of pronunciation with decoding skills in the English language setting. In collaboration with the teachers these researchers were able to implement instructional strategies which built on the students' advanced reading skills in Spanish. They changed the focus in English from decoding to comprehension on the assumption that the students' level of comprehension exceeded their level of production. And they allowed the children to demonstrate their comprehension by responding to questions in either English or Spanish or both. As a result of this intervention the children's performance in English reading advanced the equivalent of three years.[80]

Díaz, Moll, and Mehan argue that the context-specific approach used in this investigation is "pedagogically optimistic" because it assigns "a major role to specific teaching and learning conditions, as opposed to the general internal properties of children."[81] It therefore encourages positive action toward the creation of effective learning environments.

THE SOCIOCULTURAL APPROACH

The importance of the larger social context on school achievement is supported by research documenting differences in the collective achievement of similar ethnolinguistic groups according to the sociocultural context. For example, Korean students do not achieve well in Japan but are considered outstanding students in the United States; and Finnish students perform poorly in Sweden while they excel in Australia. This differential achievement is explained by Ogbu and Matute-Bianchi on the basis of the social and economic discrimination suffered by some groups in some contexts.[82] Trueba, however, argues that the categories suggested by Ogbu and Matute-Bianchi (autonomous, immigrant, and caste-like minorities) promote stereotypes and fail to account for the generational mobility typical of all immigrant groups. He suggests instead a broader perspective that takes into account the cultural context of learning.[83]

Trueba's position, as well as that of many other researchers,[84] is based on the socio-historical school of psychology led by Vygotsky. The Russian psychologist sought to explain the cognitive development of children on the basis of a close relationship between language, culture, and cognition. He argued that the cognitive and communicative functions of language form the basis for the superior form of activity that distinguishes children from animals.[85] This conceptual framework has had a major influence on research in bilingual education. Researchers of the Vygotskyan school attempt to integrate the experiences of children in *all learning environments*, including the home, the school, and the local community. Although they are particularly interested in the use of the sociocultural approach in the study of LM children in bilingual settings, they believe that this approach is crucial to understanding the learning process and academic development of all children. The research by Moll and his colleagues in a southwestern barrio in the United States, for example, is based on the principle that the students' community provides an important resource for educational change.[86]

This research is based on the premise that families and communities possess funds of knowledge which represent a potential resource for the school. Knowledge of construction techniques, herbalism, and crafts available in the community is usually dismissed by the school as irrelevant to the academic endeavor. Through this project researchers and teachers meet in after-school settings to discuss observations and to develop instructional innovations directed at gaining access to the community's funds of knowledge and incorporating that knowledge into the school curriculum. Moll describes how, as a result of this effort, one of these teachers has developed instructional activities that reach out to parents as intellectual resources in the development of lessons for the classroom. Unlike much of what passes for "parental involvement" in most schools, the classroom visits of the parents in this project are not trivial. Parents come to share their knowledge and this knowledge becomes part of the students' work or focus of study. Reading and writing in both languages gain significance as these activities, rather than being isolated exercises, become a means of analysis and expression. Furthermore, as the teacher develops her social networks in the community she becomes convinced of the valuable knowledge existing beyond the classroom and of its usefulness for academic purposes. For her students, knowledge becomes contextualized and inclusive of their personal experiences.[87]

The sociocultural approach used in this project has extended bilingual education research beyond the classroom and the traditional emphasis on learning English and acquiring basic skills. Children in these classrooms are encouraged to use either Spanish or English as tools for inquiry, communication, and thinking. The researchers, teachers, and parents collaborate in transforming the conditions for teaching and thinking through the use and development of everyone's "fund of knowledge" in a process of educational change.[88]

This approach also responds to Cummins's notion of empowerment. He has proposed that the positive effects of bilinguality on student cognition are mediated by teachers and schools and argues that students from "dominated" societal groups can be "empowered" or "disabled" by those who seek to educate them. "Educators who see their role as adding a second language and cultural affiliation to their students' repertoire are likely to empower students more than those who see their role as replacing or subtracting the students' language and culture."[89] Cummins argues that empowerment is a necessary condition for successful learning. Moll suggests that an indispensable aspect of obtaining positive change in education is the creation of supportive contexts for teachers. Within such settings teachers can collaborate with other colleagues, including researchers and parents, and receive assistance as needed in developing their thinking and teaching.[90] Moll's experiences suggest that the empowerment of LM students and their communities may well depend on the empowerment of teachers.

Researchers in bilingual education have been at the forefront of the movement to integrate social and cultural perspectives in the study of education. The psychological orientation which dominated early research in bilingual education continues, but it has been broadened by the recognition that language, culture, and cognition are interdependent. In so doing, psychology has reached and spilled over disciplinary boundaries. Three well-known cognitive psychologists (Hakuta,

Ferdman, and Díaz) argue that the study of the relationship between cognitive development and bilingual education is "a vortex of classic questions about the nature of language, mind, and society." They assert that "a complete understanding of the problem must come through a multilayered analysis that considers historical, linguistic, cognitive, socio-psychological, and sociological perspectives,"[91] to which we would add the anthropological perspective. This interdisciplinary approach is reflected in the chapters included in this volume. They are evidence of the important contribution of bilingual research to our understanding of thinking and learning.

NOTES

1. Dell Hymes, "Introduction," in *Functions of Language in the Classroom*, edited by Courtney B. Cazden, Vera P. John, and Dell Hymes (New York: Teachers College Press, 1972).

2. Wallace E. Lambert and Donald M. Taylor, *Cultural and Racial Diversity in the Lives of Urban Americans: The Hamtrack/Pontiac Study*, Preliminary Draft (Montreal: McGill University, 1986).

3. *Roll Call* 37, no. 67 (March 9, 1992): 38.

4. Rolf Kjolseth, "Cultural Politics of Bilingualism," *Society* 20, no. 4 (May/June, 1983): 40-48.

5. Ibid.

6. Lambert defines a true bilingual as an individual who has fully developed age-appropriate skills in two or more languages and can move from one language to the other with ease.

7. Jim Cummins, "Empowering Minority Students: A Framework for Interventions," *Harvard Educational Review* 56, no. 1 (February, 1986): 18-36.

8. See, for example, Richard A. Benton, "Tomorrow's Schools and the Revitalization of Maori: Stimulus or Tranquilizer?" in *Bilingual Education: A Focusschrift in Honor of Joshua A. Fishman*, edited by Ofelia García (Amsterdam: John Benjamins, 1991); and Jim Cummins, "Immersion Programs: The Irish Experience," *International Review of Education* 24, no. 3 (1978): 273-282.

9. Samuel Betances, "Understanding the Dimensions of the Problem," in *Making Schools Work for Underachieving Minority Students*, edited by Josie G. Bain and Joan L. Herman (New York: Greenwood Press, 1990).

10. Ibid., p. 26. Emphasis in the original.

11. Subtractive bilingualism is the term invented by Lambert to describe programs that seek to replace a student's vernacular with a second language. Wallace E. Lambert, "Culture and Language as Factors in Learning and Education," in *Education of Immigrant Students*, edited by A. Wolfgang (Toronto: Ontario Institute for Studies in Education, 1975).

12. Tove Skutnabb-Kangas, "Multilingualism and the Education of Minority Children," in *Minority Education*, edited by Tove Skutnabb-Kangas and Jim Cummins (Clevedon, Eng.: Multilingual Matters, 1988), p. 13.

13. Such an approach has been suggested by the Carnegie Commission and by the Academy for Educational Development. See Alan Pifer, *Bilingual Education and the Hispanic Challenge: The President's (1979) Annual Report* (New York: Carnegie Corporation, 1980); and Academy for Educational Development, "A New Direction

for Bilingual Education in the 1980s," in *Focus* (Rosslyn, VA: National Clearinghouse for Bilingual Education, 1981). They both suggested integrating bilingual and foreign language education in response to the nation's need for multilingual competence. The lack of foreign language competence in the United States has been decried by legislators as well as by business interests. A *New York Times* editorial, for example, lamented the lack of skilled translators in the country, which forced the President to rely on the host's official translations in foreign capitals (as cited in J. K. Primeau, "The Resurgence of Foreign Language Study," *Modern Language Journal* 63, no. 3 [March, 1979]: 117-122). The extent of the problem was documented by findings of the U.S. General Accounting Office, which decried the lack of linguistic competence among foreign service offices. In addition, Primeau notes how the increasing internationalization of trade has made knowledge of a foreign language, in conjunction with marketable skills, an asset in today's highly competitive market.

14. Hymes, "Introduction," in *Functions of Language in the Classroom*, p. xx.

15. Skutnabb-Kangas, "Multilingualism and the Education of Minority Children."

16. Joshua A. Fishman, "Empirical Explorations of Two Popular Assumptions: Interpolity Perspectives on the Relationship between Linguistic Heterogeneity and Civil Strife and Per-capita National Product," in *Learning in Two Languages: From Conflict to Consensus in the Reorganization of Schools*, edited by Gary Imhoff (New Brunswick, NJ: Transaction Books, 1990), pp. 209-225.

17. Shirley Brice Heath, "English in Our Language History," in *Language in the USA*, edited by Charles A. Ferguson and Shirley Brice Heath (Cambridge: Cambridge University Press, 1981), pp. 6-20.

18. Diego Castellanos, *The Best of Two Worlds: Bilingual-Bicultural Education in the U.S.* (Trenton, NJ: New Jersey State Department of Education, 1983), pp. 1-9.

19. Heath, "English in Our Language History."

20. Arnold H. Leibowitz, *Educational Policy and Political Acceptance: The Imposition of English as the Language of Instruction in American Schools* (Washington, DC: Center for Applied Linguistics, 1971).

21. Heath, "English in Our Language History."

22. Martha Montero-Sieburth and LaCelle Peterson, "Immigrants and Schooling: An Ethnohistorical Account of Political and Family Perspectives in an Urban Community," *Anthropology and Education Quarterly* 22, no. 4 (1991): 300-325.

23. Arnold H. Leibowitz, *Federal Recognition of the Rights of Language Minority Groups* (Rosslyn, VA: National Clearinghouse on Bilingual Education, InterAmerica Research Associates, 1982).

24. Jim Crawford, *Bilingual Education: History, Politics, Theory, and Practice* (Trenton, NJ: Crane, 1989).

25. Josué M. González, "Coming of Age in Bilingual/Bicultural Education: A Historical Perspective," in *Bilingual Multicultural Education and the Professional: From Theory to Practice*, edited by Henry Trueba and Carol Barnett-Mizrahi (Cambridge, MA: Newbury House, 1979), pp. 1-10.

26. Crawford, *Bilingual Education*; James Lyons, "The Past and Future Directions of Federal Bilingual Education Policy," *Annals of the American Academy of Political and Social Science* 508 (March, 1990): 66.

27. Joel Perlmann, "Historical Legacies: 1840-1920," *Annals of the American Academy of Political and Social Science* 508 (March, 1990): 27-37.

28. Ibid., p. 29.

29. Thomas P. Carter, *Mexican Americans in School: A History of Education Neglect* (New York: College Entrance Examination Board, 1970).

30. For an analysis of legislation regarding language rights see Arnold H. Leibowitz, *Federal Recognition of the Rights of Language Minority Groups* (Rosslyn, VA: National Clearinghouse on Bilingual Education, InterAmerica Research Associates, 1982).

31. *Lau v. Nichols*, 94 S.Ct. 787, 1974.

32. Walter G. Secada, "Research, Politics, and Bilingual Education," *Annals of the American Academy of Political and Social Science* 508 (March, 1990): 81-106.

33. See James Crawford, ed., *Language Loyalties: A Source Book on the Official English Controversy* (Chicago: University of Chicago Press, 1992).

34. David O. Sears and Leonie Huddy, "Bilingual Education: Symbolic Meaning and Support among Non-Hispanics" (Paper presented at the annual meeting of the American Psychological Association, New York City, 1990).

35. Crawford, *Bilingual Education*.

36. See, for example, Ann Willig, "A Meta-analysis of Selected Studies on the Effectiveness of Bilingual Education," *Review of Educational Research* 55, no. 3 (1985): 269-317; and J. David Ramírez, Sandra D. Yuen, Dena R. Ramey, and David J. Pasta, *Longitudinal Study of Structured English Immersion Strategy, Early-exit, and Late-exit Transitional Bilingual Education Programs for Language Minority Children*, Final Report, vol. 1 (San Mateo, CA: Aguirre International, 1991).

37. Diane August and Eugene García, *Language Minority Education in the United States: Research, Policy, and Practice* (Springfield, IL: Charles C. Thomas, 1990).

38. Several researchers in the U.S. setting have found that even programs which intend to deliver instruction in two languages tend to favor English, the second language, over the children's native language. In fact, researchers have consistently found about three-quarters of class time devoted to English, even in the most evenly "bilingual" programs. See Lily Wong Fillmore, "Effective Language Use in Bilingual Classes," in *Compatibility of the SBIF Features with Research on Instruction for LEP Students*, edited by William Tikunoff (San Francisco: Far West Laboratory for Educational Research and Development, 1983); and Ramírez et al., *Longitudinal Study of Structured English Immersion Strategy, Early-exit, and Late-exit Transitional Bilingual Education Programs for Language Minority Children*.

39. For a review of the position of U.S. English, see Gary Imhoff, "The Position of U.S. English on Bilingual Education," *Annals of the American Academy of Political and Social Science* 508 (March, 1990): 48-61.

40. Sears and Huddy, "Bilingual Education."

41. As of 1990, the ten states with the largest estimated numbers of LM students were California, Texas, New York, Florida, Illinois, New York, Massachusetts, Pennsylvania, Arizona, and Michigan.

42. Dorothy Waggoner, "Linguistic Minorities and Limited-English-Proficient People in the United States: Will We Be Ready to Use the 1990 Census Information?" *Numbers and Needs: Ethnic and Linguistic Minorities in the United States* 1, no. 2 (May-June, 1991): 5.

43. J. Michael O'Malley, *Children's English and Services Study: Language Minority Children with Limited English Proficiency in the United States* (Rosslyn, VA: InterAmerica Research Associates, 1981).

44. Robert E. Barnes, with the assistance of Ann M. Milne, "The Size of the Eligible Language Minority Population," in *Bilingual Education*, edited by Keith A. Baker and Adriana A. DeKanter (Toronto: Lexington Books, 1983).

45. Terrel H. Bell, *The Condition of Bilingual Education in the Nation* (Washington, DC: U.S. Department of Education, 1982); p. 3.

46. Crawford, *Bilingual Education*; Secada, "Research, Politics, and Bilingual Education."

47. Carole Edelsky, "What We Can Learn from Bilingual Children's Writing" (Paper presented at the Annual Meeting of the Teachers of English to Speakers of Other Languages, Los Angeles, CA, 1986); Kenji Hakuta, *Mirror of Language: The Debate on Bilingualism* (New York: Basic Books, 1986).

48. It should be noted that in 1992, under the editorial direction of David C. Berliner, *Educational Researcher* published a special issue on bilingual education edited by Kenji Hakuta and Lucinda Pease-Alvarez. See *Educational Researcher* 21, no. 2 (March, 1992): 4-24.

49. Daniel R. Wagner, "Perspectives on Bilingualism in Children" (Paper presented at the Biennial Meetings of the International Association of Applied Psychology, Munich, West Germany, July, 1978).

50. See, for example, Jim Cummins, "Metalinguistic Development of Children in Bilingual Education Programs: Data from Irish and Canadian Ukrainian-English Programs," in *The Fourth Locus Forum 1977*, edited by M. Paradis (Columbia, SC: Hornbeam, 1978); Edward DeAvila and Sharon Duncan, "Bilingualism and the Metaset," *NABE* Journal 3, no. 2 (1979): 1-20; Kenji Hakuta, "Degree of Bilingualism and Cognitive Ability in Mainland Puerto Rican Children," *Child Development* 58 (1986): 1377-1388; Rafael M. Díaz, "Thought and Two Languages: The Impact of Bilingualism on Cognitive Development," in *Review of Research in Education*, vol. 10, edited by Edward Gordon (Washington, DC: American Educational Research Association, 1983); and Carolyn Kessler and Mary Ellen Quinn, "Language Minority Children's Linguistic and Cognitive Creativity," *Journal of Multilingual and Multicultural Development* 8, nos. 1 and 2 (1987): 173-186.

51. Judith W. Segal, Susan Chipman, and Robert Glaser, *Thinking and Learning Skills*, vol. 1, *Relating Instruction to Research* (Hillsdale, NJ: Erlbaum, 1985); Susan Chipman, Judith W. Segal, and Robert Glaser, eds., *Thinking and Learning Skills*, vol. 2, *Research and Open Questions* (Hillsdale, NJ: Erlbaum, 1985).

52. See, for example, Kessler and Quinn, "Language Minority Children's Linguistic and Cognitive Creativity"; Stephen Díaz, Luis C. Moll, and Hugh Mehan, "Sociocultural Resources in Instruction: A Context-specific Approach," in Bilingual Education Office, California State Department of Education, *Beyond Language: Social and Cultural Factors in Schooling Language Minority Students* (Los Angeles: Evaluation, Dissemination, and Assessment Center, California State University, 1986); Díaz, "Thought and Two Languages."

53. See, for example, Lily Wong Fillmore and Concepción Valadez, "Teaching Bilingual Learners," in *Handbook of Research on Teaching*, 3rd ed., edited by Merlin C. Wittrock (New York: Macmillan, 1986); and Sylvia Larter and Maisy Cheng, *Bilingual Education and Bilingualism: A Review of Research Literature* (Toronto: Toronto Board of Education, 1984).

54. Hakuta, *Mirror of Language*.

55. Ibid., p. 33.

56. G. Richard Tucker and A. D'Anglejan, "Some Thoughts Concerning Bilingual Education Programs," *Modern Language Journal* 55 (1971): 491-493.

57. Elizabeth Peal and Wallace Lambert, "The Relation of Bilingualism to Intelligence," *Psychological Monographs* 76 (1962): 1-23.

58. Ibid.

59. Rafael M. Díaz, "Bilingualism and Cognitive Ability: Theory, Research, and Controversy," in *Children at Risk: Poverty, Minority Status, and Other Issues of Educational Equity*, edited by Andrés Barona and Eugene E. García (Washington, DC: National Association of School Psychologists, 1990).

60. Ibid.

61. Kenji Hakuta and Rafael M. Díaz, "The Relationship between Degree of Bilingualism and Cognitive Ability: A Critical Discussion and Some New Longitudinal Data," in *Children's Language*, vol. 5, edited by Keith E. Nelson (Hillsdale, NJ: Erlbaum, 1985).

62. In his "Thought and Two Languages" Díaz lists a number of studies showing the advantages of bilingualism: in measures of conceptual development, W. W. Liedtke and L. D. Nelson, "Concept Formation and Bilingualism," *Alberta Journal of Educational Research* 14 (1968): 225-232, and B. Bain, "Bilingualism and Cognition: Toward a General Theory," in *Bilingualism, Biculturalism, and Education: Proceedings from the Conference at College Universitaire Saint Jean* (Edmonton: University of Alberta, 1974); in creativity, E. Paul Torrance, Jing-Jyi Wu, John C. Gowan, and Nicholas C. Aliotti, "Creative Functioning of Monolingual and Bilingual Children in Singapore," *Journal of Educational Psychology* 61 (1970): 72-75; in metalinguistic awareness, Cummins, "Metalinguistic Development of Children in Bilingual Education Programs"; in semantic development, Anita D. Ianco-Worrall, "Bilingualism and Cognitive Development," *Child Development* 43 (1972): 1390-1400; and in analytical skills, Sandra Ben-Zeev, "The Influence of Bilingualism on Cognitive Strategy and Cognitive Development," *Child Development* 48 (1977): 1009-1018.

63. Díaz, "Bilingualism and Cognitive Ability."

64. Peal and Lambert, "The Relation of Bilingualism to Intelligence."

65. Lev S. Vygotsky, *Mind in Society: The Development of Higher Psychological Processes* (Cambridge, MA: Harvard University Press, 1978).

66. Hakuta and Díaz, "The Relationship between Degree of Bilingualism and Cognitive Ability."

67. Joshua A. Fishman, "The Social Science Perspective," in *Bilingual Education: Current Perspectives*, vol. 1, *Social Science* (Arlington, VA: Center for Applied Linguistics, 1977), p. 38. Emphasis in the original.

68. Wallace E. Lambert and G. Richard Tucker, *Bilingual Education of Children: The St. Lambert Experiment* (Rowley, MA: Newbury House, 1972).

69. G. Richard Tucker, "Implications for U.S. Bilingual Education: Evidence from Canadian Research," *Focus 2* (Rosslyn, VA: National Clearinghouse for Bilingual Education, 1980), pp. 1-4.

70. Lambert, "Culture and Language as Factors in Learning and Education."

71. Ibid.

72. Kenji Hakuta, Bernardo M. Ferdman, and Rafael M. Díaz, *Bilingualism and Cognitive Development: Three Perspectives and Methodological Implications* (Los Angeles: Center for Language Education and Research, University of California, 1986).

73. Jim Cummins, "Linguistic Interdependence and the Educational Development of Bilingual Children," *Review of Educational Research* 49 (1972): 222-251.

74. Jim Cummins, "Empowering Minority Students: A Framework for Intervention," *Harvard Educational Review* 56, no. 1 (February, 1986): 20.

75. Shirley Brice Heath, *Ways with Words: Ethnography of Communication in Communities and Classrooms* (New York: Cambridge University Press, 1983).

76. Henry T. Trueba, "The Nature and Justification for Ethnographic Research on Bilingual Education," in *Bilingual Multicultural Education and the Professional: From Theory to Practice*, edited by Henry T. Trueba and Carol Barnett-Mizrahi (Cambridge, MA: Newbury House, 1979): 157-160.

77. There are many examples of this type of research, among them: Kathryn H. Au and Joseph Mason, "Social Organizational Factors in Learning to Read: The Balance of Rights Hypothesis," *Reading Research Quarterly* 17, no. 1 (1981): 115-152; Frederick

Erickson and Gerald Mohatt, "Cultural Organization of Participant Structures in Two Classrooms of Indian Students," in *Doing the Ethnography of Schooling*, edited by George D. Spindler (New York: Holt, Rinehart and Winston, 1982); William Labov, "The Logic of Nonstandard English," in *Language and Social Context*, edited by P. P. Giglioli (London: Penguin Books, 1972); Heath, *Ways with Words*; and Susan V. Phillips, "Participant Structures and Communicative Competence: Warm Springs Indian Children in Community and Classrooms," in *Functions of Language in the Classroom*, edited by Courtney B. Cazden, Vera P. John, and Dell Hymes (New York: Teachers College Press, 1972).

78. Díaz, Moll, and Mehan, "Sociocultural Resources in Instruction."

79. Ibid.

80. Ibid.

81. Ibid., p. 199.

82. John Ogbu and María Eugenia Matute-Bianchi, "Understanding Sociocultural Factors: Knowledge, Identity, and School Adjustment," in *Beyond Language: Social and Cultural Factors in Schooling Language Minority Students* (Los Angeles: Evaluation, Dissemination, and Assessment Center, California State University, 1986).

83. Henry T. Trueba, "Culturally Based Explanations of Minority Students' Academic Achievement," *Anthropology and Education Quarterly* 19 (September, 1988): 270-287.

84. See, for example, Díaz, Moll, and Mehan, "Sociocultural Resources in Instruction"; Robert Rueda, "Social and Communicative Aspects of Language Proficiency in Low Achieving Language Minority Students," in *Success or Failure: Language Minority Children at Home and in School*, edited by Henry T. Trueba (New York: Harper and Row, 1987), pp. 185-187; Henry T. Trueba and Concha Delgado-Gaitán, *Learning through Culture* (New York: Praeger, 1988); Luis C. Moll, "Bilingual Classroom Studies and Community Analysis: Some Recent Trends," *Educational Researcher* 21, no. 2 (March, 1992): 20-24. See also the chapter by Vásquez in this volume.

85. Vygotsky, *Mind in Society*.

86. Luis C. Moll and Jim Greenberg, "Creating Zones of Possibilities: Combining Social Contexts for Instruction," in *Vygotsky and Education*, edited by Luis C. Moll (Cambridge, Eng.: Cambridge University Press, 1990); Carlos Vélez-Ibáñez and Jim Greenberg, "Formation and Transformation of Funds of Knowledge among U.S. Mexican Households in the Context of the Borderlands" (Paper presented at the Annual Meeting of the American Anthropological Association, Washington, DC, 1989).

87. Moll, "Bilingual Classroom Studies and Community Analysis."

88. Ibid.

89. Jim Cummins, "Empowering Minority Students," p. 25.

90. Moll, "Bilingual Classroom Studies and Community Analysis."

91. Hakuta, Ferdman, and Díaz, *Bilingualism and Cognitive Development*.

CHAPTER II

Symbols and the Political Context of Bilingual Education in the United States

WALTER G. SECADA AND THEODORA LIGHTFOOT

When some aspect of our American public education is found to be below par, we redouble our efforts to correct the deficiency, but when bilingual education and foreign language education are found to be unsatisfactory, we tend simply to eliminate them.

> Attributed to Joshua Fishman in
> Andersson and Boyer, *Bilingual
> Schooling in the United States*, 1978

Just because you're paranoid doesn't mean they're not out to get you.
> Variant of an anonymous quotation
> Macmillan *Dictionary of Quotations*, 1989

Bilingual education lies at the juncture of not one but two hotly contested political arenas. The first of these arenas involves language, and the second involves education. For example, no one questions that an American variant of English is de facto the official language of this country. But the implications that are drawn from this (Should English become de jure the country's national language, and if it did, what would such an action mean?) are hotly debated.[1]

Likewise, that this country's educational systems serve its children differentially as a function of their social class, language, culture, and gender backgrounds is not questioned.[2] Some have used this fact to support the setting of higher educational standards or new forms of student assessment,[3] while others have used it to argue that current reform efforts may end up by exacerbating extant inequalities.[4]

As one reads analyses of policies regarding bilingual education and the debates about how best to educate this country's growing

---

Walter G. Secada is Associate Professor of Curriculum and Instruction and Senior Researcher in the Wisconsin Center for Education Research at the University of Wisconsin at Madison. Theodora Lightfoot is a doctoral student in Curriculum and Instruction in the School of Education, University of Wisconsin at Madison.

numbers of linguistically diverse children, echoes from debates in these two larger arenas are in evidence. The focus of this chapter is on the symbolic importance of those debates. People often coalesce around issues as much because of their symbolic nature as because of theoretical or practical considerations. In this chapter, we take as given that, in order to understand the political context of bilingual education (that is, how it is situated in the politics of language and education) we must understand the symbols that frame the issues as well as the theoretical and technical debates, and how all of these find their expression in political actions.

In making this point, we do not mean to devalue the importance of any of the three—symbols, theory, or technique. Nor would we want our thinly veiled criticism of how some of these symbols are crafted to be interpreted as meaning that we are recommending that we should try to settle on some universally agreed-upon facts whose neutrality would cut across and thereby transcend these debates. Indeed, what we call facts are highly value laden and bound to theories in ways that we are just beginning to understand.[5] Moreover, any effort to settle upon universally agreed-upon facts is itself a politically contested process where the terms of discourse are themselves highly symbolic. Rather, our position is that to reduce the political context of bilingual education to any single factor, whether it be symbolism, theory, technique, facts, or political action, is to impoverish our understanding of that context.

Furthermore, we have restricted ourselves here mainly to a discussion of the national context—a practice that is consistent with most current analyses of bilingual education policy.[6] In part, this practice is a result of the symbolic importance of federal government actions which set a tone that is followed by states and localities.[7] Beyond the symbolic importance of its actions, the federal government is sometimes the guarantor of a uniform, minimal level of rights—for example, the Supreme Court's decision in 1974 in *Lau v. Nichols*.[8]

Of course, there are regional, state, and local political contexts involving bilingual education. They have always been important and have affected federal policy. Indeed, the dynamic between federal and state policy is complex. And if anything, state and regional contexts are becoming increasingly important. One outcome of the Reagan administration's efforts to scale back the federal government's role in education was to heighten awareness of the importance of states as locations for educational debates.[9] Many legal efforts and policy analyses (for example, those involving school finance, high school graduation requirements, or school reform) have shifted from the federal to the state level.[10] In addition, states have become increasingly important as sites for debates involving language policy.[11] Hopefully in the not too distant future, bilingual education policy analyses will include state and local levels as increasingly important sites for scholarly inquiry.[12]

A Dichotomy

As a heuristic, those engaged in political debates on bilingual education may be divided into cultural pluralists and assimilationists. These two opposing sides have clashed, almost incessantly, since the federal government began to fund bilingual education programs through Title VII of the Elementary and Secondary Education Act (ESEA) as amended in 1968.

CULTURAL AND LINGUISTIC PLURALISM

On the one side are people who hold values of cultural and linguistic pluralism. Historically, they have adopted what Richard Ruiz has referred to as a "language as resource orientation."[13] Cultural pluralists have argued that bilingual education should cultivate children's understanding and appreciation of their dual cultural heritages and develop their language skills to the point of complete literacy in both languages.

Construing language as a resource is based on respecting and developing children's backgrounds and the knowledge with which they enter school. In other words, cultural pluralists would be in accord with curriculum reformers who argue that children come to school possessing a vast reservoir of informal knowledge that should be tapped and developed.[14]

Many who hold cultural pluralist views also argue that bilingual education is an issue of educational equity. That is, schools have failed to fulfill the educational aspirations of those students who can be described by their language backgrounds. What is more, schools have been active in sorting students and thereby stratifying their educational and later-life opportunities along these same characteristics. Hence, it is a matter of simple justice that current efforts seek to redress those historical injustices. Bilingual education is the proposed remedy. This position is similar to the one taken in *Lau v. Nichols*, though the Court did not specify bilingual education as the sole remedy.[15]

While the idea of bilingual education as an issue of equity has some vocal proponents, others feel that this justification for linguistic and cultural pluralism in schools has significant drawbacks. Strict adherence to such a view would entail drawing some distinctions that would make many proponents of cultural pluralism uncomfortable. For example, if one were to justify bilingual education mainly on the basis that it is a remedy for previous denial of educational opportunity, it might be necessary to distinguish between (a) students who had valid claims to denial of educational opportunity either directly or through ancestry and (b) students who could not make such claims (for example, recent immigrants to this country).

The third reason for supporting pluralist goals for bilingual education is socially enlightened self-interest. According to this last view, the United States has vast, rich, and largely untapped linguistic and cultural resources that could stand it in good stead within the world's various market places, for improving cross-national understanding, and for military purposes. In terms that still ring true today, Theodore Andersson and Mildred Boyer argued that:

America's official and unofficial relations with almost every country in the world, involving diplomacy, trade, security, technical assistance, health, education, religion, and the arts, are steadily increasing. The success of these international relations often depends on the bilingual skills and cultural sensitiveness of the American representatives both here and abroad. In our country, as in every important nation, educated bilingualism is an accepted mark of the elite, an international asset.[16]

ASSIMILATIONISM

The view that is contrary to the pluralist position might be termed the assimilationist or monocultural pole. People at this pole hold that the purpose of bilingual education is to get non-English-speaking students into an all-English-speaking environment as soon as possible and to acculturate them to the norms and values of this society. While many of the most outspoken proponents of this movement are from monolingual English-speaking backgrounds,[17] others are from immigrant families.[18] In many ways, these views are part of the historical legacy of the common school which was created in part to Americanize the children of immigrants and people of non-Anglo-European descent such as American Indians and the American-born descendants of the original Spanish conquerors in the Southwest.[19]

According to assimilationist views, children who enter schools with limited English skills may need special services, but they need those services only temporarily until they learn enough English to be transferred into the school's regular all-English program. People who hold assimilationist views may grant that it is desirable for students to maintain their home languages and cultures. They would argue, however, that the development and maintenance of languages other than English are the responsibility of the parents and of voluntary cultural groups rather than of the public schools.[20] Moreover, though this country may need to develop foreign language skills among its students, they would further argue that students who do not speak English—nor read nor write it—cannot afford to try to develop their home languages while simultaneously trying to learn English. The risk in such an effort is that English or even both languages would suffer because the child had tried to do too much. This concern about the ability of children to learn two languages is usually invoked in regard to poor and minority children. Upper-class children are apparently assumed to have the intellectual potential necessary to cope with bilingualism.

Finally, many people who hold assimilationist views would argue that there are issues of equity and social justice on the other side of the coin as well. Since specialized educational services are consuming greater portions of schools' operating budgets and since these are times of diminishing resources, proponents of the assimilationist position also argue that it is unfair to students who are enrolled in the schools' regular programs when bilingual programs support goals beyond the remediation of specific language-based deficiencies.

The Shifting Debates

That there are readily identifiable opposing points of view on bilingual education does not mean that either side is static or that people hold uniformly to all aspects of a single point of view. Instead, these points of view have developed over years of protracted and often contentious debate. These debates have become particularly heated whenever the Bilingual Education Act, which is used to fund the federal program, comes up for reauthorization.[21]

When it was first passed in 1968, the Bilingual Education Act was vague enough that people at either end of the debates could pretty much read into the law what they wanted to.[22] The Act's only requirement was that federally funded programs should be designed to serve economically disadvantaged children; this was consistent with the ESEA's thrust of serving disadvantaged children in general.

People who favored cultural pluralism saw in the original Bilingual Education Act the possibility of developing bilingual competence among all children, even monolingual speakers of English.[23] Initially, there were some disagreements among the pluralists about the role that instruction in English as a second language (ESL) should play in these programs. Some proponents of bilingual education argued that children would transfer their academic skills into English as they acquired that language in everyday life; hence they did not see the need for ESL. Others argued that ESL instruction would accelerate the development of English and also encourage transfer of knowledge across languages.[24] Currently, most proponents of bilingual education would see a role for ESL instruction in the education of children.

Beginning in 1968 and continuing through most of the 1970s, people who favored assimilationist goals for the programs argued that students be moved out of bilingual programs as soon as they were able to get along with minimal support (e.g., ESL) or no support. Hence, they argued that transitional, as opposed to maintenance, bilingual programs should be funded by the government.[25] In the 1980s, some proponents of the assimilationist point of view argued that programs using *only* instruction in English as a second language should be favored over those that use both English and the child's native language. This position is opposed by the professional ESL organization, Teachers of English to Speakers of Other Languages (TESOL). Nonetheless, it has been used to try to drive a wedge between the two professional organizations for people who work with bilingual students—TESOL and the National Association for Bilingual Education (NABE).

By 1988, when the Bilingual Education Act came up for its fifth reauthorization, there had been a shift in both the law and the debate. By this time, during the original Act's twentieth anniversary, the funding law was no longer vague and flexible. Instead, it had become focused primarily on funding transitional bilingual education (TBE) programs. These are the programs that had been promoted by the assimilationist camp during the late 1960s and much of the 1970s. Ironically, in 1988, the proponents of cultural pluralism found themselves arguing to save even that much. At this point, proponents of assimilation had abandoned their earlier support for the TBE model and were arguing instead that the federal government should fund programs that were all in English.[26]

This shift is not without irony: the heirs of the cultural pluralists of 1960s found themselves defending a program that twenty years earlier they would have dismissed almost out of hand as not meeting the standards of cultural pluralism from those times. Yet this shift also symbolically captures how gains in the education of linguistic minorities that had originated during the ferment of the 1960s have been eroded over the past twenty to thirty years.

This erosion of gains is further suggested by two differing accounts of the initial passage of the Bilingual Education Act. According to Andersson and Boyer, the first passage of the Bilingual Education Act was a significant accomplishment, one that was brimming with hope and promise for developing this country's linguistic resources and for promoting cross-ethnic tolerance for diversity.[27] Yet in Stein's more recent telling of that story, the Bilingual Education Act seems to have been an afterthought of the Great Society.[28] According to Stein, the Act was passed by a somewhat distracted Congress that was losing hope in the promises of the War on Poverty and was turning its attention elsewhere on the domestic agenda.

In retrospect, this shift can be traced to a sequence of accommodations that have taken place between the pluralist and assimilationist camps in an effort to pass successive versions of the Bilingual Education Act. During each reauthorization of the funding program, the proponents of assimilationist goals have dictated the terms of the debate, and hence, they have dictated the ultimate terms of the accommodation. Indeed, each accommodation and subsequent passage of the Act has not settled the matter once and for all. Rather, each new law has merely created a new playing field on which proponents of assimilationist goals have continued to press their agendas. Thus, the inevitable result of these accommodations has been an incremental erosion of the gains made by the cultural pluralists in the 1960s. The Seidners have provided an interesting analysis of this phenomenon pursuant to the release of the original Baker and de Kanter report and to the withdrawal by the Reagan administration of rules and regulations that had been promulgated by the Carter administration to fully implement the *Lau* decision.[29]

Some writers have argued that the gains of the 1960s have generally been eroded during the past twenty-five to thirty years.[30] Hence, the losses that have been suffered by proponents of pluralist goals for bilingual education should be seen in two lights. First, those losses have resulted from the consistent attacks on pluralist goals by proponents of assimilationism. Second, these losses are part of the larger pattern of a conservative backlash and of a concerted attack on the social experiments of the 1960s. As a result, the federal government's initial support for progressive programs, which was tepid to begin with, has been replaced by indifference and even hostility.

Symbols and Their Interpretations

Recognizing that positions have changed and evolved over the years, it nonetheless helps to consider the symbols around which they have been formed. Again, we would like to note this is a dynamic process. The very act of drawing adherents to one or another position results in accommodations in that camp. Some points of view and arguments are emphasized or expanded; others are played down or narrowed; and potential oppositions if not outright contradictions among the agendas and beliefs that are held by the diverse members of those groups get silenced.[31]

The manner in which people have coalesced around different positions and how they have framed the subsequent debates has varied depending on whether the arenas of discussion have involved education or language policy. For example, debates about using English-only for voting, publishing official government documents, or other purposes often include the claim that the ability to speak and read English should be prerequisite for participation in this country's democratic and social institutions.[32] More specifically, Kathryn Woolard traced the arguments of the movement in San Francisco which arose in the mid-1980s and which succeeded in eliminating bilingual ballots. One of the arguments made was that voters whose English was limited should not have the right to vote anyway, as "knowledge of English is already required for citizenship which is a prerequisite to vote."[33] On the other hand, many non-English speakers are native-born citizens; and moreover, the knowledge of English needed to vote is different from that needed to become a naturalized citizen.

While this belief may be tacit in debates involving educational policy, it is seldom mentioned, in part because in *Lau v. Nichols* (1974) the Supreme Court explicitly rejected that line of reasoning when applied to the schooling of children. Furthermore, in any discussion concerning schooling there is a strong countervailing belief that schools should educate anyone who enters their doors, without prerequisites. Interestingly, the idea that children should possess certain abilities, skills, knowledge, or dispositions as prerequisites to entering school has found its way back into more general discourse of American educational policy. Such a view can be found in the first National Education Goal: "All children in America will start school *ready to learn.*"[34] We must wonder if proficiency in English will become an indicator of being ready to learn.

Despite such subtleties, at least three complexly intertwined themes have emerged and reemerged over the years vis-à-vis debates about the federal government's funding of bilingual education: (a) the role of the English language in American society; (b) the role of other languages and non-Anglo-European cultures in society and education; and (c) the nature and perception of competence, needs, and oppression in education. The first of these symbols, the English language, has been championed by proponents of assimilationism; and the second, not surprisingly, by proponents of multiculturalism. For example, although many articles about the importance of English have been written by proponents of cultural pluralism, these articles do not generally portray the English language as something that must be protected, and jealously guarded, in the way that proponents of assimilation often do. Similarly, proponents of assimilation rarely if ever extol the benefits to American society of multiculturalism, cultural pluralism, or bilingualism.

Though each side has claimed one of these first two symbols for itself, and seems to have ceded the other, the discourse framed around issues of students' needs—educational, social, and economic—is hotly contested by the two sides. The debates focus on how notions of need are defined and the best means for fulfilling them. This contestation relies in part on the other symbols of language and culture. In addition, it is a discourse that can be made to appeal to the American public's sense of fair play and largesse.

ENGLISH *QUA LINGUA FRANCA*

That English is the *lingua franca* and dominant language in the United States goes without saying. But English and its use are symbols around which adherents of assimilationist positions have tended to coalesce.

We use English to speak among ourselves in everyday life, commerce, the arts, the media, and numerous other venues. Together with shared democratic values and a common American heritage, English is said to be an important force that binds this vast and varied country together. As immigrants enter the mainstream of American society, they are expected to acquire English, to embrace its social and political values, and to accept that heritage. However, while many feel that learning English and understanding the values of the cultural mainstream can coexist with efforts to maintain native languages and cultural heritages,[35] assimilationists feel that acculturation is not automatic, but rather that it is somehow fragile. Hence, the language and culture of the United States (which are usually defined in terms of the Anglo-American group) should be used exclusively in both public schools and other areas of public life to assure national unity. Without acculturation and assimilation, American society would not long be unified and hence it could not stand the continued pressures that are placed on its many institutions by the many people who are admitted through its borders.

Given the de facto importance of English, many people who hold assimilationist views feel that immigrants and others should be helped in its acquisition since English makes accessible to them the range of opportunities that are said to be part of the common American heritage. Usually, they recommend all-English strategies as the favored method for learning English, and they argue that language learning should be accompanied by the renunciation of allegiance to one's former language and cultural values. This loss due to acculturation may be unfortunate, yet it is the price one pays for entry into the mainstream. For example, Richard Rodríguez wrote with great poignancy of how difficult it was for him to give up his native Spanish; but he repeatedly insisted that this sacrifice was a necessary step in his learning of English, developing a public persona, and entering the national mainstream.[36]

Nathan Glazer, a vocal and prominent proponent of assimilationism, has argued that the loss of the "folkish aspects" of one's culture—in other words, native-like command of the language and maintenance of cultural traditions—may be compensated for by the acquisition of resources that enable groups to recreate and maintain their ethnic identities at another level.

One of the interesting findings of ethnic research is that affluence and assimilation have double effects. On the one hand many individuals become distant from their origins, throw themselves with enthusiasm into becoming full "Americans" and change name, language, and religion to forms that are more typical of earlier settlers. On the other hand, however, many use their increased wealth and competence in English to strengthen the ethnic group and its associations. [For example], undoubtedly in 1975 the more folkish aspects of Ukrainian culture have weakened.... This weakening is associated with assimilation and higher income. But now there are chairs for Ukrainian studies at Harvard, supported by Ukrainian students.[37]

In other words, once Ukrainians gave up learning their native language at home, the elites among them were able to accumulate the financial and social resources necessary to study it as a foreign language and foreign culture.

Beyond the positive importance that is given to English as the key which opens the door to participation in American society, there are said to be negative consequences to the alleged diminishing of the role of English in our society. The more pervasive problems of decline in American society, according to this view, can be traced to the dissolution of the glue that binds us—loss of values, multicultural attacks on our common heritage, people's unwillingness to assimilate, and their failure to speak English.[38] In the words of Kathryn Bricker, former executive director of U.S. English:

Language is so much a part of our lives that it can be a great tool either for unity or disunity. And we are getting close to the point where we have a challenge to the common language that we share. . . . We are basically at a crossroads. We can reaffirm our need for a common language, or we can slowly go down the road of division along language lines.[39]

That the United States can have but one language as part of the glue that holds it together is said to be a lesson to be learned from Canada whose two languages (English and French) are linked to its ongoing "problems" involving Quebec, the province where French is an official language. Orlando Patterson pointed to the maintenance of ethnic ties in other countries as a force of disorder and hatred when he warned that movements such as multicultural and bilingual education in the United States are moving this country in the same dangerous direction:

There can be no doubt we are living through a period of the most intense ethnic revival. In all the continents of the earth men and women . . . now struggle with each other in murderous combat as a result of conflicting ethnic loyalties. The disastrous consequences of this revival should be obvious to anyone who reads the newspapers with any regularity. . . . In southern Africa a gang of fanatical ethnic thugs murders the minds and bodies of the native peoples with a cold-blooded efficiency that rivals that of Nazi Germany. In the Middle East, Arab fanaticism and Israeli nationalistic extremism remain at daggers drawn, resulting in the brutal displacement of a whole people. . . . But developments in the United States give the greatest cause for concern. For here, at least, was one part of the world which did seem to offer the best prospect for the universalist ideal. Here, it was hoped, was the one great refuge for all exiles, not only from specific ethnic domination, but from all ethnicities. The universalist ideal is, however, under the most serious attack in the United States, and the tragedy is that the forces combined against it come from both the right and the liberal wings of the American intelligentsia.[40]

Proponents of bilingual education and multiculturalism are being linked to groups which form particularly potent symbols of evil and intolerance for most people—supporters of apartheid in South Africa, Nazis, and terrorists. The symbolic nature of this rhetoric becomes obvious if we contrast that image of bilingualism to one which could be crafted if writers such as Patterson were to refer to countries such as Switzerland and Indonesia where multiple languages and cultures do coexist.

English is also often portrayed as uniquely suited for conveying the values of American democracy whose expression is said to be possible only through English. If one does not speak English, so this line of reasoning goes, one cannot catch the full implications, the beauty, or the fullest expression of those values. Hence, one cannot be fully American without knowing English.[41] A corollary to this argument is the assertion that English and only English can be nonethnic and the property of all. The second corollary is that the maintenance of one's native language, which is assumed to go hand in hand with the failure to learn English, represents the rejection of this common property. Thus to fail to learn English and renounce one's ancestral language is to accept the particularistic and confining life of the ghetto. Patterson asserted that English, *qua* common language, is not really an Anglo-Saxon language, but rather a "child that no longer knows its mother, and cares even less to know her. It has been adapted in a thousand ways to meet the special feelings, moods, and experiences of a thousand groups."[42]

In a 1983 editorial in the San Francisco *Examiner*, Guy Wright argued that learning English is the only remedy for escaping life as a semi-citizen: "The individual who fails to learn English is condemned to semi-citizenship, condemned to low pay, condemned to remain in the ghetto."[43] And Quentin Kopp, a San Francisco County Supervisor, was quoted in the *Bay Area Reporter, Political Supplement*, as saying that "without an impetus to learn English it is far too easy to become sequestered in a language prison."[44]

By linking English to the very fabric of American society, proponents of assimilation are able to portray any position that does not start by acknowledging the importance of English as somehow un-American. Anyone favoring a cultural pluralist position is forced to begin by agreeing with some of these basic premises, for example, the importance or beauty of English. How can anyone downplay the importance of the very language that he or she is using?

This device also makes possible the tactic of highlighting different features of the assimilationist position, depending on the group that is making the pitch and on its audience.[45] To people of non-English-speaking backgrounds, English is portrayed as the key to entry into the American mainstream; but to people who oppose such opportunity, English can be presented as a prerequisite whose mastery does not guarantee such entry but whose incomplete mastery does, nonetheless, legitimate the withholding of rights and services as well as the taking of more punitive actions. To people in the sciences and technological fields, English is portrayed as the universal language whose precision makes possible the advances in these fields; and to others, its fragile beauty becomes the reason that it needs to be protected.

One point of contention, even within the assimilationist pole, revolves around whether or not English should become the official language of the United States, as it is in many states.[46] Arguments in favor include the perceived need to protect English from (further) erosion and the fact that, since English already has de facto status as the language of this country, its status should be confirmed as a matter of law. While such arguments might appear reasonable on the surface, closer examination reveals several logical as well as practical flaws. For example, the contradictory nature of these two points is often overlooked: Why should we protect something that is already so strong that it is the country's national language?

Many adherents of the English language amendment, as this proposition is called, argue that the distinction between de facto and de jure is so slight that this step is a minor one. Of course, following their logic one could again wonder why they are putting so much energy into bringing about a change which they portray as so minor and innocuous. Indeed, and contrary to what proponents of the English language amendment seem to believe, the distinction between de facto and de jure is a crucial one. One need only consider an example with negative connotations—the segregation of school children.

Many African-American children and increasing numbers of Hispanic children attend schools that are de facto but not necessarily de jure segregated. Though in the 1970s, then Justice William Douglas urged his colleagues on the Supreme Court to blur this distinction and to create remedies for all cases of school segregation,[47] the Court was unwilling to do so—much to the relief of many school districts and to the chagrin of proponents of school desegregation. Evidence of government action to promote segregation (that is, evidence of de jure segregation) is still required for desegregation cases. Similarly, though English is de facto the language of the United States, the case must be built that government action is necessary.

One of the main reasons for opposing this amendment is that no one knows precisely what it would mean to make English the official language of this country. Under the guise of taking steps to protect the status of English, such an amendment might be used to require that people speak English as a prerequisite for having access to their rights as citizens and residents of this country. It would be surreal, to say nothing of ironic, if an action that is portrayed as opening doors to immigrants and limited English speakers instead caused such people to lose access to their rights as citizens while English-speaking criminals kept theirs. After all, there are many native-born Americans who enter school not speaking English; and there are many English speaking adults who are illiterate.

On the other hand, if an English language amendment turned out to be benign and in no way changed the status of Americans from diverse linguistic backgrounds, then the effort put into its passage would still represent a tremendous waste of time and resources. Beyond the symbolism, why pass such a law? Laws should not be used for symbolic purposes and proponents of the English language amendment have simply not built a compelling case for its necessity.

NON-ENGLISH LANGUAGES AND CULTURAL PLURALISM

Just as the English language serves as a symbol around which proponents of assimilation can coalesce and craft a core set of arguments, it is possible to identify a finite number of salient points that provide symbolic coherence for people who favor linguistic diversity and cultural pluralism. If the arguments of the former group are politically ascendant at the moment, those of the latter group may prove to be ultimately more convincing.

People are linked to this country through their homes, neighborhoods, and cultures. The values and resources found in those diverse cultures and languages, although sometimes unrecognized, are truly incredible. Such statements, again, go without saying. Yet the question remains, What should we do about this diversity?

For many people who reject assimilationist arguments, this country's cultural and linguistic diversity is not a threat to national unity, but instead a valuable resource that could help us to understand and work with people from other countries and also to compete with them in the world marketplace. People who support the nurturance and development of these resources often coalesce around multilingual and multicultural views. For example, the founders of CODOFIL, a bilingual French/English program in Louisiana, saw that state's existing bilingual heritage as a potential economic and cultural benefit given the status of French as an important language of world communication. They decided that instead of restricting bilingual education to the teaching of English to children of French-speaking backgrounds, Louisianans could instead use and expand their indigenous language traditions to make their state into a "window on the French-speaking world."[48]

Multiculturalism also preaches tolerance, that is, that we must learn to live together for the good of this diverse society.[49] Living together entails tolerance for the many languages that are spoken and the recognition of their speakers' ethnic backgrounds and heritages. As we learn to live together, we will be better positioned to live peacefully in the world community, not just because we will have better understanding of the world's diversity, but also because we will set an example for the rest of the world to emulate. Tolerance and example setting have had broad appeal in this country's history.

Moreover, given that this country will remain multilingual and multicultural because of new immigration into the foreseeable future—even if bilingual people learned English and acculturated rapidly—the types of social division and ethnic strife feared by Patterson would best be prevented not by strong pressure to assimilate, but instead by the creation of a society that was increasingly tolerant of and open to diversity.[50]

Beyond the development of resources and tolerance, multiculturalism celebrates, as an end in itself, the cultural mosaic that is this country (much as proponents of assimilation celebrate the English language for the same reason). That celebration includes acknowledging the multiplicity of contributions to this society's development from all the peoples who have come into it. In general, this view of culture includes the diverse viewpoints of all Americans, whatever their languages and ethnicity. In the words of Suzanne Ramos, a lawyer for the Mexican-American legal defense fund: "Rather than see the United States as a melting pot, we like to think of it as a salad bowl, with equal recognition for everyone."[51]

Multiculturalism can also be linked to worthwhile educational practice. Good pedagogical practice requires that we understand the children in our classrooms as well as we can. Not only should our teaching draw upon children's prior knowledge, as is recommended by people in current curriculum reform efforts; we should also recognize that such knowledge is intimately woven into our students' ethnic backgrounds and their at-home experiences. Just as schools are meant to develop students' academic and physical knowledge and skills, so too should they develop students' cultural knowledge and native language skills as worthwhile resources in and of themselves. The development of all these sources of student knowledge provides the additional benefit that students become linked more closely to their homes, extended families, and backgrounds. In fact, many outstandingly successful academic programs designed for children from diverse linguistic and cultural backgrounds incorporate strong and explicit ties to students' home culture and group ties.[52]

There are said to be negative aspects in the failure to enhance multiculturalism through schooling. (This parallels the negative consequences that are said to result from the diminished role of English in our society.) Pressure for assimilation at the expense of one's home culture forces young children to make painful personal choices which often affect their self-esteem and, in some cases, their ability to learn English and other academic skills. Grosjean quoted many bilingual and formerly bilingual people who recounted the pain that they experienced when forced to trade their home language for a school language.[53] One of these individuals recalled that his school felt "cold" and like a "boot camp." In other words, school was hardly a safe and nurturing environment for learning. In a telling counterpoint to Rodríguez's insistence that the price to pay for assimilation is necessary, the loss experienced by Grosjean's informants seems needlessly cruel:

As a child my life seemed strange and confusing. At home, which meant brothers, parents, an aunt, and an uncle . . . and grandparents, the language was Spanish, and the culture was distinctly Mexican. At school the language was a cold and distant way of being treated—like the re-molding process of an army boot camp. . . . When my parents first told me I had to learn English in order to survive in this country, the impact of the statement had little immediate effect. But later, as a young person, I began to associate my feelings of alienation with the need to identify with a group, a cultural group. My capacity to use Spanish had dwindled to nothing. Identification with the dominant group seemed impossible, but recreating my group sense seemed equally impossible without the help of Spanish. . . . My years without Spanish now appear tragic. How can I ever make up that loss? I barely communicated with my grandparents. They died, in fact, before I re-learned Spanish.[54]

The pain of this choice and loss extends beyond the personal. Ferdman has argued that the acquisition of literacy becomes easier if school knowledge and reading are consonant with a child's sense of group identity, and more difficult if not.[55] Beebe and Giles have noted that if language learning is perceived as a *subtractive process* which involves betrayal of one's own cultural group, it becomes difficult to acquire a high level of proficiency in that language.[56]

Multiculturalism and bilingualism can also be thought of as forms of social capital whose development provides students with a much needed safety net. Unfortunately, the promise of economic opportunity will not materialize for many students from linguistically diverse backgrounds.[57] Hence, the development of their ethnic backgrounds and home language competence are necessary to keep students linked to their homes and neighborhoods. Those links will empower students with access to social resources and cultural capital found in their extended families and local communities. Those resources will enable these students to survive in the larger society. Moreover, for students who do succeed in the larger society, their multicultural and dual language competence will help them to serve as links between their ethnic groups and that larger society.

Just as English can be symbolically construed to have an edge, so too are there more assertive and oppositional versions of pluralism and multiculturalism. According to some pluralists, the knowledge that schools communicate to their students and the canons of the academic disciplines themselves are based, in part, on *hiding* the contributions of this country's and the world's diverse peoples and of their languages. Multiculturalism provides a means for reclaiming those contributions, for setting the historical record straight, and for expanding the canons to include voices and perspectives that have been silenced. As the New York State Minority Task Force argued:

with a multicultural curriculum, children [of other than European backgrounds will] have higher self-esteem and self-respect, while children from European cultures will have a less arrogant perspective of being part of the group that has done it all.[58]

For example, history is often presented in schools as a linear progression of events whose flow is inevitable and is governed by natural laws. Such accounts hide the uncertain nature of historical events and render conflicts as aberrations that were dealt with quickly and efficiently by the victors, thereby granting legitimacy to their victories. This view of history does not help many students from culturally diverse backgrounds to understand that their own situations are the results of historical events that could have turned out differently. Moreover, this presentation of history does not help students to understand present-day conflicts.

The development and maintenance of non-English languages can also become a matter of cultural right and of opposition to forces that would take away people's cultural heritages and backgrounds. Not just among Hispanics but also among many American Indians, the reclamation of languages has become a matter of cultural pride in rebuilding a heritage that was forcibly taken away from them and their ancestors.

Another oppositional use of multiculturalism finds its roots in the purported trade-off between people's home cultures and languages and their access to opportunity. The promise of acculturation is that, in return, people who abandon their ethnic heritage and language are given a fair opportunity to participate in the country's social and economic systems. Yet the history of many ethnic groups demonstrates unfulfilled promises. Too many people accepted the premises of this trade-off and gave up their language and culture, but found no such opportunity. The trade was uneven: give up your language and culture and you *might* have opportunity. Practical wisdom dictates against its acceptance. Communal anger and ways of coping in the larger society have been developed in response to prior generations being duped by this promise. That anger and those coping strategies are transmitted to younger generations and they make it even more difficult for students who would like to believe this promise to act accordingly.

As John Ogbu and his associates have pointed out, many students from diverse cultural backgrounds resist academic success when it is perceived as "acting white" and weakening group identity, and if they feel that their group is trapped in a caste-like status from which there is little possibility of economic advancement.[59] School success can seem to such young people like a corrupt bargain in which they are asked to trade their ethnic solidarity for assimilation into a society which discriminates against them. Ironically, Matute-Bianchi points out that the very students who resist what they perceive as the acculturating pressures of school knowledge say, when asked, that they have high academic aspirations which they do not act upon in the context of our presently monolingual and monocultural schools. One wonders what the achievements of such students would be if their energies were liberated by an environment in which they no longer needed to trade ethnicity for school learning.

Finally, some proponents of multiculturalism point out that only in a society in which students are treated in a way which respects their diversity can we achieve equity:

Another way to emphasize equal opportunity . . . is to emphasize the differences among people—in particular, those differences rooted in culture and therefore in equal opportunity. . . . To ignore group membership is to deny an important part of the individual. Indeed, treating everyone the same can result in . . . inequities.[60]

As can be seen, multiculturalism from the perspective of dual language maintenance and pluralism is itself no less complexly woven as a symbolic construct than is English. Different people see in it different things. Some would highlight what, to the mainstream society, are its more acceptable aspects of tolerance, celebration of diversity, and the development of human resources. Others would highlight its challenging of what passes for school knowledge and academic canons, and the development of alternative resources because of the lack of true opportunity for full participation in this society. These oppositional features get highlighted by proponents of assimilation when they attack multiculturalism. At the same time, they mute the counterargument that these oppositions are a historical response to the broken promises of prior generations.

Many debates remain within the field of multiculturalism as it is supported by proponents of pluralism in bilingual education. For example, cultures are often celebrated without explicitly acknowledging their own problematic natures. Thus, how the traditional stratification of gender roles and the subsequent socialization of males and females to take on those roles can lead to conflicts with feminist conceptions for promoting gender equity are not explored. In addition, students from diverse backgrounds are often written about as if they were being socialized according to traditional, non-American cultures without acknowledging that the students' home lives and patterns of socialization have been deeply affected by their families' lives in the United States and by their networks of same-age relatives and friends who have, in fact, accepted many of the artifacts of mainstream American culture.

NEEDS VERSUS COMPETENCE

The third major area around which people have coalesced involves the perception and the reality of needs. When issues are cast in terms of student needs, it becomes possible to appeal to people's sense of good will and largesse. By casting an issue in terms of need, proponents of services for those in need have been able to sidestep questions of whether or not such special services are equitable. If someone is somehow deprived, has a special need, or in some sense is and has less than the norm, then one can appeal to people's sense of generosity while not threatening their sense of fair play—that everyone should have the same and be treated equally. For example, in 1967, when Senator Ralph Yarbrough of Texas appealed to his colleagues to expand the ESEA to include programs for Hispanic children, he asked his colleagues to:

Imagine the situation that confronts a certain youngster in my part of the country. A youngster spends his formative years in the warm, friendly environment of his family and friends—an environment in which Spanish is spoken. At age 5 or 6 he is taken to school. What a profound shock he encounters the first day, when there he is made to know in no uncertain terms that he may speak no Spanish. He must speak English, a language which he scarcely knows, both in the classroom and on the playground. If he is caught speaking Spanish, he will be punished.[61]

Obviously such a situation requires fixing. But, this vignette leaves open two questions: how needs get defined and where they are located. Was the problem that this child spoke no English upon entering school or that he was punished for speaking Spanish? Even if the school allowed the child to speak Spanish, would the problem of language discontinuity be the child's (that is, he still needs to learn English) or the school's (that is, the school needs to provide instruction in Spanish)?

The issue of how needs get defined has never really been resolved. For example, the ESEA of 1965, which was a part of President Lyndon Johnson's War on Poverty, was passed in partial response to the results of reports like the Coleman report, which documented that schools worked differentially based on the social class backgrounds of their students.[62] But rather than focusing on the schools, the programs located the problem within the children that they were intended to serve. A cornerstone of the ESEA was the belief that poor children were growing up in environments that lacked rich resources and experiences as compared to their more economically advantaged peers. Hence, these children were thought to enter school lacking intellectual and social competence because they were culturally deprived. Or, as the song of Officer Krumpke in the musical *West Side Story* put it:

"I'm depraved on account of I'm deprived!" (This song provides an interesting historical record of what were believed to be sources of young adolescents' social ills. All of them are located within the individual.)

The debate over how needs are defined and located is crucial since these items determine the types of programs that get funded. When crafting a discourse of need, there are strong pressures that should be defined so as not to characterize those in need as beyond all hope, while simultaneously their needs must be the most important and most pressing among the needs of competing interest groups.

Very often, people who support assimilationist views define needs in terms of the English language—its mastery by bilingual children and its promotion in our society. People who support pluralist views agree that needs are partly located in children, but that they are more expansive. Children must master English; but academic knowledge and skills, linkages to children's home cultures, and mastery of their native languages also need developing. Moreover, proponents of multiculturalism argue that schools must change and adapt to their diverse populations. Recently, many who support assimilationist views have adopted the view that schools need improvement, but those changes are linked more to efforts based on the rhetoric of excellence in education as found in *America 2000*[63] than to arguments about increasing the match between students' backgrounds and the organizations that are meant to educate them.

One major difficulty with framing the discourse entirely around notions of need, however, is that needs get linked almost exclusively to deficiencies—either in the child or in the school. The result is a calculus of deficiencies as proponents of various categorical programs, including those who support assimilationist goals, compete for smaller and smaller pools of money. Since it is very difficult to argue that a child's native language is a deficiency, arguments based solely on need *qua* deficiency tend to focus on bilingual children's English language and academic skills. Thus children whose first language is not English are labeled as "Limited English Proficient" (LEP). These children get defined, not by what they know, but rather by what they do not know and cannot do. In fashioning an argument based on need, people end up characterizing bilingual children as fundamentally deficient.

This stripped-down definition of need plays right into the hands of people who propose assimilation. There is a superficial agreement about need: both groups agree that bilingual children are deficient in their English language and academic skills. Hence, debates between assimilationists and cultural pluralists seem to be semantic quibbles rather than reflecting deeply oppositional points of view. In such a context, it becomes relatively easy to accept those views that seem likely to find the most widespread agreement and that will offend the fewest people. When needs get defined in terms of deficiencies, the assimilationist position provides the most direct, simplest, and easiest-to-accept political analysis. This agreement between pluralism and assimilation—that bilingual children's educational needs are at the core based on deficiencies—is why the assimilationist position has been able to dictate the terms of the debate and the subsequent accommodations in federal policy.

The recent push for educational reform[64] and developing conceptions of children as possessing vast stores of informal knowledge[65] provide another way of shaping the discourse. In that case, the argument can be cast in terms of the needs of American society for the coming century. Our society's deficiencies can be met by developing the knowledge of its children to their fullest. To build such a case, it will be necessary to draw explicit links between the goals of the education reform movement and those of bilingual education, and to overcome objections that bilingual children's needs (that is, their deficiencies) should take precedence over other goals (that is, society's deficiencies).

An Example of Symbols in Research on
Bilingual Education

As we have argued above, the fact that bilingual children's educational needs are characterized as deficiencies located in the children themselves has resulted in the superficial appearance of agreement between the two poles of the debate. Politicians are quick to forge an accommodation around any agreement, no matter how superficial. What is more, that agreement has permeated evaluation research in bilingual education.

In an earlier article, one of us argued that evaluation research in bilingual education played a major role in the political process by which the Bilingual Education Act was passed in 1988.[66] Through its subordination to the purposes of people who argued for the assimilationist pole, research was used to fashion the argument that transitional bilingual education was not working, that the federal government was mandating a single method, and that local choice in program design should be paramount.

However, that research itself represents an accommodation that was derived from need defined as deficiency. A study by the American Institutes for Research was the first large-scale evaluation of bilingual education programs.[67] Though at the time of this study, the Bilingual Education Act was vague as to the kinds of programs that it would support, the authors argued that the intent of Congress had been to develop English language skills among Spanish-speaking children. Later, in their narrative review of bilingual education evaluations, Keith Baker and Adriana de Kanter specifically rejected the use of data that had been gathered through students' native languages[68] and instead focused solely on achievement data gathered in English. More recently, in the Ramírez et al. study, achievement data were gathered in Spanish, but the federal government funded analyses only of the English language data.[69] Arguably, these are the three major studies funded by the federal government on bilingual education. They have received the lion's share of press coverage. And in all three studies, even those where native language achievement data were available, the research questions were explicitly narrowed to focus on the remediation of students' perceived deficiencies, that is, on the common understanding of need.

Other writers, especially those who support multicultural goals, have tended to craft research on bilingual education more broadly. Christina Bratt Paulston, for instance, has argued that, beyond achievement, bilingual education needs to be studied in terms of more expansive indicators such as reduced absenteeism, increased gradua- tion rates, fewer social problems among adolescents, and enhanced employment.[70] In her meta analysis of bilingual education evaluation research Ann Willig specifically brought back nonnative language indicators of academic success and also indicators of affect.[71]

Concluding Comments

Our purpose has been to lay out, in rather broad strokes, the sym- bolic nature of the political debates in bilingual education. We have presented those debates in terms of two broadly construed points of view on bilingual education—cultural pluralism and assimilation. These positions are constantly evolving and people are drawn to them for different reasons. Moreover, these debates become even more complex since they are acted out in two arenas, language and education, each having its own political processes and ways of crafting symbols.

In this chapter, we also have discussed how three symbols—English, multiculturalism, and need—are socially constructed to draw adherents. One specific symbol, that of need, has been constantly fought over by adherents of the two poles. Yet need has been defined in terms of deficiencies that get located within bilingual students. This has resulted in the superficial appearance of agreement between the two sides, making it easier for politicians to forge the accommodations that could result in the passage of funding for bilingual education programs. The terms of the discourse and the subsequent accommodation, however, have been cast so as to be more closely aligned to the assimilationist point of view. Moreover, much evaluation research in bilingual education, especially that which receives press coverage, has also reflected that accommodation.

Missing from this chapter is a discussion of how relations of power and hegemony are acted out among different groups who engage in these debates. Authors such as Michael Apple have argued that the ascendancy of the new right was based on an economic and military crisis in American society that resulted in fracturing the alliances that had given rise to the progressive movements of the 1960s.[72] The subsequent realignment led to the creation of a new, if unstable, majority who are more concerned with their property rights than with people's rights in this society. The dynamic relationship among these crises, the fragmentation of old alliances, the creation of new ones, and how symbolic politics has been enacted in the case of bilingual education merit further study.

We thank Carol Compton, Nancy Hornberger, Michael Olnek, Christine Sleeter, and the editors for their comments on an early draft of this chapter.

NOTES

1. Theodore Andersson and Mildred Boyer, *Bilingual Schooling in the United States*, 2nd ed. (Austin, TX: National Educational Laboratory, 1978); Dennis Baron, *The English-only Question: An Official Language for Americans?* (New Haven: Yale University Press, 1990); James Crawford, *Bilingual Education: History, Politics, Theory, and Practice* (Trenton, NJ: Crane Publishing Co., 1989); James Crawford, ed., *Language Loyalties: A Source Book on the Official English Controversy* (Chicago: University of Chicago Press, 1992); Joshua Fishman, "Language Maintenance in a Supra-ethnic Age: Summary and Conclusions," in *Bilingual Schooling in the United States: A Sourcebook for Educational Personnel*, edited by Francesco Cordasco (New York: McGraw-Hill, 1976), pp. 43-60; idem, *Language and Ethnicity: In Minority Sociolinguistic Perspective* (Clevedon, England: Multilingual Matters, 1989); Kenji Hakuta, *Mirror of Language: The Debate on Bilingualism* (New York: Basic Books, 1986); Nancy H. Hornberger, "Bilingual Education and English-only: A Language-planning Framework," *Annals of the American Academy of Political and Social Science* 508 (1990):

12-26; Gary Imhoff, "The Position of U.S. English on Bilingual Education," *Annals of the American Academy of Political and Social Science* 508 (1990): 48-61; Arturo Madrid, "Official English: A False Policy Issue," *Annals of the American Academy of Political and Social Science* 508 (1990): 62-65.

2. James S. Coleman, Ernest Q. Campbell, Carol J. Hobson, James McPartland, Alexander M. Mood, Frederic D. Weinfeld, and Robert L. York, *Equality of Educational Opportunity* (Washington, DC: U.S. Government Printing Office, 1966), ERIC ED 012 275; Council of Chief State School Officers, Resource Center on Educational Equity, *School Success for Limited English Proficient Students: The Challenge and State Response* (Washington, DC: The Council, 1990); Jonathan Kozol, *Savage Inequalities: Children in America's Schools* (New York: Crown, 1991); Quality Education for Minorities Project, *Education That Works: An Action Plan for the Education of Minorities* (Cambridge, MA: Massachusetts Institute of Technology, 1990); Walter G. Secada, "Agenda Setting, Enlightened Self-interest, and Equity in Mathematics Education," *Peabody Journal of Education* 66, no. 2 (1991): 22-56; idem, "Race, Ethnicity, Social Class, Language, and Achievement in Mathematics," in *Handbook of Research on Mathematics Teaching and Learning*, edited by Douglas Grouws (New York: Macmillan, 1992), pp. 623-660.

3. National Council on Education Standards and Testing, *Raising Standards for American Education: A Report to Congress, the Secretary of Education, the National Education Goals Panel, and the American People* (Washington, DC: U.S. Government Printing Office, 1992); U.S. Department of Education, *America 2000: An Education Strategy* (Washington, DC: The Department, 1991).

4. Secada, "Agenda Setting, Enlightened Self-interest, and Equity in Mathematics Education"; idem, "Race, Ethnicity, Social Class, Language, and Achievement in Mathematics."

5. Thomas S. Kuhn, *The Nature of Scientific Revolutions*, 2nd ed. (Chicago: University of Chicago Press, 1970); Imre Lakatos, *Proofs and Refutations: The Logic of Mathematical Discovery* (New York: Cambridge University Press, 1976); Charles E. Lindblom and David K. Cohen, *Usable Knowledge: Social Science and Social Problem Solving* (New Haven: Yale University Press, 1979).

6. Keith A. Baker and Adriana A. de Kanter, "Federal Policy and the Effectiveness of Bilingual Education," in *Bilingual Education: A Reappraisal of Federal Policy*, edited by Keith A. Baker and Adriana A. de Kanter (Lexington, MA: Lexington Books, 1983), pp. 33-86; Crawford, *Bilingual Education*; idem, *Language Loyalties*; Noel Epstein, *Language, Ethnicity, and the Schools: Policy Alternatives for Bilingual-Bicultural Education* (Washington, DC: Institute for Educational Leadership, George Washington University, 1977); U.S. Government Accounting Office, *Bilingual Education: A New Look at the Research Evidence*, Briefing report to the Chairman, Committee on Education and Labor, House of Representatives (Washington, DC: Government Accounting Office, 1987); Hakuta, *Mirror of Language*; Hornberger, "Bilingual Education and English-only"; James J. Lyons, "The Past and Future Directions of Federal Bilingual-Education Policy," *Annals of the American Academy of Political and Social Science* 508 (1990): 66-81; Mary McGroarty, "The Societal Context of Bilingual Education," *Educational Researcher* 21, no. 2 (1992): 7-9, 24; Frederick Mulhauser, "Reviewing Bilingual-Education Research for Congress," *Annals of the American Academy of Political and Social Science* 508 (1990): 107-118; Rosalie Porter, *Forked Tongue: The Politics of Bilingual Education* (New York: Basic Books, 1990); Walter G. Secada, "Research, Politics, and Bilingual Education," *Annals of the American Academy of Political and Social Science* 508 (1990): 81-106; Stanley S. Seidner and Maria S. Seidner, "In the Wake of Conservative Reaction: An Analysis," in *Theory, Technology, and Public Policy on Bilingual Education*, edited by Reynaldo V. Padilla (Washington, DC: National Clearinghouse for Bilingual Education, 1983); Colman B. Stein, Jr., *Sink or Swim: The Politics of Bilingual Education* (New York: Praeger, 1986).

7. Crawford, *Bilingual Education*; Seidner and Seidner, "In the Wake of Conservative Reaction."

8. Arnold H. Leibowitz, *Federal Recognition of the Rights of Minority Language Groups* (Washington, DC: National Clearinghouse for Bilingual Education, 1982).

9. David L. Clark and Terry A. Astuto, "The Significance and Permanence of Changes in Federal Educational Policy," *Educational Researcher* 18, no. 8 (1986): 4-13.

10. William H. Clune, "New Answers to Six Hard Questions from *Rodríguez*: Ending Separation of School Finance and Educational Policy by Bridging the Gap between Wrong and Remedy," *Connecticut Law Review*, in press; William H. Clune, Paula A. White, Shirley Sun, and Janice H. Patterson, *Changes in High School Course Taking, 1982-88: A Study of Transcript Data from Selected Schools and States* (New Brunswick, NJ: Consortium for Policy Research in Education, Eagleton Institute of Politics, Rutgers University, 1991); Alan R. Odden and Lawrence O. Picus, *School Finance: A Policy Perspective* (New York: McGraw-Hill, 1992).

11. Baron, *The English-only Question.*

12. For examples, see Marcelo Medina and Donald M. Sacken, "Passing Arizona's Bilingual Education Legislation," *Educational Policy* 2, no. 3 (1988): 287-305; Kathryn Woolard, "Sentences in the Language Prison: The Rhetorical Structuring of an American Language Policy Debate" (Unpublished manuscript [1988] available from the author).

13. Richard Ruiz, "Orientations in Language Planning," *NABE Journal* 8, no. 2 (1984): 15-34.

14. See, for example, Thomas P. Carpenter, "Conceptual Knowledge as a Foundation for Procedural Knowledge: Implications from Research on the Initial Learning of Arithmetic," in *Conceptual and Procedural Knowledge: The Case of Mathematics*, edited by James Hiebert (Hillsdale, NJ: Erlbaum, 1986), pp. 113-32; Barbara Means, Carole Chelemer, and Michael S. Knapp, eds., *Teaching Advanced Skills to At-risk Students: Views from Research and Practice* (San Francisco: Jossey Bass, 1991).

15. United States Supreme Court, *Lau v. Nichols*, 414 U.S. 563ff, 1974.

16. Andersson and Boyer, *Bilingual Schooling in the United States*, p. 55.

17. Thomas Bethel, "Against Bilingual Education: Why Johnny Can't Speak English," *Harper's Magazine* 258 (February, 1979): 30-33; Epstein, *Language, Ethnicity, and the Schools*; Nathan Glazer, *Affirmative Discrimination* (New York: Basic Books, 1975).

18. Porter, *Forked Tongue*; Richard Rodríguez, *Hunger of Memory: The Education of Richard Rodríguez*. (New York: Bantam, 1982).

19. Andersson and Boyer, *Bilingual Schooling in the United States*; Baron, *The English-only Question*; Joel Perlmann, "Understanding Legacies: 1840-1920," *Annals of the American Academy of Political and Social Science* 508 (1990): 27-37; Stein, *Sink or Swim*; Francesco Cordasco, "The Children of Immigrants in the Schools: Historical Analogues of Educational Deprivation," in *Bilingual Schooling in the United States: A Sourcebook for Educational Personnel*, edited by Francesco Cordasco (McGraw-Hill, 1976), pp. 23-36.

20. Glazer, *Affirmative Discrimination.*

21. See, for example, Secada, "Research, Politics, and Bilingual Education."

22. Andersson and Boyer, *Bilingual Schooling in the United States.*

23. Ibid. See also, Fishman, "Language Maintenance in a Supra-Ethnic Age"; Gary D. Keller and Karen S. van Hooft, "A Chronology of Bilingualism and Bilingual Education in the United States," in *Bilingual Education for Hispanic Students in the United States*, edited by Joshua Fishman and Gary D. Keller (New York: Teachers College

Press, 1982), pp. 3-22; William F. Mackey and Von Nieda Beebe, *Bilingual Schools for a Bicultural Community: Miami's Adaptation to the Cuban Refugees* (Rowley, MA: Newbury House, 1977).

24. James E. Alatis, "The Compatability of TESOL and Bilingual Education," in *New Directions in Second Language Learning, Teaching, and Bilingual Education*, edited by Marina K. Burt and Heidi C. Dulay (Washington, DC: TESOL, 1975), pp. 3-14; Arturo Peña, "Cooperation between Bilingual Education and TESOL: Our Children's Legacy," in *New Directions in Second Language Learning, Teaching, and Bilingual Education*, edited by Marina K. Burt and Heidi C. Dulay (Washington, DC: TESOL, 1975), pp. 15-17.

25. Bethel, "Against Bilingual Education"; Epstein, *Language, Ethnicity, and the Schools*; Orlando Patterson, *Ethnic Chauvinism: The Reactionary Impulse* (New York: Stein and Day, 1977).

26. Lyons, "The Past and Future Directions of Federal Bilingual-Education Policy"; Mulhauser, "Reviewing Bilingual-Education Research for Congress"; Secada, "Research, Politics, and Bilingual Education."

27. Andersson and Boyer, *Bilingual Schooling in the United States.*

28. Stein, *Sink or Swim.*

29. Seidner and Seidner, "In the Wake of Conservative Reaction."

30. See, for example, Michael Apple, "How Equality Has Been Redefined in the Conservative Restoration," in *Equity in Education*, edited by Walter G. Secada (Basingstoke, Great Britain: Falmer, 1989), pp. 7-25.

31. For a general discussion of how this occurs in education, see Apple, "How Equality Has Been Redefined in the Conservative Restoration." For a discussion based on San Francisco's English Language Amendment, also known as Proposition 0, see Woolard, "Sentences in the Language Prison."

32. Crawford, *Language Loyalties*; Woolard, "Sentences in the Language Prison."

33. Woolard, "Sentences in the Language Prison," p. 9.

34. U.S. Department of Education, *America 2000*, p. 1. (Emphasis added).

35. See, for example, Andersson and Boyer, *Bilingual Schooling in the United States.*

36. Rodríguez, *Hunger of Memory.*

37. Glazer, *Affirmative Discrimination*, p. 27.

38. Robert Hughes, "The Fraying of America," *Time*, 3 February 1992, pp. 44-49; Patterson, *Ethnic Chauvinism.*

39. As quoted in Richard Bernstein, "In U.S. Schools: A War of Words," *New York Times Magazine*, 14 October 1990, pp. 49-50.

40. Patterson, *Ethnic Chauvinism*, pp. 147-148.

41. This point is discussed in Baron, *The English-only Question*, and in Crawford, *Language Loyalties.*

42. Patterson, *Ethnic Chauvinism*, p. 149.

43. As quoted in Woolard, "Sentences in the Language Prison," p. 9.

44. As quoted in Woolard, "Sentences in the Language Prison," p. 16.

45. See Crawford, *Bilingual Education*, and idem, *Language Loyalties.*

46. See Baron, *The English-only Question*, and Crawford, *Language Loyalties.*

47. Gary McDowell, *Equity and the Constitution* (Chicago: University of Chicago Press, 1981).

48. Gerald Gold, "The Cajun French Debate," in *Issues in International Bilingual Education*, edited by Beverly Hartfield, Albert Valdman, and Charles Foster (New York: Plenum Press, 1982), pp. 221-240.

49. James A. Banks and Cherry A. McGee Banks, eds., *Multicultural Education: Issues and Perspectives* (Boston, MA: Allyn and Bacon, 1989).

50. Ibid.

51. As quoted in Bernstein, "In U.S. Schools: A War of Words," p. 48.

52. Jeannette Abi-Nader, " 'A House for My Mother': Motivating Hispanic High School Students," *Anthropology and Education Quarterly* 21, no. 1 (1990): 41-58.

53. Francois Grosjean, *Life with Two Languages: An Introduction to Bilingualism* (Cambridge, MA: Harvard University Press, 1982).

54. Ibid., p. 124.

55. Bernardo Ferdman, "Literacy and Cultural Identity," *Harvard Educational Review* 60, no. 2 (May 1990): 181-204.

56. Leslie Beebe and Howard Giles, "Speech Accommodation Theories: A Discussion in Terms of Second Language Acquisition," *International Journal of the Sociology of Language* 46 (1984): 5-32.

57. Calvin Veltman, *Language Shift in the U.S.* (The Hague: Mouton, 1983).

58. Bernstein, "In U.S. Schools: A War of Words," p. 52.

59. Signithia Fordham and John Ogbu, "Black Students' School Success: Coping with the Burden of Acting White," *Urban Review* 18, no. 3 (1986): 176-206; Maria Eugenia Matute-Bianchi, "Ethnic Identities and Patterns of School Success and Failure among Mexican-descent and Japanese-Americans in a California High School: An Ethnographic Analysis," *American Journal of Education* 95 (1986): 233-255.

60. Ferdman, "Literacy and Cultural Identity," p. 183.

61. As quoted in Andersson and Boyer, *Bilingual Schooling in the United States*, p. 29.

62. Coleman et al., *Equality of Educational Opportunity.*

63. U.S. Department of Education, *America 2000.*

64. National Council on Education Standards and Testing, *Raising Standards for American Education*; Quality Education for Minorities Project, *Education That Works*; Secada, "Agenda Setting, Enlightened Self-interest, and Equity in Mathematics Education"; U.S. Department of Education, *America 2000.*

65. Carpenter, "Conceptual Knowledge as a Foundation for Procedural Knowledge"; Means et al., *Teaching Advanced Skills to At-risk Students.*

66. Secada, "Research, Politics, and Bilingual Education."

67. Malcolm N. Danoff, *Evaluation of the Impact of ESEA Title VII Spanish/English Bilingual Education Program: Overview of Study and Findings* (Palo Alto, CA: American Institutes for Research, 1978); Malcolm N. Danoff, Gary J. Coles, Donald H. McLaughlin, and Dorothy J. Reynolds, *Evaluation of the Impact of ESEA Title VII Spanish/English Bilingual Education Program*, 3 vols. (Palo Alto, CA: American Institutes for Research, 1977-78).

68. Keith A. Baker and Adriana A. de Kanter, *Effectiveness of Bilingual Education: A Review of the Literature*, Final draft report (Washington, DC: Office of Planning, Budget, and Evaluation, U.S. Department of Education, September 25, 1981); idem, "Federal Policy and the Effectiveness of Bilingual Education."

69. J. David Ramírez, "Comparing Structured English Immersion and Bilingual Education: First-year Results of a National Study," *American Journal of Education* 95 (1986): 122-49; J. David Ramírez, David J. Pasta, Sandra D. Yuen, David K. Billings, and Dena R. Ramey, *Final Report: Longitudinal Study of Structured English Immersion Strategy, Early Exit, and Late Exit Transitional Bilingual Education for Language-minority Children*, vol. 2 (San Mateo, CA: Aguirre International, 1991); J. David Ramírez,

Sandra D. Yuen, Dena R. Ramey, and David J. Pasta, *Final Report: Longitudinal Study of Structured English Immersion Strategy, Early Exit, and Late Exit Transitional Bilingual Education for Language-minority Children*, vol. 1 (San Mateo, CA: Aguirre International, 1991).

70. Christina Bratt Paulston, *Bilingual Education: Theories and Issues* (Rowley, MA: Newbury House, 1980).

71. Ann Willig, "A Meta-analysis of Selected Studies on the Effectiveness of Bilingual Education," *Review of Educational Research* 55 (1985): 269-317.

72. Apple, "How Equality Has Been Redefined in the Conservative Restoration."

CHAPTER III

The Evaluation of Bilingual Education

ANN C. WILLIG AND J. DAVID RAMÍREZ

Comprehensive reviews of the effectiveness of bilingual education are readily available[1] as are commentaries on their role in shaping public policy and funding guidelines.[2] Our intent is not to replicate these reviews and discussions, which depict controversial results and disparate conclusions. Instead, our purposes are (1) to detail the complexity inherent in bilingual programs and related research and evaluation through discussion of the many research factors that affect these efforts, and (2) to emphasize the need for public policy research that addresses meaningful questions through adequate designs. Familiarity with the multitude of obstacles in evaluating bilingual programs should sensitize the reader to considerations necessary for effective planning, implementation, and evaluation of those programs. It should also foster circumspection in the interpretation of reports and discussions on bilingual education.

We begin with a discussion of the underlying assumptions of many popular notions concerning the effectiveness of bilingual education and the dangers of accepting such notions uncritically. This is followed by a review of the problems inherent in formal bilingual evaluation research and how these problems have affected evaluation outcomes. The final section summarizes and responds to a growing thrust among researchers and policymakers concerning future directions for research and evaluation in bilingual education.

Popular Notions and Pseudo-evaluations of Bilingual Programs

Popular notions regarding the effectiveness of bilingual education, with consequent effects on educational policy, have often been influenced by writers whose conclusions are based on a mixture of

Ann C. Willig is with the Multi-Functional Resource Center, Florida Atlantic University. J. David Ramírez is presently with the Wisconsin Center for Educational Research, University of Wisconsin—Madison.

information derived from their own ideology and/or gleaned from nonscientific sources.[3] At times these writers have effected what could only be termed pseudo-evaluation strategies, that is, gathering data that appear to answer a given question but which, upon examination, do not. There appear to be two basic pseudo-evaluation strategies: surveys of achievement data from the general population of language minority (LM) students and surveys of achievement data from students who are in programs that are purportedly bilingual.

Surveys of academic achievement of the general population of LM students may include data on test scores, dropout rates, or other characteristics relevant to an evaluation question. In the absence of significant general improvement on these indicators over time, conclusions sometimes are drawn concerning the effectiveness of bilingual education. A rationale based on such an approach was used by Secretary William J. Bennett in his argument to Congress to change Title VII funding priorities.[4]

The fallacy of this approach is the underlying assumption that all LM students are served in bilingual programs. In reality, the majority of LM students who are learning English are not in bilingual programs, but are served in mainstream English-only classrooms or special programs that use only English.[5] Hence, data from the general population of LM students answer no questions about bilingual education since most of these students are not in bilingual education programs.

The second pseudo-evaluation approach to estimating the effectiveness of bilingual education has been through the analysis of survey data pertaining to students who have participated in programs that are labeled "bilingual" with no checks on the actual nature of the program. The "bilingual program" label alone carries little meaning, since programs are defined and operationalized in many ways and frequently the label is applied to programs that provide little or no instruction in the native language. All-English programs sometimes have been labeled bilingual merely because the program has a bilingual classroom aide or contains students who are bilingual.

Programs vary widely in the amount, duration, and nature of instruction in the home language. Programs may provide instruction in the home language from ten minutes per day to 80 percent of the day and may range from one to more than seven years. Some bilingual programs provide for oral use of the native language but no native language reading while still others may include both oral and written use of the native language. Programs also vary considerably in the length of time they serve students before exiting them to the regular classroom. Studies have documented that most of the transitional bilingual programs for elementary school LM students provide instruction primarily in English, with limited or infrequent use of the native language.[6]

The lack of correspondence between the program label and program operation was most recently noted by Ramírez and his colleagues in their efforts to identify study sites for their national longitudinal study of programs for LM students.[7] Key individuals throughout the United States were supplied with specific program criteria and asked for nominations of programs that had these specific characteristics. Telephone interviews followed by site visits revealed that only nine of over three hundred nominated programs exhibited the specified program features. Less than half of the programs nominated as late-exit bilingual programs actually provided the 40 percent primary-language instruction that had been described as a minimal criterion for such programs. Thus even when a strong and clear operational definition is provided, one can expect a mismatch between the program label and the program in practice.

When expectations for student performance are based solely on the label of the program in which the students have been instructed, the consequent misinterpretations may affect not only the results of program evaluation,[8] but also individual students. This is illustrated by one district's testing policy where, instead of testing in English, the district's annual achievement tests were given in Spanish to all students who were in the bilingual programs. However, the district's bilingual programs provided no reading instruction in Spanish and only minimal oral use of that language. Consequently, the children were totally frustrated because they could neither read nor comprehend the questions on the Spanish-language versions of the tests.[9]

In sum, survey data on the success of LM students in the general population or on programs merely labeled "bilingual" are misleading unless the characteristics of the programs are documented—and they seldom are. Moreover, survey data do not reveal characteristics of the students that allow for meaningful interpretation of the survey results. Although formal evaluations attempt to overcome these difficulties, these studies also face obstacles that frequently invalidate findings.

Formal Evaluation Research on Bilingual Programs

Formal research on bilingual programs, such as has been reported in professional documents and journals, has yielded controversial results and little definitive information. This has been due to a plethora of methodological problems that include issues in program definition, documentation of instructional and contextual variables, inability to equate treatment and comparison groups on important background characteristics, difficulties in the assessment of language and achievement, and problems with selection and attrition and consequent changes in the composition of treatment and comparison groups. Elaboration of these issues may help the reader to understand the complexities of bilingual education and why evaluations of bilingual education have failed to produce definitive information.

PROGRAMMATIC VARIABLES AND CONTEXTUAL FACTORS

Issues surrounding the definition of bilingual programs are of concern in formal research and evaluation studies because few researchers have used operational definitions of the programs under study. Careful documentation of treatment and comparison conditions ensures adequate differentiation of these conditions and the identification of specific characteristics that may be responsible for any observed effects of a treatment. When documentation concerning the exact nature of the treatment and comparison programs is not available, little sense can be made of discrepant research findings.

Adequate documentation of program characteristics must include, among other things, the amount (percent) and duration (years) that each language in a program is used and the nature of the language use, reported for each academic subject. There may be large differences in the effects of two programs where both provide 50 percent native language instruction. One program may provide native language instruction in art classes, while the other may offer science instruction through the primary language. Alternatively, one program may use the native language only for oral instruction while another program may include instruction in reading and writing the native language.

Instructional variables other than the language of instruction also should be documented for both the treatment and comparison conditions in order to avoid confounding instructional quality with the language of instruction. Variables indicating instructional quality include such things as time on task, the frequency and type of student language use by language (speaking, reading, and writing), the nature of student-teacher interactions (both verbal and affective), the relative mix of students with various language proficiencies, classroom size, grouping strategies, degree to which active learning activities are provided, and so on.

An additional problem related to the documentation of instructional characteristics has been a lack of attention to background variables that indirectly influence the nature of instruction in programs, such as the backgrounds and characteristics of teachers and principals in both the treatment and comparison programs. With two notable exceptions, most evaluation studies fail to provide such data. In one instance where such documentation was provided,[10] the linguistic background, language use, experience in teaching bilingual programs, and extracurricular interests of the teachers in the comparison (nonbilingual) program suggested that the comparison programs may have had many elements in common with the bilingual programs. Ramírez et al. found teachers across three types of programs for LM students differed markedly by program on a number of characteristics that need to be considered in the analyses of academic achievement.[11] These characteristics included similarity of teachers' and students' backgrounds, teachers' fluency in the students' primary language, amount of advanced training teachers had in meeting the needs of language-minority students, attitudes toward how best to instruct them, and use of grouping strategies.

A number of contextual factors for any given program may also influence the outcomes of instruction, and it is crucial that these, too, be documented and accounted for in any interpretation of results. Stern is one of the few researchers who has provided such documentation in bilingual program evaluation.[12] She described high teacher turnover rates, disorganization, lack of interest, and hostile attitudes of nonbilingual teachers and staff toward the bilingual program. Stern's evaluation showed no positive effects for the bilingual program, but these and other conditions she describes (which will be recounted later) readily account for the evaluation findings. Had there been no documentation of these factors, the evaluation findings could have led to misinterpretations and false conclusions regarding the bilingual programs studied.

Anecdotal information depicting deleterious program contexts is known to many bilingual program staff members and administrators across the country. Bilingual program personnel still describe programs that are hidden in basements or out-of-sight areas or tell of hostile, prejudicial comments or treatments by nonbilingual program teachers or administrators. Given the existence of such conditions, the importance of documenting problems of program implementation in evaluations of bilingual programs cannot be overemphasized.

Although bilingual program evaluations per se are notable for lack of such documentation,[13] research on patterns of language use and effective teaching behaviors in second language programs has begun to shift from simplistic comparisons of students' achievement under different treatments to more complex studies incorporating documentation of fidelity of treatment.[14] This shift reflects growing awareness that program effects can be understood only after the program treatment has been defined operationally and observed systematically to confirm fidelity of treatment in the implementation of the program.[15]

INCLUDING PROGRAMMATIC AND CONTEXTUAL VARIABLES IN BILINGUAL EVALUATIONS

Bilingual program evaluations have seldom included detailed documentation of classroom processes as an integral part of the study. However, such documentation is not only possible in evaluation research; it is necessary if such research is to provide information that can contribute to the design and implementation of bilingual programs.

Research design that includes essential documentation requires careful planning with attention to the nature and focus of the documentation. The design would necessarily draw upon and adapt methods from other types of studies as was done in one of the few examples of research that provided such detail.[16] In designing the study by Ramírez et al., Ramírez and Merino identified four types of approaches that have been used in bilingual research to examine classroom processes and identify critical variables and/or questions related to bilingual programming. The approaches were drawn from literature on teacher effectiveness[17] and represent primarily descriptive, stand-alone studies. However, they illustrate observational approaches that would be well worth integrating into comprehensive evaluation studies as one or more of many components. These approaches merit elaboration both as examples of ways in which programs can be documented and as illustrations of the types of variables that might surface through such observations.

OBSERVATIONAL APPROACHES FOR CONFIRMING PROGRAM IMPLEMENTATION

The approaches drawn from teacher effectiveness literature which have been used in the study of bilingual programs include: (1) process studies, (2) process/context studies, (3) process/process studies, and (4) process/product studies. Examples of each of these follow.

Process studies are observational studies which simply describe a particular process. They do not allow for establishing a clear relationship between observed classroom processes and student outcomes, and since they are labor intensive and require large expenditures of resources, they cannot be used with a large number of classrooms nor are their results generalizable. Their value is in the identification of critical questions and/or processes that should be examined through more intensive and controlled studies.

This type of study, which represents much of the early work on bilingual classrooms, often took the form of case studies that described how language was used in one classroom or program. For example, through ethnographic techniques used to describe the nature of classroom discourse in a Boston bilingual classroom,[18] it was observed that teachers tended to favor the use of English for instruction, using Spanish principally to control student behavior. Mackey used a similar approach to describe language use patterns in a Berlin school.[19] This type of information highlights the nature of variables that are essential to include in any evaluation of bilingual programs.

Process/context studies describe the relationship of process to context, such as the distribution of language use in the context of different program models. An example of a process/context study is that of Legarreta,[20] who was the first to study systematically the relationship of language use and program model. Legarreta coded the language used by a total of five French teachers in two different contexts in Montreal: French immersion programs in English schools and programs in all-French schools. She found that regardless of the program model, the teachers used similar patterns of questioning, reinforcement, and error correction. This study is important in that reliable observation procedures were used and differences were analyzed across programs. However, the small sample size limits the generalizability of such findings and makes it difficult to differentiate teachers and programs.[21] Inclusion of such variables in program evaluations would be useful in documenting crucial similarities and differences between programs under study.

Process/process studies describe the relationship of one process to another, such as how certain teacher behaviors (e.g., feedback) can affect the responses of students.[22] Process/process studies in bilingual education have attempted to understand the language use patterns of teachers and students and how they affect one another. Gaies and Chaudron found that teachers adjust the complexity of their speech to ESL students to accommodate to their students' level of proficiency in

English.[23] Increasing the wait time when asking second language learners a question was found to increase the number of correct responses.[24] Schinke-Llano found that some bilingual elementary teachers interacted differently with fluent and limited-English-proficient students.[25] For example, teachers directed fewer academically related utterances to limited-English-proficient students than they did to English-proficient students. Other research efforts examined the relationship of instructional strategies in ESL classrooms to student engagement[26] or to student perception of effectiveness.[27] The value of process/process studies is that they attempt to understand the teaching process itself (that is, the nature of the treatment) rather than its relationship to outcome. While this emphasis on process is critical to understanding the nature of the instructional treatment (that is, what actually happened), it does not help us to understand the effect of treatment on achievement or other outcomes. Bilingual program evaluation designs that incorporate information and modified techniques from process/process studies such as these could produce results much more meaningful for program improvement.

Process/product studies describe the relationship of a process to a product or particular outcome measure. Process/product studies in bilingual education have frequently related teachers' and students' language behaviors to an outcome measure such as student achievement.[28] In a study by Ramírez and Stromquist, eighteen bilingual elementary teachers teaching ESL were recorded on videotape.[29] Student gains were related to specific teacher behaviors. Student oral production was found to improve when teachers: (a) required students to manipulate concrete objects following a teacher command; (b) questioned students regarding information previously presented by the teacher; (c) explained the meaning of new words; (d) corrected students' grammatical errors directly by providing the correct structure; and (e) varied the type of teacher behaviors. In contrast, student oral production decreased when teachers modeled or corrected pronunciation errors.

Rating scales also have been used in process/product studies to record the frequency of classroom behaviors by categorizing them from low to high. Wong-Fillmore et al. used such a measure to analyze seventeen bilingual and English-only classrooms.[30] Third- and fifth-grade classrooms were observed during a period of one year through the use of video, audio, and live recordings. Student gains on oral language and achievement tests were used to identify successful and unsuccessful classrooms. Gains in English production skills were found to be related to interactional opportunities (that is, fair allocation of turns) and quality of instructional language (for example, clarity of instructional goals). These variables were found to affect Chinese and Hispanic students differently. For example, opportunities to interact with other students helped Hispanic students but were not helpful to Chinese students. The advantage of a rating approach is that it allows one to observe high-inference and more complex behaviors. The procedure is limited in that it is subjective and interrater reliability may be difficult to achieve.

The studies by Ramírez and Stromquist and by Wong-Fillmore et al. both lacked clear operational definitions of instructional models, and there was a great deal of variability of instruction both within and between classrooms. Wong-Fillmore et al., for example, observed that teachers used students' primary language from zero to 24 percent of the time. With such diversity in treatment, it is extremely difficult to identify effective bilingual classroom techniques.[31]

The value of process/product studies is that they directly relate specific instructional practices to student gains. However, since these studies are correlational, results are limited to statements of co-occurrence rather than causality.[32]

While each of these alternative approaches to documenting instructional treatments is helpful, the limitations of each necessitate an evaluation design that incorporates each approach as a complementary component. The recent study by Ramírez et al. is one such effort to integrate alternative data collection procedures into a single evaluation design.[33] Both quantitative and qualitative data collection procedures were used to document the characteristics of students, parents, families, teachers, principals, and project directors, as well as homes, classrooms, schools, districts, and community through questionnaires, focus groups, standardized and nonstandardized tests, and observational inventories.

All the problems discussed above, that is, failure to document program characteristics and other factors that directly and indirectly affect the quality of instruction in any program, are surmountable by careful research with adequate funds for collecting the essential information. Problems that are more difficult and perhaps impossible to overcome are those that concern the equating of treatment and comparison groups. We now turn to a discussion of those problems.

EQUATING TREATMENT AND COMPARISON GROUPS

Traditionally, equating treatment and comparison groups is accomplished through random assignment of students to the respective groups. However, contrary to calls for a "true randomized design,"[34] random assignment is not possible when its consequence might deprive a child of a service or program which he or she truly needs or which might retard the child's achievement. In lieu of random assignment, researchers often attempt to use nonrandom groups for comparison by selecting groups that are equated on as many variables as possible and/or by using statistical adjustments. Statistical adjustments pose many problems and discussions of these appear elsewhere.[35] Equating groups of bilingual students is a problem since the major variables on which they must be equated for bilingual research (that is, language variables) are the very determinants of a student's need for the program. A consequence of the difficulty in equating treatment and comparison groups in bilingual program evaluation has been that almost every evaluation study to date has compared bilingual program students to students who differed from them in ways that would have significant effects on the outcomes of the evaluation. In a meta-analysis of evaluation research on bilingual programs, Willig found that effect sizes (that is, magnitude of results) from evaluation studies were strongly influenced by a failure to equate experimental and comparison groups on language dominance and other language-related variables.[36]

It is primarily the cluster of variables related to language that differentiates the problems inherent in bilingual program research and evaluation from the problems of research on other types of educational programs. Discussion of these variables and the problems they pose for research and evaluation will further illustrate the complexities of bilingual programs and bilingual program evaluation.

Language variables. One of the most crucial variables on which treatment and comparison groups must be equated in bilingual program research is proficiency in each of the relevant languages. Any attempt to accomplish such equating, through matching or other procedures, would typically require language assessments and testing in both languages.

Problems in language assessment. A major problem in language assessment is that tests of language proficiency generally have low reliability and low convergent validity.[37] This is mostly accounted for by two major factors: variations in the language use of individuals[38] and variations in the nature of the tests.

At the individual level, each individual possesses a variety of language skills, and competence and performance vary depending on the context of language use, the interactants, their relationships and relative statuses, the domain of the communicative intent, and the topic. Although this is true of monolingual individuals, bilingual individuals have an even more varied repertoire of language uses that complicates attempts to equate groups on language proficiencies. For a child who lives in a dual language environment, certain topics of conversation with certain types of individuals in certain kinds of settings may call forth one language, while very different topics with different individuals in different settings might usually be dealt with in the other language. For example, conversations concerning topics discussed in the home versus those discussed in school or church might normally be conducted in different languages. Furthermore, in any dual language community or neighborhood, the patterns of language use will vary from individual to individual. The almost infinite variety of language uses and the variations in reactions and motivations to language settings are real obstacles to the development of valid and reliable language tests.

Variations in language tests *per se* also contribute to divergence of scores. Several paradigm shifts in linguistics and psycholinguistics over the past twenty-five years[39] have each led to tests that measure different aspects of language. In defining language proficiency, differential emphasis has been placed on phonology, grammar, meaning and vocabulary, or the myriad of skills necessary for communicative competence. The result has been a plethora of tests that demonstrate low convergent validity.[40]

Sequence of language skills. Also important in reporting evaluation data is documentation of the language modalities used in any testing or examination situation. Second language modalities may develop in different sequences depending upon the context in which the language is learned. In most bilingual program settings, with students who have not had prior literacy experiences in the second language, comprehension will usually precede language production. Adults and students who have studied a language primarily through books may be literate in the language but lack oral skills. Yet, Willig found that researchers seldom differentiated between comprehension and production in describing language assessments used in studies.[41]

Controlling for language exposure. The nature of language exposure in the neighborhood of residence and in the school setting can further complicate problems with group comparisons. In Willig's meta-analysis, when the neighborhood language was approximately the same for both the experimental and comparison groups, regardless of whether the language was English or not, effects were positive for the bilingual program groups. On the other hand, when the neighborhood languages differed, program effects were not detected.

The impact of neighborhood differences may be produced by exposure to differential vocabulary that can cause differences between program groups and reduce group overlap on various scoring systems. For example, vocabulary can be affected in the classroom by student aggregation or segregation. Campbell and Boruch point out that since some vocabulary is learned from classmates, children whose classmates have a lower level of vocabulary would learn less.[42] Lower student vocabulary also lowers the vocabulary used by the teacher in classroom interaction and in reading assignments, as was noted earlier in this chapter. Neighborhoods and play groups have a similar effect.

The complexity of controlling for language proficiencies, language exposure, and other language-related variables may perhaps be illustrated by Mackey's typology of bilingual programs,[43] which is based on the language patterns used both in the bilingual programs and in the broader context of the programs. Mackey's typology consists of a 9 by 10 matrix, wherein each of the 90 cells represents a different combination of language patterns for the different types of bilingual programs and for the different community contexts in which the programs are found. The contextual variations indicate not only the specific patterns of language use for the languages of the child, but also those used in the home, the bilingual program, the school, the neighborhood or area, and the nation as a whole. Furthermore, the relative status of each of the languages used in each setting influences the motivational factors in language learning. Each segment of the ever-widening pattern of linguistic context ultimately impinges on the child.

The difficulties in establishing experimental control for the innumerable language-related considerations in bilingual evaluation research makes comparisons of treatment and nontreatment groups extremely problematic.

OTHER DIFFICULTIES WITH BILINGUAL PROGRAM
EVALUATION RESEARCH

Attrition and changes in group composition in bilingual programs present additional challenges for bilingual program evaluation. For example, children in transitional programs usually are exited from the bilingual program and moved into mainstream English-only programs as soon as their English skills are thought to be adequate. The bilingual program slots vacated by these children are then filled with new children who know less English. These policies guarantee that the level of English proficiency in the nonbilingual program comparison groups will be higher than that of the experimental group.

For example, Stern studied the differential impact of transitional bilingual programs and submersion (all English, regular classroom) programs for grades one to six.[44] Results from every measure favored the comparison groups. Fortunately, Stern had documented that many of the children in the comparison groups previously had been in the bilingual program and were among the highest scorers in the "control" group. Stern also found that at every grade level, more than 50 percent of the children in the bilingual program had been placed in the bilingual program *during the year of the evaluation.*

The problems associated with nonrandom assignment are illustrated quite convincingly in a nationwide evaluation of the Follow Through programs. Stebbins et al. evaluated many program models from different areas of the country and used three different comparison groups for each bilingual program.[45] They concluded that the analyses using local comparison groups seemed to have the most reliable results, even when the "best matched" group was not the local group. Such results illustrate the problems involved in trying to compensate for nonrandom assignment through attempts to match experimental and comparison groups.

In Willig's meta-analysis of bilingual research, failure to compensate adequately for nonrandom assignment was revealed by a large number of uncontrolled differences that had a substantial impact on the magnitude of the effect sizes in the analyses. Willig found that the variance of the effect sizes was dominated by factors in research design and research quality, resulting in little information concerning substantive issues related to bilingualism and bilingual education.

In sum, a multitude of problems have plagued bilingual program evaluation efforts. Most of these can be overcome by careful research design that documents program processes and contexts and incorporates indicators of instructional quality. The problem of equating students in the programs studied, however, is more difficult. Although perfect control over variables in field research will probably never be attained, careful documentation of student characteristics in each of the programs studied can, over time, provide cumulative indicators concerning student characteristics that correlate with success in various contexts.

Partly because of the difficulties with bilingual program evaluation that have been described above and the consequent failure to produce meaningful and relevant information, researchers are expressing concern over the nature of bilingual program evaluations that stem from federal efforts to obtain information for policy development. These concerns are not only due to frustrations with the methodological problems, but also with the focus of the questions being asked by the policymakers who determine funding priorities. Many researchers would like to abandon efforts at comparative program evaluation and redirect the focus of bilingual education research.

Future Directions

There is a growing perception among researchers that large-scale efforts to demonstrate the general effectiveness of bilingual education have been misdirected. They assert that several decades of failed attempts at such demonstration have made obvious the futility of expending valuable resources to attempt well-controlled comparative evaluation studies.[46] Proposals for redirection focus on two central issues: (1) broadening the scope of questions addressed in bilingual research studies, and (2) shifting from large-scale public policy studies and the use of summative evaluation methodology to a series of smaller studies with increased emphasis on case studies and the use of ethnographic methods.

With regard to the issue of research questions, there is definitely a need to investigate issues that concern all levels of program design and implementation. At the program level, studies are needed to address the variations in program implementation and their corresponding rationale, and why there are or are not differential effects. Detailed descriptions of the programs also are essential and these should address classroom processes in detail, including the nature and quality of instruction in bilingual programs, the knowledge base and needs of teachers, and how to optimize classroom instruction for students from many linguistic backgrounds.[47]

At the student level, researchers have elaborated on the need to identify individual differences in bilingual students, the cognitive growth of students in the programs, the linguistic and knowledge resources that bilingual students bring to school and how these can be used as a base for knowledge building. A major call in many of these proposals is for increased focus on the role of native language development in furthering cognitive and second language growth in bilingual students, as opposed to placing sole emphasis on the acquisition of English.

There is also a call to expand research efforts to develop and test theory relating to bilingualism and bilingual education, including both cognitive and linguistic aspects of bilingualism, learning strategies employed by bilingual learners, and other basic issues. Hakuta and Pease-Alvarez summarize these arguments by stating that future research efforts in bilingual education should be directed toward (1) conducting basic research which contributes to our theoretical understanding of how children learn and how we can facilitate their learning; (2) providing detailed descriptions of instructional programs, settings, staff, students, and communities; and (3) gathering information that is relevant to teachers and students.[48]

The failure to address crucial questions such as the above stems partly from public policy regarding education for language minority students and the consequent channeling of research funds. For example, a single-minded and simplistic focus on the rapid acquisition of English and an unwillingness to deal with the complexity of factors that promote second language and cognitive development has precluded the funding of much research that could investigate the relationships between first and second language development and test theory that could point to more effective ways to achieve educational goals. The recent national study by Ramírez and his colleagues, in which language and achievement data were collected on a nationwide sample of students in varying program models, illustrates this point. Although funding sources allowed limited collection of first-language data, funds were not provided for analysis of those data on the basis that such analysis was not relevant to existing policy which only considers English language development.

Crucial research questions are also ignored when contracting officials' methodologists, who review or design policy research, consider *only* basic design issues and not the substantive questions that should impact the real world. For example, the recent review by the National Academy of Science[49] of the Ramírez et al. study concurred with the investigators' expressed limitation that the lack of a completely crossed design precluded answering the question of relative effectiveness for two of the three programs. However, while the issue of relative effectiveness had been the evaluation question contracted for by federal officials, Ramírez et al. argued that the more fundamental policy question was which, if any, of the three alternative instructional programs helped the "limited-English proficient" students "catch-up" to the norming population. Answers to that question should be the determining factor in making decisions about program types and needs for services. Although the Ramírez et al. study provided information regarding this latter question, the relevance of that information was largely ignored in the National Academy of Science review of the study.

Broadening the scope and types of research questions to be investigated should result in a concomitant increase in the variety of research methods used to investigate these questions. Each question can best be answered with specific methodologies, ranging from intensive ethnographic studies to large-scale cross-sectional evaluation studies. We believe that each type of research question and each research method has a crucial place in a knowledge-building cycle that includes theory development and testing, design of programs based on theoretical research, implementation of programs, and feedback for revision. Each component of this cycle provides valuable information for specific audiences and ignoring any one component can only retard the process of development of optimal educational programs for LM students.

The present situation in educational research on bilingual education and programming for LM students represents an imbalance in this cycle. Since the major impetus for the development of bilingual programs came from civil rights and political issues, policies that direct research funding have focused almost entirely on program evaluation to the exclusion of research that would ground program design in well-researched theory. The consequence has been a great deal of frustration with the large number of programs that are not achieving intended goals because they are not theoretically grounded.

If this situation is to be rectified, it is crucial that policymakers balance the research agenda to include research that addresses issues discussed here. However, abandoning standard evaluation efforts and methods in order to accomplish the above would also create an imbalance that would preclude obtaining valuable feedback for the improvement of program implementations and would ignore the needs of makers of public policy.

Public policy research is concerned with the implementation of policy across the widest range of contexts. Experience with meta-analyses of studies has shown the myriad problems that arise with lack of consistency across studies regarding the variables considered and how they are defined, collected, and analyzed. The strength of a single research design implemented across a number of contexts, while admittedly challenging, provides the consistency needed to identify commonalities and differences across and within program implementations.

Additionally, when properly designed and supported, large-scale studies can successfully address a range of research questions deemed critical to any successful bilingual evaluation and relevant to practitioners and learners. The Ramírez et al. sudy is an example of a theory-driven study which incorporated a range of quantitative and qualitative data collection procedures in an integrated design to document critical characteristics of the instructional treatment, students, their families, and instructional staff and communities.[50] The results are directly related to day-to-day instruction. For example, this study has provided information on prevalent verbal behaviors of teachers that minimize opportunities for language production on the part of students. Further research is needed to demonstrate methods that maximize such opportunities and that train teachers to use the new methods.

Although no comparative quantitative research study can ever account for all possible variations of program implementation, this limitation is even greater for ethnographic studies with their limited sample sizes. While the richness of an ethnographic study provides a wealth of information and understanding in a given setting, it provides an extremely limited view of implementations across settings. Large-scale comparative research can do a much better job at delineating a range of variability across program implementations.

Rather than call for the exclusive use of either a comparative evaluation or an ethnographic research agenda, we would strongly argue for a middle-of-the-road approach that asks a variety of essential questions to be addressed by a variety of appropriate methodologies.

We would also argue against confounding issues concerning research methods and types of studies with issues concerning the nature of the questions addressed. Although the Ramírez et al. study illustrates successful adaptation and integration of a number of methodological approaches, it also illustrates the role of existing policy in determining, through the restrictions on analysis of first-language data, which questions will be addressed. As described earlier, a major criticism of existing evaluation research is the failure to address the contribution of native language abilities to second language and cognitive development. However, it is not evaluation methodology that has restricted the range of questions, but priorities in existing policy.

In spite of the frustrations and failures of many of the large-scale evaluation studies and criticisms of standard methodologies, a few studies that used standard methodologies (in addition to Ramírez et al.) have provided relevant and useful information that can contribute to the direction of future research. For example, Cziko, who questions the use of standardized testing,[51] cites the successes of the San Diego bilingual immersion programs[52] when suggesting the use of Runkel's paradigm, the "method of possibilities." The bilingual immersion programs have been successful in developing proficiency in two languages but the data that indicate success consist only of scores on standardized achievement tests (taken in both English and Spanish) in reading and mathematics. This type of success calls for further research to examine the characteristics and variations of such models and to determine the key instructional and contextual factors that account for the successes.

Similarly, Hakuta and Pease-Alvarez[53] cite Collier's study as basic research which shows that students acquire English in two to seven years. Yet Collier's data were summative data based on standardized test scores in language and content areas across large samples of students in a large metropolitan district.

Studies such as the above illustrate that it is possible to ask relevant questions and address them with standard evaluation methods. Without evaluation research, we would have no checks on what really works or has been effective in various contexts. Suggestions such as Cziko's, that we use the "method of possibilities" to identify what is possible to include in the goals of other programs are worthwhile, but they cannot be the end point. Once implemented, it is necessary to determine whether the possibilities are indeed attained in other programs, and this calls for evaluation research. Such research can incorporate relevant questions concerning native language just as it can address those relevant to learning English.

In sum, we would argue for a balanced research agenda that includes a variety of types of studies to address a range of questions relevant to various audiences who have a role in the education of LM students. Evaluation studies, whether large-scale or for single programs, should be designed to assure that they include both product and process issues.

It appears that some federal policymakers have begun to move in more meaningful directions. In *The Condition of Bilingual Education in the Nation*, the following conclusion appears:

Bilingual education research should direct its energies toward questions such as, What are the characteristics of successful approaches and how can they be replicated? For too many years research in bilingual education has centered on determining whether bilingual education works and which methodologies work best. There are two reasons for redirecting research efforts toward a focus on successful approaches and techniques. First, it is unlikely that there can be a single, nationally representative impact study that will provide a single, definitive answer to the question of "what works" that would be accurate for every local context. . . . Second, twenty-two years after the passage of the Bilingual Education Act and the implementation of programs funded under the act, enough is known to identify effective, even exemplary programs, to determine why they work, and to use this information to improve other programs.[54]

Hopefully, the above represents a shift in the focus of federal efforts toward encouraging meaningful and productive research that will yield practical benefits for the potentially bilingual children of our country. As Padilla writes, "We need to bring together the best researchers and practitioners to explore how to optimally implement bilingual programs so that all students acquire linguistic skills in English while retaining their home languages."[55]

NOTES

1. See Theodore Andersson and Mildred Boyer, *Bilingual Schooling in the United States*, 2nd ed. (Austin, TX: National Educational Laboratory, 1978); Keith Baker and Adriana de Kanter, "Federal Policy and the Effectiveness of Bilingual Education," in *Bilingual Education: A Reappraisal of Federal Policy*, edited by Keith Baker and Adriana de Kanter (Lexington, MA: Lexington Books, 1983), pp. 33-86; Christina B. Paulston, *Bilingual Education: Theories and Issues* (Rowley, MA: Newbury House, 1980); James Crawford, *Bilingual Education: History, Politics, Theory, and Practice* (Trenton, NJ: Crane, 1989); Jim Cummins, *Empowering Minority Students* (Sacramento, CA: California Association for Bilingual Education, 1990); Kenji Hakuta, *Mirror of Language: The Debate on Bilingualism* (New York: Basic Books, 1986); Barry McLaughlin, *Second Language Acquisition in Childhood*, vol. 2, *School Age Children*, 2nd ed. (Hillsdale, NJ: Erlbaum, 1985); Ann C. Willig, "A Meta-analysis of Selected Studies on the Effectiveness of Bilingual Education," *Review of Educational Research* 55 (1985): 269-317.

2. See Walter G. Secada, "Research, Politics, and Bilingual Education," *Annals of the American Academy of Political and Social Science* 508 (1990): 81-106.

3. Richard Rodríguez, *Hunger of Memory* (Boston: David R. Godine, 1982); Christine Rosselle, "Nothing Matters?" *Bilingual Research Quarterly* 1 (1992): Rosalie Porter, *Forked Tongue: The Politics of Bilingual Education* (New York: Basic Books, 1990); Noel Epstein, *Language, Ethnicity, and the Schools: Policy Alternatives for Bilingual-Bicultural Education* (Washington, DC: George Washington University, 1977).

4. U.S. General Accounting Office, *Bilingual Education: A New Look at the Research* (Washington, DC: U.S. General Accounting Office, 1987).

5. J. Michael O'Malley, *Children's English and Services Study: Educational and Needs Assessment for Language Minority Children with Limited English Proficiency* (Rosslyn, VA: InterAmerica Research Associates, 1982); California State Department of Education, *Annual Census* (Sacramento, CA: California State Department of Education, 1991); R. Willner, *Ten Years of Neglect: The Failure to Serve Language-minority Students in the New York City Public Schools* (New York: Educational Priorities Panel, INTERFACE, 1985).

6. Development Associates, Inc. and Research Triangle Institute, *LEP Students: Characteristics and School Services* (Arlington, VA: Development Associates and Research Triangle Institute, 1985); O'Malley, *Children's English and Services Study*.

7. J. David Ramírez, Sandra D. Yuen, Dena R. Ramey, and David J. Pasta, *Longitudinal Study of Sheltered English Immersion, Early-Exit, and Late-Exit Transitional Bilingual Education Programs for Language Minority Children* (Washington, DC: United States Department of Education, 1991).

8. Malcolm N. Danoff, Gary J. Coles, Donald H. McLaughlin, and Dorothy J. Reynolds, *Evaluation of the Impact of ESEA Title VII Spanish/English Bilingual Education Programs* (Palo Alto, CA: American Institutes for Research, 1978).

9. Ann C. Willig, Cheryl Y. Wilkinson, and Eloussa E. Polyzoi, *Interim Report for the Development of Teaching Strategies for Use with Limited English Proficient Children Who Are Receiving Services for LD or Mild MR* (Austin, TX: Handicapped Minority Research Institute on Language Proficiency, 1986).

10. Danoff, Coles, McLaughlin, and Reynolds, *Evaluation of the Impact of ESEA Title VII Spanish/English Bilingual Education Programs*, vol. 3, *Year Two Impact Data, Educational Process, and In-depth Analysis*.

11. Ramírez et al., *Longitudinal Study of Sheltered English Immersion, Early-Exit, and Late-Exit Transitional Bilingual Education Programs for Language Minority Students*.

12. Carolyn Stern, *Final Report of the Compton Unified School District's Title VII Bilingual-Bicultural Project: September 1969 through June 1975* (Compton City, CA: Compton City Schools, 1975).

13. Willig, "A Meta-analysis of Selected Studies on the Effectiveness of Bilingual Education."

14. J. David Ramírez and Bárbara Merino, "Classroom Talk in English Immersion, Early-Exit, and Late-Exit Transitional Bilingual Education Programs," in *Language Distribution Issues in Bilingual Schooling*, edited by Rodolfo Jacobson and Christian Faltis (Clevedon, England: Multilingual Matters Ltd., 1990), pp. 61-103.

15. Keith A. Baker and Adriana A. de Kanter, *Effectiveness of Bilingual Education: A Review of the Literature* (Washington, DC: Office of Planning, Budget, and Evaluation, U.S. Department of Education, September 25, 1981); Willig, "A Meta-analysis of Selected Studies on the Effectiveness of Bilingual Education"; Lily Wong Fillmore and Concepción Valadez, "Teaching Bilingual Learners," in *Handbook of Research on Teaching*, 3rd ed., edited by Merlin C. Wittrock (New York: Macmillan, 1986).

16. Ramírez et al., *Longitudinal Study of Sheltered English Immersion, Early-Exit, and Late-Exit Transitional Bilingual Education Programs for Language Minority Students*.

17. M. J. Dunkin and B. J. Biddle, *The Study of Teaching* (New York: Holt, Rinehart and Winston, 1974); Michael H. Long, "Inside the 'Black Box': Methodological Issues in Classroom Research on Language Learning," in *Classroom Oriented Research in Second Language Acquisition*, edited by Herbert W. Seliger and Michael H. Long (Rowley, MA: Newbury House, 1983).

18. Henry Trueba and Pamela Wright, "A Challenge for Ethnographic Researchers in Bilingual Settings: Analyzing Spanish/English Interaction," *Journal of Multilingual and Multicultural Development* 2 (1981): 243-257; J. Schultz, "Language

Use in Bilingual Classrooms" (Paper presented at the Annual Convention of Teachers of English to Speakers of Other Languages [TESOL], Los Angeles, CA, 1975).

19. William Mackey, *Bilingual Education in a Binational School* (Rowley, MA: Newbury House, 1972).

20. Dorothy Legarreta, "Language Choice in Bilingual Classrooms," *TESOL Quarterly* 11 (1977): 9-16.

21. Ramírez et al., *Longitudinal Study of Sheltered English Immersion, Early-Exit, and Late-Exit Transitional Bilingual Education Programs for Language Minority Students.*

22. Craig Chaudron, "A Descriptive Model of Discourse in the Corrective Treatment of Learner's Errors," *Language Learning* 27, no. 2 (1977): 29-46.

23. S. J. Gaies, "The Nature of Linguistic Input in Formal Second Language Learning: Linguistic and Communicative Strategies in ESL Teachers' Classroom Language," in *On TESOL, '77, Teaching and Learning English as a Second Language: Trends in Research and Practice*, edited by H. D. Brown, C. A. Yorio, and R. H. Crymes (Washington, DC: TESOL, 1977); Chaudron, "A Descriptive Model of Discourse in the Corrective Treatment of Learner's Errors."

24. Andrew Cohen, *A Sociolinguistic Approach to Bilingual Education* (Rowley, MA: Newbury House, 1975).

25. Linda Schinke-Llano, "Foreigner Talk in Content Classrooms," in *Classroom Oriented Research in Second Language Acquisition*, edited by Herbert W. Seliger and Michael H. Long (Rowley, MA: Newbury House, 1983).

26. A. Nerenz and C. Knop, "Allocated Time, Curricular Content, and Student Engagement Outcomes in the Second Language Classroom," *Canadian Modern Language Review* 39 (1983): 222-232; William Tikunoff and José A. Vázquez-Faría, "Successful Instruction for Bilingual Schooling," *Peabody Journal of Education* 59 (1982): 234-271.

27. A. Omaggio, "The Relationship between Personalized Classroom Talk and Teacher Effectiveness Ratings: Some Research Results," *Foreign Language Annals* 15 (1982): 255-259.

28. Robert Politzer, "Foreign Language Teaching and Bilingual Education: Implications of Some Recent Research Findings" (Paper presented at the ACTFL Annual Conference, San Francisco, 1977).

29. Arnulfo G. Ramírez and Nelly Stromquist, "ESL Methodology and Student Language Learning in Bilingual Elementary Schools," *TESOL Quarterly* 13 (1979): 145-158.

30. Lily Wong Fillmore, Paul Ammon, Barry McLaughlin, and Mary Ammon, *Learning English through Bilingual Instruction, Final Report to the National Institute of Education* (Berkeley, CA: University of California, 1985).

31. Ramírez et al., *Longitudinal Study of Sheltered English Immersion, Early-Exit, and Late-Exit Transitional Bilingual Education Programs for Language Minority Students.*

32. Ibid.

33. Ibid.

34. Michael M. Meyer and Stephen E. Feinberg, eds., *Assessing Evaluation Studies: The Case of Bilingual Education Strategies* (Washington, DC: National Academy Press, 1992).

35. Donald T. Campbell and Robert F. Boruch, "Making the Case for Randomized Assignment to Treatments by Considering the Alternatives: Six Ways in Which Quasi-experimental Evaluations in Compensatory Education Tend to Underestimate Effects," in *Evaluation and Experiment: Some Critical Issues in Assessing Social Programs*, edited by

Carl A. Bennett and Arthur A. Lumsdaine (New York: Academic Press, 1975); Donald T. Campbell and A. E. Erlebacher, "How Regression Artifacts in Quasi-experimental Evaluations Can Mistakenly Make Compensatory Education Look Harmful," in *Compensatory Education: A National Debate*, vol. 3, *Disadvantaged Child*, edited by John Hellmuth (New York: Brunner/Mazel, 1970).

36. Willig, "A Meta-analysis of Selected Studies on the Effectiveness of Bilingual Education."

37. G. Gillmore and A. Dickerson, *The Relationship between Instruments Used for Identifying Children of Limited English Speaking Ability in Texas* (Houston, TX: Region IV Education Service Center, TEA, November 1979); Daniel Ulibarri, Maury Spencer, and George Rivas, *Comparability of Three Oral Language Proficiency Tests and Their Relationship to Achievement Variables* (Sacramento: Office of Bilingual Education, California State Department of Education, September, 1980).

38. Shirley Brice Heath, "Sociocultural Contexts of Language Development," in *Beyond Language: Social and Cultural Factors in Schooling Language Minority Students* (Los Angeles: Bilingual Education Office, California State Department of Education, Evaluation, Dissemination and Assessment Center, California State University, 1986), pp. 143-186.

39. See, for example, Leonard Bloomfield, *Language* (New York: Holt, Rinehart and Winston, 1933); Noam Chomsky, *Syntactic Structures* (The Hague: Mouton, 1957); idem, *Aspects of the Theory of Syntax* (Cambridge, MA: MIT Press, 1965); C. J. Fillmore, "The Case for Case," in *Universals in Linguistic Theory*, edited by E. Bach and R. T. Harms (New York: Holt, Rinehart and Winston, 1968); William Labov, *The Study of Nonstandard English* (Urbana, IL: National Council of Teachers of English, 1970); Robert Lado, *Language Testing* (London: Longmans, Green, 1961); Roger Shuy, "Quantitative Language Data: A Case for and Some Warnings Against," *Anthropology and Education Quarterly* 8, no. 2 (1977): 73-82.

40. Willig, "A Meta-analysis of Selected Studies on the Effectiveness of Bilingual Education."

41. Ibid.

42. Campbell and Boruch, "Making the Case for Randomized Assignment to Treatments by Considering the Alternatives."

43. William F. Mackey, "A Typology of Bilingual Education," in *Bilingual Schooling in the United States*, vol. 2, edited by Theodore Andersson and Mildred Boyer (Austin, TX: Southwest Educational Development Laboratory, 1970).

44. Stern, *Final Report of the Compton Unified School District's Title VII Bilingual-Bicultural Project.*

45. Linda B. Stebbins, Robert G. St. Pierre, Elizabeth C. Proper, Richard B. Anderson, and Thomas R. Cerva, *Education as Experimentation: A Planned Variation Model*, vols. IVA-IVC (Cambridge, MA: ABT Associates, April, 1977).

46. Kenji Hakuta and Lucinda Pease-Alvarez, "Enriching Our Views of Bilingualism and Bilingual Education," *Educational Researcher* 21, no. 2 (1992): 4-6; Gary Cziko, "The Evaluation of Bilingual Education: From Necessity and Probability to Possibility," *Educational Researcher* 21, no. 2 (1992): 10-15; Walter Secada, "This Is 1987, Not 1980: A Comment on a Comment," *Review of Educational Research* 57, no. 3 (1987): 377-384; Amado Padilla, "Bilingual Education: Issues and Perspectives," in *Bilingual Education: Issues and Strategies*, edited by Amado M. Padilla, Halford H. Fairchild, and Concepción Valadez (Newbury Park, CA: Sage, 1990).

47. Stebbins et al., *Education as Experimentation.*

48. Hakuta and Pease-Alvarez, "Enriching Our Views of Bilingualism and Bilingual Education."

49. Meyer and Feinberg, *Assessing Evaluation Studies.*

50. Ramírez et al., *Longitudinal Study of Sheltered English Immersion, Early-Exit, and Late-Exit Transitional Education Programs for Language Minority Students.*

51. Cziko, "The Evaluation of Bilingual Education."

52. Kathryn J. Lindholm, "Bilingual Immersion Education: Criteria for Program Development," in *Bilingual Education: Issues and Strategies*, edited by Amado M. Padilla, Halford H. Fairchild, and Concepción Valadez (Newbury Park, CA: Sage, 1990).

53. Hakuta and Pease-Alvarez, "Enriching Our Views of Bilingualism and Bilingual Education."

54. U.S. Department of Education, Office of Bilingual Education and Minority Languages Affairs, *The Condition of Bilingual Education in the Nation* (Washington, DC: U.S. Department of Education, 1991).

55. Amado Padilla, "Bilingual Education: Issues and Perspectives."

Section Two
PRACTICE AND RESEARCH

CHAPTER IV

Bilingual Education and English as a Second Language: The Elementary School

ROBERT D. MILK

Bilingual education stimulates widely contrasting associations and signals a variety of meanings to different people. This should not be surprising, given the diverse goals of various advocacy groups who have promoted a bilingual approach to education in recent decades, not to mention the sharply divergent sociopolitical agenda of parents and families who have stood to benefit from this approach. In a similar vein, English as a second language (ESL) is understood differently by different persons, whether they are participants or nonparticipants in bilingual education. Sometimes these differences are based on lack of knowledge about schools, programs, and multicultural communities; sometimes they are not, as highly informed professionals may differ significantly on the appropriate role of ESL in bilingual education.

In reflecting on bilingual education and ESL in the elementary school, I will first attempt to capture meaningful distinctions in usage with regard to these terms, particularly in reference to implicit assumptions not clearly understood by decision makers and by mainstream educators whose specialties lie outside of this area. I will then discuss current practice in bilingual education at the elementary school level in the United States, particularly as it relates to the education of language minority children in the public schools. "Language minority children" may be simply defined as referring to "children from homes in which English is not the predominant language of communication between parents and children."[1] These children may or may not be

---

Robert D. Milk is Professor and Director of the Division of Bicultural-Bilingual Studies, University of Texas, San Antonio.

88

"limited English proficient" (LEP), a term commonly used in the literature as well as in legislation pertaining to bilingual education. In this chapter, I shall avoid the latter term because it erroneously implies that children who acquire a language other than English in their home may have linguistic deficits. My goal is to capture the essence of what is known about effective practices in bilingual education based on current research, with particular attention to recent trends in (a) second language instruction and (b) language minority education at the elementary school level.

Bilingual Education: Background

If we were to trace the roots of the modern bilingual education movement in the United States, we would find a number of intertwining strands, each representing different conceptions of bilingual education articulated by advocates who have widely divergent reasons for persistently arguing in favor of a bilingual approach to education. Any attempt to create a discrete list of these different conceptions is essentially arbitrary, since historical movements typically evolve within a dynamic interactive context that makes it difficult to assess to what extent any one perspective may have operated in total isolation from parallel movements that were developing concurrently. Nevertheless, at the risk of oversimplification, it is helpful to understand at the outset that bilingual education in the elementary schools has been advocated for different reasons, and by different groups. One strand that can be readily traced is tied to the ongoing desire of important segments in many ethnic groups in the United States to maintain their culture and heritage (including language) in the face of intense pressures to assimilate. In the context of the 1960s and early 1970s, the goal of ethnic revitalization and/or cultural maintenance was an important motivator for a significant number of advocates of bilingual education.[2]

A second strand represents language educators and parents who, in the face of disappointing results following efforts to teach a foreign language to students at the elementary school through direct instruction with conventional foreign language methods, looked to bilingual education as an alternative approach for obtaining more effective outcomes in the teaching of foreign languages in elementary schools. A third strand represents the perspectives of many mainstream educators regarding the primary rationale for bilingual education. These educators see it as an effective way to obtain solid, academically grounded English proficiency for language minority children in elementary schools in the United States.

A fourth strand represents the primary focus of most minority educators who are actively involved in bilingual education. They see this approach as one means through which equal educational opportunity can be pursued for language minority children in public schools. These advocates have come to bilingual education out of a historical legacy within which public schools failed miserably in their obligation to meet the educational needs of children whose home language was other than English. The legal foundations driving this strand include Title VI of the Civil Rights Act of 1964, as well as the Equal Educational Opportunities Act of 1974, which states that "no state shall deny equal educational opportunity to an individual . . . (through) failure of an educational agency to take appropriate action to overcome language barriers that impede equal participation by its students in its instructional programs."[3] Typically, educators operating from this perspective stress that the outcomes of an elementary school education must include a great deal more than proficiency in English, in particular, strong academic achievement and full-scale cognitive and social development. It goes without saying that these goals cannot be achieved if children drop out of school; hence, an additional set of goals for these educators, operating within the strong civil rights tradition of recent decades, is to challenge societal and institutional obstacles that have impeded the educational progress of children growing up in language minority communities in this country.

It is helpful to keep these four strands in mind during any discussion of bilingual education. For the purposes of this chapter, the perspectives of the latter two groups will be held foremost in mind, since the interplay between these two strands is what has driven much of the policy debate within bilingual education in recent years. Nevertheless, in discussing the ultimate potential of bilingual education, as well as current trends in the more highly successful innovative projects in this area, it will be necessary to connect back to all four strands, because taken together they form the basis for a full-scale understanding of the enrichment potential of fully implemented bilingual-bicultural education.

Definitions and Key Distinctions

Bilingual education programs are common throughout the world, and they exist in substantially different forms in various international contexts. In many nations, "bilingual education" refers rather broadly to any educational approach that leads to bilingual outcomes, that is, students who are proficient to some degree in two or more languages. In the United States, for historical and political reasons, modern conceptions of bilingual education emphasize the instructional use of two languages in the classroom as the essential defining characteristic for this approach. In 1971, the U.S. Office of Education defined bilingual education as "the use of two languages, one of which is English, as mediums of instruction for the same pupil population in a well-organized program which encompasses all or part of the curriculum and includes the study of the history and culture associated with the mother tongue."[4] A decade later, the common federal definition had been shortened: "Bilingual education means instruction given through two languages, one of which is English."[5]

Over the years, a number of distinctions have been drawn to emphasize various program alternatives. In the 1970s, a distinction was often drawn between *transitional* programs, which emphasize relatively rapid transition from an instructional program with native language support accompanied by English language development into the all-English curriculum, and *maintenance* programs, which stress preservation of the child's home language and culture, with a more gradual easing into English and a continuation of native language instruction throughout the upper elementary grades.

An additional distinction has commonly been made between one-way bilingual education, where only the language minority group is schooled bilingually, and two-way bilingual education, where "speakers of both languages are placed together in a bilingual classroom to learn each others' language and work academically in both languages."[6] In a similar vein, *enrichment bilingual education* refers to "bilingual instruction for all members of society, rather than for minorities alone."[7]

The success of Canadian immersion programs since 1965 has encouraged some policymakers to promote this approach in the United States. In these programs, language majority students learn a second language through a process of total immersion in that language (L2). In the Canadian context, English-speaking Canadians were schooled in and through French for the major part of their elementary school education. In this program, the second language of the students (French) is not only a subject which they are learning, but is also the medium through which subject matter instruction is delivered.[8] Language educators do not generally consider immersion approaches to be appropriate for language minority students:

Immersion-type education through the second language has been notably unsuccessful with language minority children where there is inadequate input and support for continued mother tongue development, such as in some programs in English for native Americans and Canadians on reservations. It is also unlikely to be an appropriate alternative for young immigrant children learning the dominant language of their new country in school if it is not accompanied by first language instruction.[9]

Creative efforts to meet the separate needs of language minority and language majority students under one umbrella have been pursued over the past decade in a number of innovative programs. *Bilingual immersion education* refers to a whole set of programs in the United States which "combine the most significant features of bilingual education for language minority students and immersion education for language majority students."[10] In these programs, second language learners are purposefully mixed with native language speakers in order to encourage natural contexts for second language acquisition which lead to two-way interaction among students. Through this process, "the language majority student receives foreign language instruction within the school setting and the language minority student benefits from the opportunity to maintain the native or home language while concurrently acquiring a second language, English."[11]

Additional terms have been introduced into bilingual education discussions over the past decade as a result of ongoing policy debates at the national level. One highly publicized longitudinal study, conducted between 1983 and 1991 with U.S. Department of Education research funds, compared three alternative programs using new terms to describe generic program options: (a) "late-exit bilingual program" (substantial instruction in the home language with services provided through grade six); (b) "early-exit bilingual program" (less than forty minutes each day of instruction in the home language, offered for no more than two to three years); (c) "structured English immersion program" (almost all of the instruction in English with services offered for no more than two to three years).[12] Further clarification of these terms can be gained from examining table 1, which is adapted from a recent evaluation study.[13]

English as a Second Language (ESL) for Language Minority Students

Based on the definition of bilingual education cited earlier, it is clear that all bilingual education programs in the United States necessarily *must* have an English as a second language (ESL) component. Because this component can be developed in so many different ways within individual programs, it is difficult to arrive at an accurate, all-encompassing definition of ESL. As a general statement, however, ESL might be described as "a second language instructional approach in which the goals, teaching methods and techniques, and assessments of student progress are all based on" and oriented toward development of that student's English proficiency. Some ESL methods may define progress more in terms of "abilities to communicate messages in the target language," whereas other methods (in particular, older "conventional" methods) may focus more heavily on "abilities to produce grammatically correct utterances in the target language."[14]

ESL instruction may take place either in the context of a functioning bilingual education program, or outside that context when bilingual programs are not available. The latter option is particularly common in settings where many different language groups exist and in settings where there are only small numbers of a particular language minority group, making bilingual instruction difficult to implement. In any case, it is important to note that English as a second language is not a form of bilingual instruction; rather, it is an instructional approach which is designed to meet special needs of students who are in the process of acquiring English as an additional language. Under ideal circumstances, ESL appears as an integrated component within a bilingual curriculum; in other circumstances, it may appear as a separate strand within a mainstream all-English curriculum. ESL may be found in various forms within bilingual programs: (a) "pull-out ESL," which takes the student out of the classroom to a separate class taught by a different teacher during a part of the day; (b) a separate ESL lesson taught by the classroom teacher within the classroom during a specific instructional period each day; (c) a fully integrated mode wherein the classroom teacher develops ESL objectives as an interconnected strand within regular content-area and language arts instruction. This latter mode of delivery is commonly referred to as "content-based instruction." It reflects a strong trend within the ESL profession which can be, if properly implemented, particularly compatible with major community-based goals for bilingual education, such as achievement orientation within a strong cognitive focus.

Content-based ESL. Language teaching at all levels has for many years experienced a strong push for "contextualized language

TABLE 1

Design and Implementation Issues of Models for "Language Minority" Education

Issue/Model	Bilingual Late Exit	Bilingual Early Exit	Double Immersion	Sheltered English	ESL Pull-out
Use of native language	yes	yes	yes	no	no
Goal of bilingualism	yes	no	yes	no	no
Bilingual communication with parents built in	yes	yes	yes	no	no
Special instruction in English as a subject	yes	yes	yes	yes	yes
English taught in teaching other subjects	yes	yes	yes	yes	no
Core subjects taught in native language	yes	yes	yes/no	no	no
Access to curriculum	Full access in native language with gradual increase in English	Full initial access in native language, later in English	Full access in both native language and English differentiated	Reliance on English for access	Reliance on English for access

TABLE 1—(Continued)

DESIGN AND IMPLEMENTATION ISSUES OF MODELS FOR
"LANGUAGE MINORITY" EDUCATION

Issue/Model	Bilingual Late Exit	Bilingual Early Exit	Double Immersion	Sheltered English	ESL Pull-out
Applicable demographic conditions	Concentration of single non-English language minority (LM) group	Concentration of single non-English language minority (LM) group	A mixture of language minority (LM) and non-LM groups, with varying language proficiency backgrounds or profiles.	Multiple language groups or single group	Multiple language groups or single group
Potential advantages	Promotes full bilingualism for language minority (LM) students.	Makes efficient use of limited bilingual teachers by concentrating them at early grades Allows for native language oral fluency in early grades	Promotes full bilingualism for all students of various language backgrounds. Built-in integration	Response to multiple language groups and small concentrations	Flexible in accommodating small numbers of LM students with diverse languages

Source: Adapted from Paul Berman et al., *Meeting the Challenge of Language Diversity: An Evaluation of Programs for Pupils with Limited Proficiency in English*, vol. 1, Executive Summary (Berkeley, CA: BW Associates, 1992). Used with permission.

lessons," where the focus of what is presented and studied in the classroom is something other than isolated language structures presented out of the contexts in which the language is actually used. Adult learners who have very specific reasons for learning a second language can often have their needs met more effectively within a "special purpose" course than in one which is designed to meet general proficiency goals, such as speaking or reading the language. Common examples of this approach are "Spanish for Medical Personnel," or "ESL for Hotel Workers." When instructional goals are essentially academic in nature, as in elementary and secondary schools, one way in which contextualized language teaching can be delivered is by basing the second language curriculum on the content of required courses. This approach has a number of advantages that are fairly obvious. First, because it is tied in to ongoing learning activities, it relates directly to immediate needs experienced on a continuing basis by the learner. Second, because the second language instruction is relevant to immediate needs, motivation is strengthened. Third, because content area instruction, in order to be effective, is based on an existing knowledge base, a meaningful context is provided for the target language. Generally speaking, the more background knowledge that is tapped into, and the richer the context within which the language is presented, the easier it is for the learner to capture meaning. By focusing on meaning, learners appear to progress more rapidly in the acquisition of a second language. Finally, presenting ESL to learners in an authentic interactional context enables them to acquire discourse features and interaction patterns which are typically not easily taught and learned in conventional second language classrooms.[15]

Content-based instruction has a number of clear implications for ESL practice. First, *instructional planning* has to take into account both language goals and content-area goals, and some kind of link has to be made between the two in the overall planning process. Second, *materials* which are used for ESL lessons should be "authentic texts" in the sense that they have been created and are drawn on for purposes other than teaching language. Third, *activities* must be appropriate for the specific subject matter and be "geared to stimulate students to think and learn through the use of the target language."[16] Fourth, *assessment* procedures need to reflect adequately the dual set of goals addressed in content-based lessons. This means that conventional tests may often be inappropriate, and informal assessment procedures may need to be explored in order to enable learners to demonstrate what they are able to do with the language while engaged in content-area activities.

Many of the characteristics just described tend to appear in creative contemporary ESL teaching, regardless of whether or not the teacher sees herself as engaged in "content-based instruction." An example of this is provided by a currently popular model for organizing ESL instruction at the elementary school level—the "theme-based approach." Many teachers following this approach are enthusiastic not only because of positive results they are obtaining with students, but particularly because of the creativity it allows them in planning ESL lessons that are linked to content drawn from across the curriculum and not directly tied to a rigid ESL curriculum that has been predefined by a set of adopted ESL materials.[17]

Finally, content-based ESL instruction can be seen as part of a broader trend within elementary education toward integrating language and content instruction in all areas of the curriculum. This can sometimes lead to confusion, since it is in fact possible for both ESL specialists and content area teachers to be actually engaged in delivering ESL instruction. Consequently, for the sake of clarity it is helpful to differentiate between content-based approaches to second language instruction, where the ESL teacher is drawing on subject matter of the curriculum as the basis for an ESL lesson, and situations where a subject area teacher is pursuing explicitly stated ESL goals within the context of a regular lesson in the content area. The term "sheltered instruction" is commonly used in referring to the latter case.

Bilingual Education in the Elementary School: Examples from Different Settings

What is it like to be a student in a bilingual education classroom in the United States? Obviously, given the diversity of language minority students, local circumstances, and program alternatives, there is no such thing as a "typical" experience in bilingual education. Nevertheless, certain commonalities are evident across diverse settings. One of the best ways to get a sense of the issues and complexities of this educational approach is to look at a few of the ways through which learners might receive bilingual instruction. A sampling of the literature on different kinds of bilingual programs provides a sense of the extent to which community contexts for bilingual programs vary, as well as a rich contrast in approaches to bilingual instruction.

Schools that are in border areas often operate in bilingual contexts where program goals may be strongly influenced by language use patterns in the community:

El Paso's Ysleta School is only five blocks from Mexico. The principal . . . has created a bilingual program that makes students fluent in oral and written Spanish and then in English. . . . Children learn to move back and forth naturally between Spanish and English.[18]

Schools that are located in multilingual multicultural contexts may emphasize the social interaction that occurs across ethnolinguistic groups participating in the program. In addition, the bilingual methodology used must be appropriate for all the children in the program. For example, Oyster Elementary School in Washington, D.C.

strives for parity between the two languages of instruction, with English and Spanish used in roughly equal proportions, and with majority and minority children mixed throughout the day. The school's enrollment is 60 percent Hispanic, 20 to 25 percent non-Hispanic white, 15 percent black, and 2 percent other language minority. Each subject is taught in both English and Spanish—not concurrently, but on alternate days, periods, or semesters— giving students an immersion experience and also a chance to develop conceptually in their native tongue. Since children are mixed, teachers must work hard to make instruction comprehensible to one group and still interesting to the other. . . . Children are taught initial literacy in English and Spanish at the same time. By the middle of the first grade, they are reading in both languages.[19]

Some programs include students from different socioeconomic backgrounds, and must provide, under one umbrella, separate program strands to meet the unique needs of each group:

In San Diego, one program simultaneously "serves native Spanish-speaking (60 percent) and native English-speaking students (40 percent). . . . The program combines primary language development for minority-language students (native Spanish speakers) with second language immersion for majority-language students (native English speakers)." In preschool through grade three, instruction begins all in Spanish, with one period of ESL; instruction in English is increased until, "by the upper elementary grades, the instructional day is divided equally between Spanish and English. . . . The program enables both groups of students to become fully bilingual by the completion of elementary school, while attaining academic skill levels equivalent to or higher than those of their grade-level peers in the regular school program. . . . (The) inclusion of two linguistic groups in one classroom" allows each group to assist the other in the acquisition of the two languages of the school.[20]

Many bilingual programs that have been deemed successful by participants have not been accompanied by comprehensive evaluation efforts that effectively document the extent to which they are achieving their goals. The final example describes one school which has been accompanied by a substantial research effort:

Eastman Avenue School in Los Angeles is located in a neighborhood that is stable, lower socioeconomic, and composed nearly entirely of Hispanic students. The program, revised in 1983, now develops literacy in the primary language. "Beginning students receive solid subject matter instruction in Spanish; as the child progresses, subject matter is gradually introduced in English. Math is the first subject to be taught in English, with social studies coming later. ESL is taught from the beginning. . . . Limited English proficient children are mainstreamed with fluent English speakers in art, physical education, and music right from the beginning."[21]

These four examples, taken together, provide a glimpse of the wide variety of contexts and approaches to bilingual education in the United States and explain why it is often problematic to lump together "bilingual education programs" under one all-encompassing label.

Bilingual Education: Instructional Issues

Rationale for bilingual education. Other chapters in this volume have documented the substantial role which political agendas at both local and national levels have played in defining and ultimately constraining the full implementation of bilingual education programs. Despite competing political and ideological viewpoints, however, the fundamental rationale for bilingual education has achieved remarkable consistency among educators who have taken on advocacy roles on behalf of language minority children. Simply stated, for this group, bilingual education is not just a quick route to English proficiency, but something much more profound: it is an educational alternative which provides the strongest route to academic achievement through L1 (a non-English language) as a means for attaining the paramount long-term goal of academic achievement in L2 (English). Seen from this perspective, the goals for bilingual education as presented by Zamora, are typical:

- [To] improve the historically low academic achievement levels of students of limited English proficiency;
- [To] help students of limited English proficiency to become fluent in English and capable of functioning in an all-English curriculum;
- [To] improve the positive self-concept of students of limited English proficiency;
- [To] increase the holding power of the school; that is, to reduce the high dropout rate of students of limited English proficiency.[22]

Undergirding this rationale is a firm conviction that native language instruction provides the most effective means to achieve desired outcomes with language minority students: "Research evidence and a deeper consideration of the factors impinging on educational success shows that . . . native language instruction for language minority children promotes their educational success *in English* in a variety of ways, while at the same time preventing the alienation from the school culture that can undermine their educational achievement."[23]

Curriculum. From a curriculum perspective, this set of goals has some very clear implications for a bilingual classroom. Over the years, conventional approaches to the bilingual education curriculum for English learners have commonly included four categories. These categories are overlapping in some parts and different stages of language acquisition, as well as different grade levels, may require a slightly different curriculum focus.

I. Languages
   A. Reading/language arts in L1
   B. Reading/language arts in English

II. Content areas

III. Second language learning
   A. ESL
   B. Second language instruction in non-English language[24]

IV. Culture and heritage[25]

In a later section of this chapter I discuss current trends in bilingual education and will note how the field is currently moving toward more holistic conceptions of the curriculum. As this occurs, conventional categories may be de-emphasized to reflect instructional approaches that are grounded in full integration of language and content instruction.

Instructional alternatives. At one level, alternative program models reflect substantially different ideological perspectives as well as often conflicting political goals. This must always be borne in mind in discussing issues relating to curriculum and instruction. Nevertheless, if we address the specific instructional needs of the bilingual learner, as seen from the perspective of a classroom teacher, the fundamental curriculum decisions for bilingual education involve critical issues of language distribution. Simply stated, for the bilingual teacher the starting point for instruction involves a set of questions which revolve around language choice: "When do we use L1 and when do we use English in this classroom? For what subject areas? For which children? For which grouping structures? How much English and how much L1 should I use at the beginning of the school year, and how much should I use at the end? Should I alternate languages based on instructional period/day of the week, based on curriculum considerations, or based on some other factor? Should I always maintain strict separation of the two languages during instruction?"[26] Clearly, these are fundamental issues related to bilingual methodology, and they merit careful consideration by practitioners and program developers alike. Conventional wisdom has often taken one of two alternative positions: (1) always maintain strict separation of the two languages, and structure your program in ways which will encourage this; or (2) maintain strict separation of the two languages during periods which are focusing on language instruction (for example, language arts and ESL), but during content area instruction develop a consistent pattern for using the two languages of the classroom based on reasonable pedagogical considerations.

The first option uses an explicit, highly salient feature (for example, time of day or day of the week) to cue which language may be appropriately used at any given moment. One example here is the "alternate day" model, where one language is used on certain days and the other language is used on alternate days. In a similar vein, one language might be used in the morning, and the other language after the lunch period. These models offer highly structured support for maintaining consistent use of both languages in the classroom, something which tends not to happen when the two languages are used concurrently without specific guidelines within a given time period. When a more "laissez-faire" approach to language choice is followed, there is a tendency for English to totally predominate in the classroom, and in many cases an unconscious neglect of the other classroom language results.[27]

The second option for classroom language distribution stresses encouraging students to use the non-English language of the bilingual community in the manner which feels most natural when they are engaged in learning activities in the content areas. One of the key points raised here is that bilingual children engaged in cognitively demanding academic learning must be allowed to access their entire scope of linguistic resources in order to achieve full potential. Artificially restricting students to their "weaker language" based on arbitrary criteria (such as time of day) is pedagogically unsound, particularly when the primary focus of an activity is cognitively oriented.

Each of these two options has demonstrated success in specific documented cases. As in much of educational research, it seems likely that there is an interaction effect present with respect to alternative bilingual methods, and that other factors are ultimately more important in determining what will prove effective in any given context. Nevertheless, despite important differences in viewpoints with regard to these issues, a consensus has emerged among most bilingual educators with regard to a number of key points:

• Translation is both ineffective and inappropriate as a bilingual method of instruction. This procedure not only wastes time (by repeating the same content in the two languages), but it does not allow for the development of elaborated language. Moreover, it is extremely boring for students and runs counter to basic pedagogical principles related to motivating learners and contextualizing lesson content.

• Bilingual teachers need to be trained to "self-monitor" their language use, and to make conscious decisions about language choice in the classroom. As a rule, failure to make conscious choices regarding language distribution leads toward a replication of societal patterns, which in most cases means heavy neglect of the child's primary language in the learning process.[28]

• Full implementation of bilingual education requires substantial use of the primary language as a medium of instruction. *Programs that do not provide significant amounts of instruction in the non-English language should not, in fact, be included under the rubric of "bilingual education."* This is an important point to keep in mind when examining evaluation results with respect to alternative approaches to educating language minority children.

• Preserving the home language of language minority children is valuable in its own right, but it is also sound educational practice.[29]

This principle provides a fundamental point of unity between bilingual education for language minorities in the United States and vernacular education movements worldwide. In Great Britain, common arguments for mother tongue teaching include: (a) to support continuity of learning and avoid a "learning freeze"; (b) to instill confidence (an essential prerequisite to learning); (c) to validate the home culture; (d) to accord "equality of opportunity" to ethnic minority pupils; (e) to promote cognitive and social growth; (f) to enhance a positive sense of identity; (g) to facilitate communication between parents, children, and relatives by maintaining linguistic competence in the home language; and (h) to enrich cultural life of country as a whole.[30] Each one of these arguments is applicable to the United States context. Taken as a whole, they provide a basis for linking bilingual education in the elementary schools in the United States to a broad range of international contexts where instructional practices may contrast sharply, yet the basic principle of affirming home language enhancement during the early years of schooling persists.

Further complicating the discussion related to classroom language is the presence of different varieties of Spanish within bilingual speech communities. Fortunately, all Spanish varieties in the United States are mutually intelligible, and formal written Spanish is remarkably consistent despite important regional variations in actual spoken use. An important point to keep in mind when discussing bilingual methodology is that spoken varieties used by students during early years of schooling are likely to differ from the variety modeled by their teacher in the classroom. This should not be seen as a problem, since students are embarked on a developmental journey which will ultimately lead them to full acquisition of a more formal variety of Spanish, to be used when they write and, in certain cases, when they speak.

Different program models clearly imply different "rules" for classroom language use; in some cases, these alternatives imply fundamentally different philosophical orientations, particularly with respect to the desirability of encouraging bilingualism in our society. Much of the literature on this subject appears to be contradictory and, at times, somewhat contentious. One statement that seems reasonable, however, based on our current state of knowledge, is that different models appear to be effective in different contexts, and some models which are effective in one context (for example, close to a border area, or in a community which has a high concentration of one specific language minority group) may not be particularly effective in other contexts. It is clear that bilingual contexts vary widely in the United States, and that the sociolinguistic features of a particular language situation (including such things as attitudes toward the use of English or toward the home language; the degree to which a home language may be used for reading and writing; the extent to which languages are mixed or not mixed when used by bilingual individuals in a community) impact deeply the desirability or effectiveness of alternative language distribution models.

Current Trends in Education of Language Minority Students

Over the past decade, widespread public dissatisfaction over perceived failures within the nation's educational system have led to strong calls for greater accountability by schools. Accompanying the often strident attacks on educators has been a call for increased testing and evaluation of teachers and students at all levels. While strict accountability and appropriate assessment of student progress are highly desirable, there has been a growing consensus among many educators that minority students—and in particular language minority students—may often be adversely affected by some of the "backwash effects" of inappropriate mandated testing programs. One of the greatest concerns that has been voiced increasingly in recent years is that schools serving minority students, which have historically not obtained good results in achievement outcomes, have begun to treat the test as the starting point for classroom instruction rather than as a mere assessment of outcomes. This serious distortion, which leads teachers and students to focus on test-taking skills and on mastering discrete points which have been taken from the curriculum out of context, denies students the kind of contextualized, language-rich learning environment that most enhances comprehension, language acquisition, and cognitive development. Ironically, this type of test-centered curriculum focusing on "minimum skills" is most likely to occur precisely in settings where students can be most harmed, that is, settings with students who are in the process of acquiring a new language (English), and who need to learn how to use that language for new purposes (such as thinking and solving problems).[31]

Contemporary instructional practice in bilingual education is extremely varied, yet much of what is commonly alluded to in the literature as representing the best of current innovative approaches seems to share a common interest in countering the negative and potentially harmful pressures of test-driven curricula that focus excessively on highly specific, narrowly defined minimum skills. Indeed, when this literature is carefully examined, certain common underlying themes tend to emerge which suggest quite a contrasting approach to language minority education. I will highlight some of these trends that appear particularly significant:

• Greater attention to language minority students' *cognitive* development. Although it is typically the students' language background that will trigger their involvement in transitional bilingual education, it is an error to lose sight of the overall necessary final outcome of public schooling, that is, full achievement in all the subject areas. In order for students to be successful in the upper elementary grades and beyond, there needs to be strong emphasis on the development of thinking skills in all areas of the curriculum from the very beginning of formal instruction. In practice, this means rejection of techniques and procedures that rely on drill and practice or repetition out of context, and abandonment of activities that rely heavily on lower-order cognitive functioning with little need for learners to draw on their intellectual resources. It means, further, organizing the curriculum heavily around activities that promote a great deal of interaction and which demand high levels of cognitive involvement by learners as they complete assigned tasks.[32]

• Insistence on attending to language goals from a holistic perspective, with stronger emphasis on process and on interconnecting oral/written language, as well as reading/writing instruction. The trend in creative practice is clearly away from treating language development goals in isolation from other learning goals. As a consequence, the *integration* of language and content area instruction emerges as a primary theme with regard to both native language instruction and second language teaching. This important current development in bilingual education is not unrelated to parallel trends in mainstream education that are challenging conventional assumptions regarding the teaching of reading and writing, and which are leading to thorough reexamination of elementary school language arts curriculums in many parts of the country. In practice, this emphasis leads to intensive and extensive literacy activities across the curriculum and throughout the day, and very often puts the act of writing at the heart of instructional activity throughout the curriculum.

• Not unrelated to the first two trends is an increased attention to *interaction* as a fundamental requirement for successful attainment of both linguistic and cognitive goals. In practice, this means organizing the classroom physically in ways that will increase interaction among students (e.g., clustering students instead of placing them in parallel rows) and selecting methods (e.g., small-group instruction) which maximize opportunities for interaction.[33]

• *Cooperation* has not been a prevalent principle in U.S. education, where goals have typically been defined in relation to individual achievement. A contemporary trend which has received a great deal of attention is cooperative learning. In this approach, students operate out of small groups where collaboration in solving problems is valued and actively promoted, while maintaining individual accountability for learning outcomes. Cooperative learning creates interdependence among group members through a broad variety of strategies, but a unifying thread that is common to all procedures is student-centered instruction with a high degree of face-to-face interaction within small groups. The approach appears promising for a number of reasons, not the least of which is that it appears to be quite effective.[34] In addition, cooperative learning appears to be highly compatible with learning preferences of many students whose needs are not currently being met under conventional classroom practices. It also encourages hetero-geneous grouping in classrooms, which sets up naturally occurring student-student learning environments that enhance student self-confidence and self-esteem as individual contributions are rewarded through the achievement of group goals.[35] Finally, as we will note below, cooperative learning also holds tremendous promise as a vehicle through which ESL goals can be effectively pursued.

• As dissatisfaction with pedagogically counterproductive, exter-nally imposed testing programs increases among educators in general, bilingual educators have begun to stress the importance of developing *alternative assessment* procedures for measuring student outcomes. Language assessment issues have always been at the heart of bilingual education policy formulation, and many unresolved issues remain related to the measurement of language proficiency among bilingual children at young ages. Some of these issues may never be fully resolved to the satisfaction of policymakers and/or measurement specialists. There is an increasing trend in bilingual education to supplement formal procedures for measuring language proficiency by adopting informal assessment procedures which allow classroom teachers to track students' language development in both academic and social/interpersonal settings. Included in the broad array of procedures available are oral and written language samples, checklists for observing language use in context, and anecdotal records.[36] With current interest in "portfolio assessment" receiving a great deal of attention as an effective evaluation tool for all educators, it seems likely that the long-term interest in bilingual education in avoiding excessive reliance on single measures for arriving at important decisions about students will receive strong external validation as an appropriate stance toward comprehensive evaluation in general.

Implications for ESL instruction. The themes outlined above are highly compatible with current trends in ESL instruction. In recent years, ESL specialists working with LM children have moved away from discussions focusing on "alternative second language teaching methods" toward a discussion of classroom-based features that can be manipulated by teachers in an effort to maximize the potential for second language acquisition within that context.[37] Of particular interest here are the current trends toward greater use of cooperative learning approaches within small groups. This approach to learning in elementary classrooms introduces a number of factors which, based on current research on second language acquisition, are highly favorable for effectively pursuing ESL goals. Specifically, cooperative learning is beneficial for second language acquisition because it allows for more frequent talk among students, encourages natural language use in a meaningful setting, integrates academic learning with language learning, draws on primary language resources of the children, and develops social skills for increased interaction.[38] Although there are tremendous individual differences in how children go about the task of acquiring a second language,[39] classroom contexts which provide multiple opportunities for negotiation of meaning through two-way interaction are increasingly seen as important elements for enhancing the process of second language acquisition among LM students.

Implications for bilingual instruction. Taken as a whole, current trends identified above offer substantial promise for improved outcomes in language minority performance. Of particular significance is emergence of research evidence that innovative approaches following these themes appear to be effective when found in well-implemented programs. One recent study collected data on four innovative demonstration models built around these themes, and found support for "the value of using teaching and learning approaches that promote participation and cooperation among students, and that recognize the contribution that students can bring into the classroom. . . . [In addition], the models showed the importance of providing language minority students with instructional content that is challenging and that is culturally and personally relevant to the students."[40]

One trend that poses an interesting challenge for bilingual instruction is the increasing reliance on integrative approaches to developing language goals within the context of content area goals. In some instances, the adoption of holistic approaches to literacy instruction, combined with a blurring of distinctions between specific classroom periods for native language and second language instruction, can lead to unintended outcomes, such as premature discontinuation of efforts to help the child achieve literacy in his or her primary language. Based on sociolinguistic research on the relationship between minority languages and English in the United States, it is clear that, in most cases, when students are left to their own devices and not firmly guided in the process of acquiring literacy skills in their native language, they will tend to drift away from further developing reading and writing in that language. Yet a great deal of research evidence suggests that, for language minority children, a firm grounding in native language literacy is an important contributing factor for successful achievement outcomes in bilingual education.[41] This suggests that bilingual educators working within whole language approaches will need to incorporate strategies and procedures to counter sociolinguistic pressures existing within schools and communities that often lead students and parents to neglect full development of literacy in the primary language. This is not to say that whole language instruction does not support L1; to the contrary, the underlying principles that have guided the whole language movement are wholly compatible with the philosophy of bilingual education, and, indeed in many areas of the nation, whole language practitioners have been at the vanguard of redirecting bilingual education in ways that strengthen native language proficiency of LM children. Rather, the point being made, simply stated, is that teachers must recognize that children's language choices are also subject to social pressures which propel them to L2. Olga Vásquez, in chapter 8 in this volume, provides an example of how this may occur in even the most supportive of environments.

Conclusion

Bilingual education programs do not exist in a vacuum—the same forces and external conditions which profoundly affect so-called "mainstream education" invariably influence the direction in which bilingual educators will move. As we head toward the twenty-first century, many of the external events that are altering our nation's perceptions of its role in the world are also going to influence the course which bilingual education will choose to take. For too long has there been a disregard in the nation for learning about other peoples, as well as a notorious reluctance to commit time and resources to the task of becoming proficient in languages other than English. This societal failure, which is often unfairly blamed completely on the schools, must be juxtaposed with something which schools *are* in a position to do something about, that is, ending a long tradition of neglect with regard to the valuable linguistic and cultural resources that already exist in the nation. A new sense of urgency is emerging that the nation can no longer afford to overlook or to waste these precious human resources, and from this comes a renewed interest in examining ways through which our educational system might promote more effectively the study of other languages and cultures.

For some policymakers, a linkage is being made for the first time between concerns related to the nation's economic future in an interdependent global economy, and bilingual education, which possesses strong potential for attaining high levels of achievement in foreign languages as well as cross-cultural abilities not currently emphasized in the curriculum. The four strands identified at the outset of this chapter provide a strong clue as to how bilingual education is well-equipped—from both a philosophical and historical perspective—to provide leadership in this effort. Historical roots tied to ethnic revitalization movements provide hundreds of excellent examples of successful efforts to preserve and enhance existing language and cultural resources residing within the nation's multicultural communities. A second strand, which is tied to ongoing efforts of foreign language educators to stimulate interest in the study of language and culture as an indispensable element within every general education, represents a valuable teaching resource that needs to be tapped as an ally in efforts to redirect the public's priorities toward these common goals. Finally, bilingual educators who are currently working within the framework of conventional bilingual education, focusing heavily on the primary needs of language minority children (that is, equal educational opportunity, English proficiency, full academic achievement, and empowerment through culturally relevant education) need to become linked to efforts aimed at fulfilling a vision of the United States as a committed multicultural nation operating effectively within a global family. This goal can be achieved through umbrella projects which allow for program variation according to diverse student needs within the common enterprise.

Above all, however, the educational interests of our most vulnerable student population—those children whose home language is not English—must be carefully protected within joint ventures. The needs of these children must never be secondary to the enrichment goals of others who have little to lose and a great deal to gain from this enhancement of the elementary curriculum. In other words, the needs of LM students must remain the primary goal of any language enrichment program that includes monolingual English-speaking children. The promise of fully inclusive, broadly defined bilingual education is that it provides a curriculum enhancement which could eventually lead to full achievement of bilingualism for all elementary school children in the nation. This multicultural vision is not only attainable through bilingual education, but, at some point, may become a national imperative for economic survival.

NOTES

1. Lily Wong Fillmore, "Language and Cultural Issues in the Early Education of Language Minority Children," in *The Care and Education of America's Young Children: Obstacles and Opportunities*, edited by Sharon L. Kagan, Ninetieth Yearbook of the National Society for the Study of Education, Part 1 (Chicago, IL: University of Chicago Press, 1991), p. 33.

2. See Joshua A. Fishman, *Language Loyalty in the United States: The Maintenance and Perpetuation of Non-English Mother Tongues by American Ethnic and Religious Groups* (The Hague: Mouton, 1966).

3. Colman B. Stein, *Sink or Swim: The Politics of Bilingual Education* (New York: Praeger, 1986), p. 66.

4. As cited in Carlos J. Ovando and Virginia P. Collier, *Bilingual and ESL Classrooms: Teaching in Multicultural Contexts* (New York: McGraw-Hill, 1985), p. 2.

5. *Federal Register*, vol. 45 (152), August 5, 1980, pp. 52064-65.

6. Ovando and Collier, *Bilingual and ESL Classrooms*, p. 40.

7. Ibid., citing Joshua A. Fishman.

8. David P. Dolson, *The Application of Immersion Education in the United States* (Rosslyn, VA: National Clearinghouse for Bilingual Education, 1985), p. 5.

9. Donna Brinton, Marguerite A. Snow, and Marjorie B. Wesche, *Content-Based Second Language Instruction* (New York: Newbury House Publishers, 1989), p. 8. See also, Office of Bilingual Bicultural Education, *Studies on Immersion Education: A Collection for United States Educators* (Sacramento, CA: California State Department of Education, 1984).

10. Kathryn J. Lindholm, *Directory of Bilingual Immersion Programs: Two-Way Bilingual Education for Language Minority and Majority Students*, Publication ER8 (Los Angeles: Center for Language Education and Research, University of California, Los Angeles, 1987), p. 5.

11. Marguerite A. Snow, *Innovative Second Language Instruction: Bilingual Immersion Programs*, Publication ER1 (Los Angeles: Center for Language Education and Research, University of California, Los Angeles, 1986), pp. 2-3.

12. David Ramírez, *Longitudinal Study of Structured English Immersion Strategy, Early-exit, and Late-exit Bilingual Education Programs*, Final Report. (Washington, DC: U.S. Department of Education, Contract No. 300-87-0156, 1991). A discussion of this study is included in chapter 3 of this volume.

13. Paul Berman, Jay Chambers, Patricia Gándara, Barry McLaughlin, Catherine Minicucci, Beryl Nelson, Laurie Olsen, and Tom Parrish, *Meeting the Challenge of Language Diversity: An Evaluation of Programs for Pupils with Limited Proficiency in English*, vol. 1 (Berkeley, CA: BW Associates, February 1992), p. 5 of Executive Summary, R-119/1.

14. Office of Bilingual Bicultural Education, *Schooling and Language Minority Students: A Theoretical Framework* (Sacramento, CA: California State Department of Education, 1981), p. 216.

15. Brinton, Snow, and Wesche, *Content-Based Second Language Instruction*, pp. 3-4.

16. Ibid., p. 2.

17. For further discussion on coordinating the learning of ESL with content area subjects, see Bernard Mohan, *Language and Content* (Reading, MA: Addison-Wesley, 1986).

18. Stein, *Sink or Swim: The Politics of Bilingual Education*, p. 66.

19. James Crawford, *Bilingual Education: History, Politics, Theory, and Practice* (Trenton, NJ: Crane, 1989), p. 168.

20. San Diego Unified School District, *An Exemplary Approach to Bilingual Education: A Comprehensive Handbook for Implementing an Elementary-Level Spanish-English Language Immersion Program* (San Diego, CA: San Diego Unified School District, 1982), p. 1.

21. Stephen Krashen and Douglas Biber, *On Course: Bilingual Education's Success in California* (Sacramento, CA: California Association for Bilingual Education, 1988), p. 36.

22. Gloria Zamora, "Understanding Bilingual Education: A Texas Perspective," *IDRA Newsletter* (November, 1979): 6-8.

23. Catherine E. Snow, "Rationales for Native Language Instruction: Evidence from Research," in *Bilingual Education: Issues and Strategies*, edited by Amado Padilla, Halford Fairchild, and Concepción Valadez (Newbury Park, CA: Sage, 1990), p. 72.

24. This is offered for non-LEP participants, and typically exists in two-way programs (which includes English proficient students). Many transitional bilingual education programs do not include this kind of instruction in the curriculum.

25. This category varies widely depending on program model, but for programs that seriously address the third and fourth goals listed earlier (i.e., positive self-concept and reduced dropout rates), this is a critical part of the curriculum.

26. These issues are discussed at length in Rodolfo Jacobson and Christian Faltis, eds., *Language Distribution Issues in Bilingual Schooling* (Clevedon, England: Multilingual Matters, 1989).

27. See Arnulfo G. Ramírez, *Bilingualism through Schooling: Cross-Cultural Education for Minority and Majority Students* (Albany, NY: State University of New York Press, 1985), pp. 154-174, and Lily Wong Fillmore and Concepción Valadez, "Teaching Bilingual Learners," in *Handbook of Research on Teaching*, edited by M. C. Wittrock (New York: Macmillan, 1986).

28. Dorothy Legarreta-Marcaída, "Effective Use of the Primary Language in the Classroom," in Office of Bilingual Bicultural Education, *Schooling and Language Minority Students: A Theoretical Framework* (Sacramento, CA: California State Department of Education, 1981), pp. 83-116.

29. Nadine Dutcher, *The Use of First and Second Languages in Primary Education: Selected Case Studies*, Staff Working Paper No. 504 (Washington, DC: World Bank, 1982).

30. Paula Tansley, *Community Languages in Primary Education: Report from the SCDC Mother Tongue Project* (Windsor, Berkshire: NFER-NELSON, 1986), pp. 16-18.

31. See, for example, Jim Cummins, *Bilingualism and Special Education: Issues in Assessment and Pedagogy* (Clevedon, England: Multilingual Matters, 1984).

32. For an illustrative example, see Roland G. Tharp and Ronald Gallimore, *Rousing Minds to Life* (Cambridge, England: Cambridge University Press, 1988).

33. See, for example, Robert A. DeVillar and Christian J. Faltis, *Computers and Cultural Diversity: Restructuring for School Success* (Albany, NY: State University of New York Press, 1991).

34. See Robert Slavin, *Cooperative Learning: Theory, Research, and Practice* (Boston: Allyn & Bacon, 1990).

35. Luis C. Moll, Carlos Vélez-Ibáñez, and James Greenberg, *Community Knowledge and Classroom Practice—Combining Resources for Literacy Instruction: A Handbook for Teachers and Planners* (Arlington, VA: Development Associates, 1990).

36. Celia Genishi and Anne H. Dyson, *Language Assessment in the Early Years* (Norwood, NJ: Ablex, 1984).

37. See Pat Rigg and D. Scott Enright, eds., *Children and ESL: Integrating Perspectives* (Washington, DC: Teachers of English to Speakers of Other Languages, 1986).

38. Mary McGroarty, "The Benefits of Cooperative Learning Arrangements in Second Language Instruction," *NABE: Journal of the National Association for Bilingual Education* 13, no. 3 (Winter, 1989): 127-144. See also Carolyn Kessler, ed., *Cooperative Language Learning: A Teacher's Resource Book* (Englewood Cliffs, NJ: Prentice Hall Regents, 1992).

39. Lily Wong Fillmore, "Individual Differences in Second Language Acquisition," in *Individual Differences in Language Ability and Language Behavior*, edited by Charles J. Fillmore, Daniel Kempler, and William S. Wang (New York: Academic Press, 1979), pp. 202-228.

40. Charlene Rivera and Annette M. Zehler, "Assuring the Academic Success of Language Minority Students: Collaboration in Teaching and Learning," *Innovative Approaches Research Project* (Arlington, VA: Development Associates, 1990), p. 15.

41. Jim Cummins, *Empowering Minority Students* (Sacramento, CA: California Association for Bilingual Education, 1989).

CHAPTER V

Secondary Schooling for Students Becoming Bilingual

TAMARA LUCAS

Students in U.S. secondary schools who are not native speakers of English face serious challenges in their quest to succeed in school and beyond. They must develop their oral and written abilities in English to the extent that they can understand and express complex concepts in various subject areas. They must learn the ins and outs of the United States educational system quickly enough to take the appropriate and necessary classes so that they can graduate and, ideally, be prepared for postsecondary education. If they are new to the United States, they must develop an understanding of the local and national cultural values and customs in order to participate successfully in schooling and related activities. For the most part, secondary language minority (LM) students must face these challenges with little support from the schools and the educational system. They are expected to be able to fend for themselves in a system with which they are assumed to be familiar and for which they are assumed to be prepared.

How well does this system serve secondary LM students? Overall, the assessment is gloomy. Students who enter secondary schools without adequate English skills to succeed in regular classes are generally not familiar with the system and are not fully prepared to participate in it. Because of the fragmented departmental structure and the subject-matter orientation of secondary schools, few of them provide a cohesive program to address the complex needs of LM students. Secondary schools lack sufficient numbers of staff with applicable training and experience as well as appropriate materials and curricula.[1] In fact, most of the energy and resources spent on developing programs for LM students in the last two decades has been concentrated on elementary programs. As a result of these factors, for most or all of every school day, secondary LM students find them-selves struggling to understand a minimum of academic material with

Tamara Lucas is Project Director for Art, Research, and Curriculum Associates of Oakland, California.

little effective assistance, and rarely engaging in cognitively sophisti-
cated thought and communication.

Despite this generally gloomy picture, LM students do participate
and achieve in some secondary schools. Much of the information and
many of the examples in this chapter are drawn from three research
projects focused on such schools. In one study, my colleagues and I
identified and examined six effective high schools in California and
Arizona which were taking concrete steps to promote the academic
success of Latino LM students.[2] These schools were nominated by
educators at state, county, and district levels and the schools provided
quantitative evidence of their success (for example, attendance rates,
dropout rates, postsecondary education attendance, and/or test
scores). Another study identified and examined nine exemplary
programs in six states, including seven secondary programs, in which
instruction was provided primarily through modified instructional
approaches in English rather than in students' native languages.[3]
Again, programs were selected through a process of nomination and
subsequent collection of evidence of student success. A third study
examined the efforts of school districts to continue programs for LM
students after having received federal funding to provide such services
under Title VII of the Elementary and Secondary Education Act
enacted in 1968.[4] (Title VII provides for grants to school districts to
establish programs for students with limited proficiency in English.)
As part of this latter study, case studies were conducted of twenty
school districts in sixteen states which had been successful in
continuing such programs after federal support ended.[5]

Although I draw from these studies, the chapter is not a report of
research. It is a compilation of factors that have practical influences on
the success of LM students in secondary schools. At times I appeal to
the authority of my own and the reader's experience with schools and
schooling; at other times, I appeal to the authority of research. The
chapter synthesizes information gathered in different studies and
projects with diverse purposes, presenting issues that are relevant to
secondary schools serving LM students and are of practical concern to
educators. Although many of the issues discussed apply to most
secondary LM students, the primary focus is on Hispanic students,
the largest group of LM students in U.S. schools.

This chapter is also not a description of a "model" or "models" of
secondary practices that can be summarily adopted by schools. There
is no one model of effective secondary schools or programs that will
work everywhere for LM students in general or for Hispanic LM

students in particular. While secondary schools have some striking similarities, each school and program in which Hispanic LM students achieve has characteristics that set it apart from all others. Although "schooling has a common set of characteristics, . . . school-to-school differences result from the sum total of how these characteristics manifest themselves in each school."[6]

Schools and programs exist within different contexts. Indeed, "multiple embedded contexts . . . define the secondary school workplace and shape teaching and learning within them."[7] One of the key findings of the study of exemplary programs using English as the primary language of instruction (called Special Alternative Instructional Programs, or SAIPs) was that "the form an exemplary SAIP took and the nature of its success built upon and was influenced by its context."[8] Contextual factors such as the following determine what program elements are appropriate and effective in any given school: the backgrounds and training of school and district staff; the nature, size, stability, educational backgrounds, countries of origin, and recency of arrival of the LM students and their families; the history of and attitude toward linguistic and cultural diversity in the community, the district, and the school; the history of programs for LM students in the district and the school.

Effective programs for LM students are most likely to result when conscious attention is given to the existing contextual factors within particular communities and schools. As Goodlad has pointed out, "Improvement is essentially a school-by-school process, enlightened by the degree to which those associated with each school and trying to improve it have the data required for building a useful agenda"[9]—data which must include information about contextual factors like those listed above. Efforts at school improvement should "reflect . . . local contexts, histories, and organizational cultures."[10]

While existing contextual factors influence which program elements will be effective, the context itself can, at the same time, be adapted to support the success of the program and of the LM students it serves. Secondary LM students have "a complex array of academic and social needs which go far beyond lack of skills in the English language."[11] Programs that are most effective with these students are embedded within larger environments that are supportive of LM students' learning and achievement in a broad sense. The study of exemplary SAIPs found, for example, that these were not isolated programs and were not the only support available to LM students. In fact, it proved difficult in most cases to determine where the SAIP left off and "regular" school programs began.[12]

Some of the activities and services in the larger context surrounding effective programs for secondary LM students are as follows:

• LM students have access to counseling and tutoring services as needed.

• They have a variety of extracurricular activities available to them (for example, newspapers, sports, activities, clubs).

• The nonbilingual and non-ESL classes in which LM students enroll incorporate modified instructional approaches to some degree. In the electives they take while enrolled in the special programs and in the regular content classes they take after being exited from special programs, the instruction takes into account their linguistic and cultural diversity.

• Their families find extensive support networks in the schools, districts, and communities.

• Value for their languages and cultures is manifested throughout the schools and districts in a variety of ways: learning about students' cultures, learning students' languages, hiring bilingual staff with the same cultural backgrounds as the students, offering advanced as well as basic and lower-division content courses in the students' primary languages, encouraging students to develop their primary language skills, allowing students to speak their primary languages.[13]

The chapter is divided into two parts. In the first part I examine school and program structure, presenting four different organizational configurations of programs for LM students. In the second part I present some common features across secondary programs that are successful with Hispanic LM students. Although these aspects of secondary programs will be discussed separately, in reality they are all interrelated. In attempting to adapt these features to other schools, we should keep in mind that "efforts at improvement must encompass the school as a system of interacting parts, each affecting the others."[14]

Organizational Configurations of Secondary Schools Serving LM Students

One of the key features of secondary schools is their fragmented structure. They are departmentalized according to subject areas, and the school day is divided into short (usually forty-five to fifty-five minutes) time blocks in which students take classes focused on specific subject areas. This fragmentation and "structural rigidity . . . [appear to be] particularly unsuited to the educational needs of LEP [limited English proficient] students."[15] The resulting superficial coverage of subjects, which works against serious learning for all students,[16] is even more superficial for LM students, who have difficulty with English as well as with the content being presented. Just as the school is fragmented, so is the approach to educating LM students. When different departments are responsible for meeting the needs of LM students in their subject areas, the effectiveness and comprehensiveness of the approach in the different subjects may vary considerably. For example, LM students may be well served in mathematics and poorly served in science and social studies.[17] In addition, the division of the school day into short periods makes it impossible for teachers to provide extended and in-depth instruction on challenging topics.

In fact, it is difficult to imagine that this fragmented approach to instruction and to time allocation is the most effective way to organize secondary schools for any students. "A number of structural features of secondary schools" such as departmentalization and a subject-based focus may inhibit collaboration and interaction among faculty members as well as student learning.[18] Some restructuring appears to be called for.

Restructuring is, of course, not an either-or phenomenon. It occurs along a continuum encompassing programs which depart less radically from the traditional and programs which depart more radically. At the same time, school restructuring "is not a destination; it is a process,"[19] a dynamic rather than static phenomenon, requiring constant monitoring and adjusting to changes in staff, students, goals, needs, problems, and successes. It is not yet clear which kinds of organizational configurations work best in programs for LM students. No research focused on this question has been conducted, and practical experience has not been sufficiently varied and extensive to provide clear guidelines. Therefore, while the examples described here are for the most part from programs that have been identified as being successful with LM students, it is not clear whether their success derives partly or at all from their structures.

The organizational configurations of secondary schools and programs serving LM students may be categorized according to four different types along a continuum from more traditional to less traditional, as illustrated in figure 1.

STRUCTURE A: SPECIAL COURSES WITHIN THE LARGER SCHOOL STRUCTURE

The most traditional organization for secondary schools serving LM students provides special courses within a standard school

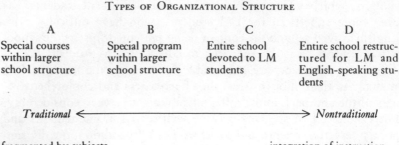

Fig. 1. Structures of secondary programs serving LM students

structure. In these schools, some combination of ESL classes, native language content classes, ESL content classes,[20] and native language development classes (for example, Spanish for Spanish speakers) are offered for LM students, just as regular English and content classes are offered to native speakers of English. LM students follow the same schedules as the English-speaking students, but they take classes designed specifically to address their language differences. LM students and English-speaking students are usually integrated for some portion of the day, the amount of integration depending upon such factors as students' levels of proficiency in English and the availability of specially trained staff. The number of special classes, the qualifications of those who teach them, the content areas covered, and the quality of instruction vary radically from school to school. The teachers of these special classes are affiliated only with their subject area departments and may not communicate with each other any more than they communicate with the mainstream staff. While many schools approach the education of LM students in this way,[21] I know of no schools with this structure that have been identified as effective or exemplary with respect to the education of limited English proficient students.

STRUCTURE B: A SPECIAL PROGRAM WITHIN THE LARGER SCHOOL STRUCTURE

Other schools have cohesive programs for LM students that exist within the larger school structure. In this arrangement, someone is responsible for coordinating the program across subject areas and grade levels. The comprehensiveness of the program and the extent to which it is an autonomous unit vary. Some programs offer special courses in all subject areas and have their own full-time administrators and their own building or space within a building. Others offer courses in only some subject areas, are run by a part-time coordinator, and hold classes in various locations within a school facility. In all these programs, however, the goal is to help LM students become proficient enough in English so that they can be mainstreamed as quickly as possible.

A Texas school district in 1990 had a school-within-a-school program where the middle schools and high schools were organized by interdisciplinary teams, with the LM program staff constituting one team that shared the same students. In addition to having their own preparation periods, they had a common planning period every day to discuss students and to coordinate their teaching. In one middle school, for example, four teachers and a paraprofessional taught a group of one hundred sixth, seventh, and eighth grade students in a section of the school that had once been the science department and was separated from the main part of the second floor by double doors. In the morning, students were grouped according to four levels of English proficiency—novice (for students with weak literacy skills in any language as well as very little English ability), beginning, intermediate, and advanced. In the afternoon, they were grouped by grade level for classes in mathematics, science, and social studies. The teachers were affiliated with their content area departments in the school and met with those departments as well as with their team. One of the teachers was the team leader, acting as a liaison with the principal and district administrators. The team, with the guidance of the team leader, made decisions about scheduling and assigning students to the different program levels.

A second type of program that functions within the larger school structure would be more accurately described as a school-outside-a-school. These programs have their own buildings separate from other schools, but they are not comprehensive schools and students do not attend them for the whole day. Another Texas district had a center for LM students in middle and high schools. Teachers at the center had students for blocks of time (two to three periods), which allowed them flexibility in the types of activities they could do as well as giving them extended time with the students. Middle school LM students were bused to the center from their home schools and spent the morning there. High school students were bused to the center from their home schools in the afternoon. The center provided ESL classes for all students, social studies for middle school students, and fundamentals of mathematics, pre-algebra, and algebra I for high school students. At their home campuses students also were in ESL and ESL content classes, depending upon their level of English proficiency, and students in some schools were in classes in Spanish for Spanish speakers.

Having a special program within a larger school structure, like those described above, makes efficient use of staff. Those who are educated to work with LM students and committed to working with them can work exclusively with LM students in an environment designed to serve non-native speakers of English. Coordination of the program is greatly facilitated by having most of the services for LM students in one location.

STRUCTURE C: AN ENTIRE SCHOOL
DEVOTED TO LM STUDENTS

In the two program structures (A and B) described above, classes or cohesive programs for LM students exist within larger school structures designed for speakers of English. The norm in these schools is the native English speaker—even if LM students constitute a very large proportion of the student population—and the goal is to see that LM students are "transitioned" into regular classes as soon as possible. Departing more from the traditional school structure, the third type of program (Structure C) consists of an entire school designed just for LM students, a school in which the norm is a non-native speaker with limited proficiency in English. This type of program is, of course, even more cohesive than that described above because the LM program is the school and vice versa. Within this category, there are two subcategories: (1) schools which LM students attend for a limited period of time before enrolling in a regular school; and (2) schools which LM students can attend for all four years of high school.

Most schools which LM students attend for a limited amount of time are designed specifically for newcomer students, that is, LM students who have been in the United States for two years or less.[22] Almost all these programs provide English language development classes and orientation to U.S. schooling and culture. Many also provide some content classes in students' native languages and/or in English, and some provide native language development classes. The amount of time students may stay in such programs varies. However, since these students are linguistically segregated from native English speakers, most school districts require that they be sent to a regular school after a period of time. This type of structure, like the school-outside-a-school, makes efficient use of staff and gives recently arrived LM students a chance to become acclimated to U.S. schools and culture in a safe environment before being thrust into a regular high school.

For example, in 1991 LM students could attend one newcomer school in the San Francisco Bay Area for only six months, after which they had to enroll in a regular district high school, vocational school, or community college. To attend the school, students could not have been in the United States for more than two years. The school offered four levels of ESL classes and native language content classes in several different languages (Spanish, Chinese, Vietnamese, Filipino, Cambodian). Preliterate students with no proficiency in English took a two-semester orientation course which taught them about the school, the neighborhood, the city, and the surrounding area as well as providing practice in basic communication skills and access to some information about U.S. culture.

I am aware of only one school that is devoted entirely to LM students and which they can attend for all four years of high school. This school, established in 1985 in New York City, is a comprehensive high school specifically for LM students. It is one of two alternative high schools located on the campus of a community college, the other school having been previously designed for students who were at risk for dropping out. In 1990, when my colleagues and I visited the school, students were admitted based on years of U.S. residency (fewer than four years), low scores on a standardized test (below the 21st percentile on the Language Assessment Battery), and/or recommendation by junior high school guidance counselors. The school's students had full access to all the facilities of the community college and could enroll in college courses if they were proficient enough in English.

In addition to enrolling only LM students, this high school also departed from the traditional secondary school in its curriculum and its decision-making structure. Besides having access to courses that met all state guidelines and requirements for a fully comprehensive high school, students took a three-course sequence which helped to facilitate their adjustment to U.S. schools and society and a three-course sequence on personal and career development and decision making. They worked in an out-of-school unpaid internship program for which they earned credit, and attended a weekly seminar during their internship to discuss their work experiences. The school did not offer separate ESL classes because all teachers integrated English language development in all classes, regardless of the content focus of the class. Four days a week, the students followed the traditional pattern of attending classes in fifty-minute time blocks. But on two half-days a week, the traditional fragmented structure was modified. On Wednesday afternoons, students went to their work internships or club meetings while the staff participated in development activities and committee meetings. The school was organized into "houses"— groups of fifteen to eighteen students and a staff member (teacher, counselor, administrator, and/or paraprofessional) who met every Tuesday morning for seventy minutes throughout the entire school year. House meetings were devoted to addressing students' nonacademic needs through discussions and other types of activities.

The school's approach to decision making also distinguished it from most others. Collaboration was emphasized throughout the school—between teachers and administrators, among teachers, between teachers and students, among students—and the decision-making structure of the school reflected this emphasis. School governance was largely in the hands of the staff rather than the principal. Each faculty member served on one of four committees that made recommendations to the administration and then worked on the implementation of negotiated changes. The committees were: Personnel/Peer Support; Curriculum; Staff Development; and Immigration Concerns.

STRUCTURE D: RESTRUCTURING OF ENTIRE SCHOOL FOR LM STUDENTS AND FOR SPEAKERS OF ENGLISH

Some entire schools have been reorganized to provide more flexibility and autonomy to teachers and more opportunity for individualized learning and collaboration among students, as the following two examples illustrate.[23] While the population of students in these schools is more traditional than the all-LM population in the schools in structure C, the structural elements (integration of subject areas, scheduling, and decision making) are less traditional. I am aware of no secondary school in any structural configuration that has abandoned the departmental structure.

While sharing some features of the New York high school (for example, "families" similar to the high school's "houses" and shared decision making), a middle school in the San Francisco Bay Area departed to a greater extent from the traditional school organization. "Families" were fundamental to this school's operation, providing a structure for the curriculum and a home-base within which students could learn such skills as cooperation and responsibility as well as academic skills and content. (In contrast, at the New York high school, the houses met only one morning a week and teachers did not work in teams with specific groups of students otherwise.) There were two heterogeneously grouped families per grade level, each consisting of approximately one hundred students and four teachers. Content was taught through an integrated thematic approach whenever possible, which meant that the departmental structure was less rigid than in traditional secondary schools. The teachers met four hours per week to do team planning, to work on integrating their teaching of different subjects, and to make decisions about themes they would teach. The schedule was arranged according to time blocks. The teachers on each team negotiated among themselves about how the time would be divided up within each block. For example, if the science teacher needed three hours for two mornings one week because her students were doing laboratory activities that required extended time, she could negotiate with the social studies teacher to give her some social studies time on two mornings and then take more time from science on two other mornings. Within this overall structure, there were "bilingual" families in which support was provided in Spanish and Chinese. Students who spoke various native languages were grouped together for content instruction in English with Spanish or Chinese support. Students were separated for language arts instruction, the LM students receiving ESL and the native English-speaking students receiving regular language arts. The administration and faculty had developed a shared decision-making plan in which they had agreed who would make what decisions. Decisions made by faculty which the principal could not veto related to school scheduling, curriculum development and design, financial priorities for school budgets, and hiring of personnel.

Another high school in New York City had also restructured its entire program. The first step was to establish a special program for LM students within the larger school (Structure B in figure 1) and the next step was to restructure the entire school for speakers of English as well as for LM students (Structure D). The first Title VII project funded in the school had helped set up a bilingual program which took the form of a "mini school"—a smaller, more personal program within the larger high school similar to the school-within-a-school program in Texas described above. All LM students were placed in this program and all ESL and bilingual content area teachers taught within this department. The "mini school" provided the staff development and coordination for a wide variety of services for LM students. From the beginning, the bilingual program concerned itself with all aspects of a student's life—academic, emotional, and social—and developed an integrated approach to meeting the needs of LM students.

In fact, the "mini school" concept was so successful in meeting students' affective needs that it caught the attention of the rest of the school. As the school struggled to find solutions to its increasingly serious dropout problem, the bilingual program became the model for a schoolwide restructuring effort aimed at developing more personalized and integrated programs for all students. Known as "designated houses," these programs built on the nurturing and sense of identity which was evident in the bilingual mini school. This restructuring shifted bilingual services in the content areas to the academic departments in the school, which, according to the school staff, resulted in increased capacity for meeting the needs of LM students in the mainstream program. In 1990-91, staffing in the departments included six bilingual mathematics teachers, six bilingual social studies teachers, four bilingual science teachers, two bilingual business teachers, and two bilingual/ESL aides. Bilingual materials were available in all subject areas. Bilingual students—including many Hispanic students—were said to be among the top students in the school.

As the examples above illustrate, some adjustments are being made in secondary school structure and organization in order to better meet the needs of LM students. Primary among these adjustments are:

• Organizing schools according to groups called "families" or "houses" to facilitate integration of instruction and content and to provide more support for LM students. Teacher teams work with the same group of students and are allotted a common preparation time so they can coordinate the curriculum. They are usually affiliated both with a family or house and with their subject area department.

• Establishing some form of shared decision making among faculty and administrators.

• Grouping LM students together for longer blocks of time rather than having them change classes every period. In some cases these blocks are used to integrate the teaching of core subjects such as social studies and English language arts, thus making the departmental structure less rigid.

• Establishing a cohesive program for LM students with which all,
teachers of classes for LM students are affiliated in addition to their
regular subject affiliations.

Successful Practices in Secondary Schools with LM Students

Schools identified as being successful in providing programs that
promoted the achievement of LM students in the three research
projects upon which I am drawing here fall into the B, C, or D types
of organizational configurations shown in figure 1. Regardless of the
particular school and program organization, however, some features
of curriculum, instruction, staffing, and family involvement have
consistently emerged across the successful schools and programs. In
discussing these features here, I provide an overview of key elements
in such schools, but these comments are not to be interpreted as a
comprehensive account of all necessary elements of secondary schools
that are successful with LM students.

CURRICULUM

Most secondary schools face serious obstacles to providing quality
education.[24] Secondary schools with large numbers of LM students
grapple with added difficulties such as large and often sudden growth
in the LM population, continuous arrival of LM students throughout
the year, and insufficient staff experience with LM education.[25]
However, some secondary schools have found ways to provide a
challenging and comprehensive curriculum for LM students. Schools
which prepare LM students for success in school and beyond provide
instruction that facilitates the development of multiple skills: (1)
English skills, (2) content area skills and knowledge, and (3) native
language abilities. The exact nature of these classes is determined by
various contextual factors such as the size, backgrounds, and recency
of arrival of the population; staff skills and qualifications; community
attitude and history.

The curriculum in an Illinois high school where LM students are
succeeding provided opportunities for development of multiple skills.
The curriculum consisted of two hours of ESL per day for all LM
students; content classes in Spanish and in Lao; content classes,
including electives and English literature classes, taught through
modified (ESL) approaches; and native language development classes
for Spanish speakers. All classes required for graduation at the high

school were offered in Spanish and Lao, although not every class was offered every year.

At the secondary level there is great variety in the extent and nature of the subject area offerings. The major difference between different models of programs for LM students in Minicucci and Olsen's sample of California secondary schools was the approach to academic content instruction. They found four different models of content area instruction (ESL content only, primary language only, primary language combined with ESL content, and mainstream placement) and three degrees of content coverage (full, partial, and sparse).[26] Not all schools can provide full content coverage every semester, but, like the Illinois high school described above, successful secondary schools make it a priority for LM students to have access to required courses and to basic as well as advanced content classes. They provide classes designed to meet the needs of the LM students and to be consistent with the staff qualifications in their schools. Recognizing that many students enter U.S. middle and high schools with limited English skills and that students "get far less out of [subject matter] instruction presented in a language they are just learning than they [do] if it [is] given in a language they already [know],"[27] secondary schools are increasingly offering content courses in the students' native language.

Instruction to promote native language development also varies with respect to its extent and method of presentation—whether it is provided through formal classes (for example, Spanish for Spanish Speakers) or through other less formal means (for example, the use of instructional aides, peer tutoring, or community resources). Table 1 shows some of the ways students' native languages were used in the nine exemplary SAIPs in which English was the primary language of instruction. As this table shows, there are many ways to facilitate the use and development of students' native languages inside and outside the classrooms, even when formal instruction is provided in English.

INSTRUCTION

It is often said that elementary teachers teach children while secondary teachers teach their subjects. This cliché is usually taken to mean that elementary teachers adapt their teaching strategies to students' needs, actively engaging them in learning, while secondary teachers adopt a transmission model of instruction through which they concentrate on presenting subject matter and assume that the students will learn it. In fact, evidence suggests that instruction at all levels has a way to go in order to promote active learning and to teach

TABLE 1
Use of Native Language (L1) by Students and Teachers across Nine Exemplary Special Alternative Instructional Programs

	SITES								
	A	B	C	D	E	F	G	H	I
Use of Native Language (L1)									
By students									
To assist one another	x	x	x	x		x	x	x	x
To tutor other students							x		
To ask/answer questions	x	x	x	x		x		x	
To use bilingual dictionaries		x	x	x				x	
To write in L1	x	x		x	x	x		x	
To interact socially	x	x	x	x	x	x	x	x	x
By teachers									
To check comprehension	x	x				x		x	
To translate a lesson		x							
To explain an activity	x	x	x			x		x	
To provide instruction	x	x							
To interact socially	x	x	x		x	x	x	x	
In the larger school context									
Content instruction in L1	x	x	x				x		x
Instruction in L1 culture, history, language arts	x	x	x			x	x		x
Library books in L1	x	x			x			x	x
Communication to parents in L1	x	x	x		x	x			
Parents encouraged to read to students in L1	x	x			x				

Note: x = presence of this use of L1 at the site.
      Sites B and C do not include secondary students.

Source: Tamara Lucas and Anne Katz, "The Roles of Students' Native Languages in Exemplary SAIPs" (Paper presented at the Annual Meeting of the American Educational Research Association, Chicago, April 1991).

complex linguistic and cognitive skills and knowledge. Goodlad's research in K-12 classrooms containing a wide range of students found an "extraordinary sameness of instructional practices in the more than 1,000 classrooms observed" in which "teachers lectured and questioned, students listened, [and] textbooks were the most common medium for teaching and learning."[28] More recent research focusing on three types of programs for elementary LM students found similar results: teachers provided "a passive language learning environment, limiting student opportunities to produce language and develop more complex language and thinking skills."[29]

In successful secondary programs for LM students teachers adapt their teaching strategies to the students' needs and engage students in active learning. A principal of a secondary school in New Jersey said, "One difference between my LEP teachers and my non-LEP teachers is that they teach kids *and* subject matter. Other secondary teachers teach subject matter only." In fact, strategies used by successful secondary teachers in ESL classes, in content ESL classes, and in native language content classes are not unique to the secondary level. They are very similar to what we know to be characteristic of good elementary teaching for LM students.

Instructional practices used by successful teachers of secondary LM students are the following:

• Rather than relying solely on language to facilitate learning, these teachers use a variety of activities and learning opportunities for students, for example, visuals, physical activity, and nonverbal clues.

• When using language, they do not rely solely on English, but allow and encourage students to use their native languages as needed to facilitate learning and participation.

• When these teachers use English, they modify its complexity and content so that students understand and can participate in classroom activities.

• They also do not rely solely on themselves as the sources of knowledge and learning, but encourage interaction among students. They bring in older and younger, more proficient and less proficient, students from other classes, and involve paraprofessionals and community members in classroom activities.

• They encourage authentic and meaningful communication about course content.

• They hold high expectations of their students, challenging them and requiring them to think critically rather than eliciting a preponderance of one-word responses.

• They recognize student success overtly and frequently.

STAFF CHARACTERISTICS

No program, regardless of how innovative it might be, will succeed unless the teaching and administrative staff supports it and participates wholeheartedly. In all schools that are successful in addressing the needs of LM students, the staff is crucial. The following staff characteristics have emerged in our studies focusing on secondary programs (as well as in the parts of our studies that focused on elementary programs) as especially important for the success of students, programs, and schools.

Staff members are knowledgeable. Staff members know about approaches and strategies for educating LM students. Teachers and other school staff know how to provide the challenging curriculum and effective· instructional approaches that facilitate students' development of multiple skills. Schools acquire such knowledgeable staff by hiring people who are already educated and experienced in working with LM students. Some school districts search far and wide for well-prepared bilingual staff members. They offer stipends to attract and keep such teachers.

Schools also provide extensive, high-quality staff development focused on bilingual instruction, ESL, and modified instructional approaches in teaching English; on issues pertaining to cultural diversity; and on cross-cultural counseling. "The critical importance of ongoing staff development is one of the most consistent and significant findings in the effective schools research."[30] Many districts with large numbers of LM students have developed long-term relationships with teacher education institutions or other technical assistance organizations and have established ongoing staff development. The attitude of the bilingual coordinator in a district in New Mexico reflects that of many others in districts with strong staff development components: "Our primary goal was to teach students, and our second goal was to teach the teachers. If you don't teach the teacher, nothing happens. You need to teach the teacher in order to [insure a quality program for LM students]." A major focus of an Illinois district's first Title VII project was "baseline training" for personnel in cultural awareness, ESL strategies, understanding bilingual education, and other basic issues in the education of LM students. The "baseline training" that was done for all staff helped them to become more open about diversity and helped to develop an understanding of what bilingual education was all about. It marked "the beginning of acceptance of the students and of bilingual education," according to a high school bilingual program staff member. In the words of an assistant superintendent, it "set the stage for the belief that people who don't speak English are valuable." Thirty-nine of the teachers at the high school received training through this program from 1981 to 1987.

Staff members hold high expectations for LM students and take concrete actions to demonstrate their expectations. Most studies of effective schools indicate that high expectations of students constitute one key ingredient for success. At schools where LM students succeed, they are expected to succeed. Not only do staff at these schools expect LM students to succeed, they take concrete actions to demonstrate their expectations and to help students meet them.[31] Some of those actions are:

- Hiring minority staff in leadership positions to act as role models;
- Providing a special program to prepare LM students for college;
- Offering advanced and honors bilingual/ESL classes in the content areas;
- Challenging students in class and providing guidance to help them meet the challenge;
- Providing counseling assistance (in the primary language if necessary) to help students apply to college and fill out scholarship and grant forms;
- Bringing in representatives of colleges and college students of diverse cultural and linguistic backgrounds to talk to students;
- Working with parents to gain their support for students going to college;
- Recognizing students for doing well.

In successful schools many examples can be found to indicate that teachers and administrators hold high expectations for students. However, a school's counseling program plays an especially important role in communicating expectations. High school counselors are "gatekeepers" who make decisions that have lasting effects on students' lives.[32] The courses students are encouraged and, in many cases, allowed (or not allowed) to take determine their preparation for life after high school (for example, vocational courses ostensibly to prepare them for trades; general education courses that might allow them to enter a community college but not a major university; college preparatory courses). Students who are not proficient in English and do not yet fully understand the U.S. educational system are particularly dependent upon their counselors to advise them about the path most appropriate and beneficial for them in the short term and in the long run.

Many secondary schools that serve native speakers of Spanish effectively have counselors who speak Spanish and are knowledgeable about students' cultural backgrounds and experiences. They may have participated in staff development programs or taken courses in cross-cultural counseling. They communicate with parents and other family members about students' school work and their future plans and opportunities. They are well informed about educational opportunities and financial assistance for LM students in postsecondary institutions. They bring in members of the community, representatives from colleges and universities, and business people of various ethnic backgrounds, including Hispanics, to speak to students about their futures. These schools also insure that LM students have access to the counselors who can best communicate with them rather than assigning them to a counselor arbitrarily.

Staff members show that they are committed to programs for LM students and to the students themselves. Staff at these schools and in these districts show through their actions that they sincerely believe in the programs and want to do what they can to insure that LM students succeed in school and beyond. Consistent with Wilson and Corcoran's findings, "the energy, commitment, and vision of the professionals working in these schools are central to their success."[33] Their "fearless and empathetic regard"[34] for LM students is evident in their attitudes and actions. They are eager to learn how to work more effectively with the students. They put in many extra hours and participate in activities over and above what their jobs call for. In some schools and districts, the staff is described as generally committed; in others, particular people are credited for their singular dedication to making the program work. The ESL curriculum specialist in a district in North Dakota, for example, was described as doing "three people's work." A teacher in a district in Indiana said that, for the program coordinator there, working for bilingual and multicultural education "is a belief, not a job." A former bilingual/ESL staff member and current high school principal in a Virginia district said that commitment was one of the main contributors to the district's success in its programs for LM students:

[One] aspect of [the district's] success, very frankly, has been the unusual dedication and commitment and creativity of the staff in these programs. I've never found another staff like them. . . . The [bilingual/ESL] department here and in every school in the county spends more time together and individually preparing, reviewing, and working with kids than any department that I have ever found anywhere.

This commitment is manifested in various ways by people in a multitude of roles: teachers, paraprofessionals, community/school liaisons, secretaries, counselors, principals, project directors, district bilingual coordinators, superintendents, school board members. For example, a principal at a New Jersey middle school said the teacher commitment was the key reason for the district's success with LM students:

Obviously, no program is going to work unless you have concerned and caring teachers. . . . The ESL/bilingual [teachers] buy into the learning of their kids more than any of the other areas. . . . And I can see this just looking at their attendance. They're here every day. They're never absent.

Such commitment does not come only from the bilingual or ESL staff. At a New Mexico high school, for example, a teacher who was the English department chair and the state's teacher of the year asked the ESL coordinator at the school to come to her class for nine weeks to show her how to teach LM students. She set an example that made it easier for others to ask for assistance with LM students.

The commitment of bilingual coordinators and program directors is also given credit for program success in many schools and districts. The Supervisor of Secondary Bilingual/ESL programs in a New Jersey district described the efforts of the district-level bilingual staff as follows:

If we weren't strong enough, if we didn't open up our mouths, we wouldn't be included in certain things. A program sometimes is set up and it's scheduled and all for everybody except the LEP students. So you just have to be on your toes. And we fight this all the time. But you have to continually fight for what you believe in.

Staff commitment to students goes beyond providing effective curriculum and instruction and beyond holding high expectations. It leads staff members to try to understand and communicate with their students and to take part in a political process that challenges the status quo. In the words of Jim Cummins, "minority students can become empowered only through interactions with educators who have critically examined and, where necessary, challenged the educational (and social) structure within which they operate."[35] Some of the ways in which this staff commitment is manifested are:

• Giving extra time and energy after school and during lunch or preparation time to counsel as well as teach students.

• Providing activities outside the classroom that promote participation and leadership of LM students (for example, Movimiento Educacional Chicano de Atzlan [MECHA] chapters, Latino clubs, Spanish language newspapers and newsletters, soccer teams, Ballet Folklorico groups, multicultural events and celebrations). In some districts in

California, teachers are exploring the ways in which the Foxfire approach can be adapted to facilitate learning and empowerment of LM students.

• Participating in community activities, attending meetings, and holding elected and appointed positions in their communities through which they act as advocates for LM populations.

Administrators and nonprogram staff actively support the program. While commitment to providing services and to empowering students comes primarily from staff members directly involved with LM students, support must come from outside the programs if they are to thrive. The active support of district policymakers such as superintendents and school board members, district and school site administrators, and nonprogram staff can be crucial to the development and maintenance of effective programs for LM students.

At the school level, the support of principals, who have the power to make or break a program just as teachers do, is crucial to the success of programs. As a supervisor for special programs in Tennessee said, "If you don't have the principal's support, you can write the most fantastic proposal or have the most wonderful program but it's going to just die on the vine because they're going to view it as just something else that you're asking their teachers to implement." Principals in schools that are successful with LM students are described as actively supporting programs for those students, as sensitive to the needs of LM students, as valuing native languages and cultures of LM students by enrolling in classes to learn those languages. Actions that show a principal's support include: encouraging parents of LM students to participate in school activities; promoting staff development focused on LM students; including LM program staff on meeting agendas; working with the district bilingual staff to design school curriculum; allowing district bilingual staff to plan with the whole school staff.

In many schools, the support of mainstream staff plays a key role in the establishment and maintenance of successful programs. Nonprogram staff support adds credibility to what the program staff might say about the effectiveness of and need for the program. The principal of the Illinois high school whose curriculum was described above said, "I can't say enough about our staff and their support of bilingual education." Vocational teachers in this school were willing to be trained to teach sheltered courses. Twenty-three mainstream staff at the school in the fall of 1991 wanted to take a three-credit graduate course in teaching ESL. In a district in North Dakota with a small

number of LM students and few special services for them, the support
of mainstream staff was seen as absolutely necessary for continuation
of the program. Regular classroom teachers who had "credibility"
with others were described as "cheerleaders" for the program.

Staff members actively promote the program. If staff members,
administrators, and community members are to become committed to
programs for LM students, they must understand and believe in them.
People involved with the programs need to keep others informed
about their "good work." Thus, in schools with strong ongoing programs staff members—especially administrators—actively promote
them. In some cases, they strongly emphasize program successes; in
other cases, the strategy is simply to inform people about program
components and activities.

The superintendent in a Virginia district described the situation
well:

What I think is important is we keep the program in the public eye. We
provide the board with . . . a constant flow of information. The overall
strategy is keep people informed, keep the programs visible, take the heat so
people don't think you're spending too much money. I guess the primary
strategy is information, information, information. Just keep pounding away.
And I think that builds understanding, the belief system that there's a real
need, the sophistication that says you've got to do these things if you're going
to make a constructive difference. All those things go together to make for
continuing support. . . . You've established a strong awareness and an
information base that makes it possible to accept the responsibility to fund
those programs after the feds cut and run.

Communication about the program was also identified by the
administrators in a district in Mississippi as a key factor in the success
of their program. The program director said, "Networking is the
most important strategy [for keeping our program going]. We talk to
anybody and listen to everybody." A curriculum specialist elaborated: "We communicate by phone, face to face, in memos, in meetings, in passing informally, at Chamber of Commerce meetings, at
professional organizations of various sorts. . . . Give us a box to stand
on and we'll talk to them." The program director frequently went
to faculty meetings to present information about the program, and
one of the bilingual/ESL staff members attended the principals' meetings to keep abreast of what was happening in the district. The
Title VII project newsletter went out four times a year to district
offices, schools, other projects, and the community. The project

director was very visible in the community, coordinating many joint activities with other agencies such as churches, social service agencies, and adult education programs.

The LM program coordinator had also been instrumental in promoting the program in a small urban district in Tennessee. The district supervisor of special programs said that the coordinator had done an "extremely good job at keeping the positive aspects of the programs in the press" and "in the forefront." For example, she had been on the radio as Educator of the Week and had talked about the ESL program, had been instrumental in getting the Chamber of Commerce to include a piece about the ESL program in its newsletter, and had had the local newspaper interview our visiting research team.

Many staff members are fluent in Spanish and are members of the local Hispanic community or are involved with that community. Staff availability is a major problem for most school districts trying to develop programs for LM students. There are simply not enough certified teachers who are bilingual and/or members of the ethnic/ cultural groups of the LM students in the schools, including Hispanics. Schools where LM students are succeeding have given priority to hiring teachers who are bilingual and to providing financial support and incentives for others to become knowledgeable about the language and culture of the students. One California district made it a priority to hire role models for its large number of Hispanic students. It was district policy to interview any Hispanic who applied. If a Hispanic was among the top three candidates for a position and was not hired, the hiring committee had to justify its decision.

Hispanics in various school and district positions play key roles. The first Hispanic board member in a Florida school district was credited with changing the district's focus from an ESL department to a department that encompassed academic needs and social services as well as language needs. She was also viewed as playing a key role in convincing the board to expand from a bilingual staff of two district-wide positions in 1988 to the 1991 staff of 80. One administrator said, "Having someone who is a former LEP student herself, able to talk to community and parents in their own language, has been a tremendous help." The principal at an Arizona high school described that district's policy with regard to staffing:

When we hire teachers, we try to look for the best teachers, number one, but number two and most importantly, we try to get teachers that relate to our type of kids, and number three, if we can get teachers who are from this area, who have graduated from this high school, and who have had to go through these problems, the growing up problems and the educational problems from here, and have gone out and have become successful, then we have provided role models for our kids that are essential.

A counselor at a California high school described the benefits of having a number of bilingual Hispanic staff members at the school:

Parents and students see us [i.e., bilingual Latinos] in leadership positions, not just in the cafeteria or as janitors. People in the school understand problems in the community and have lived it themselves. . . . For example, I understand if a student has to stay home all week to take care of kids. . . . Parents come in because I speak Spanish and can understand their problems. I'm not from a middle-class, elite, intellectual background.

In many districts, community members serve as home/school liaisons. These home/school liaisons are especially visible to members of the non-native English speaking communities and are seen as key people in getting the word out about the programs and the need to actively support them. A Hispanic home/school liaison in an Illinois district with a strong home/school program explained why people like her were so important to the program: "We came from the people who needed the service. We're in contact with people who are in the community. The home/school liaisons and the aides know the needs; we have children enrolled in the program, so we know the needs that way."

People playing different district and school roles provide strong leadership. Strong leadership is generally recognized as an important factor in school success. However, leadership in secondary schools that are successful with LM students appears to be more complex and multidimensional than what is described by the effective schools literature and by my colleagues and me in our study of six successful high schools.[36] People playing different district and school roles provide different types of leadership at different stages in the process of developing, implementing, and maintaining effective secondary programs for LM students. Their leadership is manifested in various ways, many of which I have already discussed.

The principal's leadership often takes the form of support for staff and programs for LM students. When the principal actively supports a program, as described above, other staff and community members are more likely to treat it as a valuable, accepted part of the school's offerings. Some secondary principals have developed knowledge and expertise in issues relevant to LM students, taking their leadership beyond support to active development, promotion, and monitoring of program components and instructional approaches. A Latino high school principal in California became very involved in curriculum design.[37] He eliminated all remedial classes and added advanced content classes in Spanish (e.g., algebra, economics, chemistry). In a small rural Arizona school district, most people attributed the development of the program to the leadership of principals. Principals were primarily responsible for writing Title VII grants and bringing bilingual education to the district. The elementary and middle school principals responsible for writing their respective Title VII grants were described as having fought "tooth and nail for years" to get the program in their schools.

While principals such as these play leadership roles in programs for LM students, bilingual/ESL coordinators or directors at district and school levels often take more active leadership roles than principals. Their actions are key to the shape and success of these programs. They provide the vision for the program, provide expertise in LM issues, help design program components, officially and unofficially recruit staff, monitor the progress of programs and of students, provide staff development, promote the program in the community and the district, and function as consultants and sounding boards for program staff. They are described as "go getters," as the "driving forces" behind successful programs.

An ESL teacher in a Mississippi district said: "I think [the ESL/bilingual director] is probably the key person. . . . She has taken charge and given us goals to work for." A principal also described her leadership ability: "[The ESL/bilingual director] coordinates and monitors everything. She monitors test scores. She [offers suggestions] when test scores are low. She secures extra funding. She does staff development." She also coordinated activities with other agencies in the district and community to avoid duplication of services.

In some districts, the leadership of superintendents also plays a direct role in shaping and maintaining programs for LM students. In a rural California district, the superintendent's involvement was pivotal in creating the structures leading to the extensive program in place in 1990. As a result of his efforts, Title VII was funded in the fourth year of his term as superintendent. He initiated the networking that created a consortium of districts which wrote and administered the Title VII grant; recruited the project director; provided funding for additional costs connected with the project not covered by the grant; helped to generate support for the project throughout the district, including among members of the school board and school staff. At the end of funding, he took steps to insure that the majority of Title VII project staff continued with the district.

The leadership of teachers in developing and maintaining quality LM programs has not emerged in these studies as strongly as that of program directors or coordinators, school principals, superintendents, and school board members. The fact that teachers are overburdened with work, coupled with the rigid and fragmented structure of secondary schools, leaves most teachers with little time, energy, or opportunity to exert a great deal of influence beyond their own classrooms and departments. Of course, some teachers do lead by example, like the New Mexico teacher of the year described earlier.

FAMILY INVOLVEMENT

Common sense tells us and some evidence suggests that families and students alike benefit when families are involved in their children's schooling.[38] Yet levels of family involvement in children's schooling remain low, and parents and parental figures are generally less likely to be involved in their children's schooling at the secondary level than at the elementary level.[39] Several factors contribute to the lack of family involvement in middle and high schools: the fragmented structure of the secondary school day means that no one teacher is responsible for each student and that each teacher is responsible for 150 or more students; few schools take concrete steps to encourage family members to get involved in school activities, especially at the secondary level; adolescents are beginning to establish their own identities apart from their parents; parental figures tend to have less direct influence on their children's behavior as the children get older; as the content of classes becomes more advanced, family members feel less equipped to help students with school work. The families of LM students are even less likely to become involved in schooling than are those of English-speaking students because they generally do not speak English proficiently, do not understand how the educational system works and what is expected of family members, and have different customs and values with regard to education and the roles of educators and families.

Some federally funded programs require the establishment and maintenance of committees involving parents or family members. For example, when a district receives Title VII funding for a bilingual program, it must set up a Parent Advisory Committee. While many of these committees provide only *pro forma* family involvement to meet federal regulations, others have provided the impetus for family involvement which has continued after federal funding ended. Some schools have made it a priority to encourage and support the involvement of the families of LM students whether or not they are required to do so by federal regulation. They send letters and newsletters to families in their native languages, include students on programs as performers and honorees, hold meetings at times and in places that are convenient for family members, maintain full-time home-school liaisons who can speak the families' native languages and understand their cultures.[40] The following examples illustrate steps taken by some districts to involve LM students' families.

In a Texas district, family members interested in getting involved with the schools could do so in a variety of ways. For instance, the community liaison offered well-attended dance classes for parents and community members. The district offered classes for parents in computers, literacy, and ESL. The take-home computer program was particularly successful. Some programs brought in speakers from the community to address parents. The district sponsored a yearly parent symposium to provide information about legal assistance, adult literacy programs, local health organizations, and other community services. Attendance at these events was reported to be good.

In a Virginia district, the Family-School Partnership Project, funded by the Fund for the Improvement and Reform of Schools and Teaching (FIRST), provided community resource assistants for the Spanish-speaking and the African-American communities. The Parent Education Project provided community resource assistants who spoke Khmer, Lao, and Spanish. Through these projects, the district offered workshops for parents on the educational needs of their children, orientation sessions on the school system and community services, and activities for home learning provided by teachers for use by parents and their children. Similarly, in a New Jersey district, the bilingual Community-School Coordinators provided information and training and served as a crucial link between the schools and the parents. According to an administrator, the activities for parents help them "improve their self worth. . . . Parents have to feel good about what is going on in the schools to support their children in school and get involved."

Conclusion

Hispanic students bring with them to schools in the United States their diverse educational, social, academic, linguistic, personal, and cultural experiences. To prepare these students for success in school and beyond, some educators are thoughtfully developing secondary programs and are adapting middle and high schools to address a variety of needs in ways that are appropriate within local contexts. They are examining ways in which school structures promote and hinder students' success and they are adjusting organizational configurations accordingly. They are designing curricula that challenge LM students and provide them with access to skills, abilities, and content knowledge. They are using instructional approaches that engage students and challenge them to use and develop their minds. They are becoming knowledgeable about issues in the education of LM students, dedicating time and energy to educating LM students, promoting programs for LM students, and hiring bilingual Hispanic staff members. People in various roles are providing leadership in different ways and at different stages in the process of developing and maintaining secondary programs for LM students. They are encouraging families of LM students to become involved in school activities and are providing opportunities for them to get involved.

These educators are role models for those of us who work in the field of bilingual education. While our paths will not be identical to theirs because situations, students, backgrounds, and needs differ, we can learn from the directions they have taken. This chapter has identified key issues which those who design, deliver, suggest, study, and critique secondary education for native speakers of Spanish (and other languages as well) need to consider to achieve quality education for these students. Ultimately, educational "quality is the hard won result of dedicated work by competent, committed people."[41]

My sincere thanks go to the staffs of the many middle and high schools that were visited and examined by myself and others in these various projects. The following people contributed to this chapter: my colleagues in the study of successful California and Arizona high schools—Rosemary Henze and Rubén Donato; the staff of the study of exemplary SAIPs—William Tikunoff, Migdalia Romero, Beatrice Ward, David von Broekhuizen, Lillian Vega Castañeda, and Anne Katz; the staff of the study of Title VII Capacity Building—Yungho Kim, Sofía Aburto, Timothy Beard, Ivonne González, Rosemary Henze, Anne Katz, Leticia Pérez, Katherine Ramage, and Lauren Vanett. I also thank Steven Athanases and Suzanne Wagner for their comments on earlier drafts of this chapter.

NOTES

1. For an examination of California secondary schools with LM students, see Catherine Minicucci and Laurie Olsen, *An Exploratory Study of Secondary LEP Programs*, vol. 5, *Meeting the Challenge of Diversity: An Evaluation of Programs for Pupils with Limited Proficiency in English* (Berkeley, CA: BW Associates, 1991).

2. Tamara Lucas, Rosemary Henze, and Rubén Donato, "Promoting the Success of Latino Language-minority Students: An Exploratory Study of Six High Schools," *Harvard Educational Review* 60, no. 3 (1990): 315-340.

3. William Tikunoff, Beatrice A. Ward, David von Broekhuizen, Migdalia Romero, Lillian V. Castañeda, Tamara Lucas, and Anne Katz, *Final Report: A Descriptive Study of Significant Features of Exemplary Special Alternative Instructional Programs* (Los Alamitos, CA: Southwest Regional Educational Laboratory, 1991); idem, *Final Report: A Descriptive Study of Significant Features of Exemplary Special Alternative Instructional Programs*, vol. 2, *Report for Practitioners* (Los Alamitos, CA: Southwest Regional Educational Laboratory, 1991).

4. Yungho Kim and Tamara Lucas, *Final Report: Descriptive Analysis of Bilingual Instructional Service Capacity Building among Title VII Grantees* (Oakland, CA: ARC Associates, 1992).

5. Tamara Lucas, *Successful Capacity Building: An Analysis of Twenty Case Studies, Phase III Report: Descriptive Analysis of Bilingual Instructional Service Capacity Building among Title VII Grantees* (Oakland, CA: ARC Associates, 1992).

6. John I. Goodlad, *A Place Called School* (New York: McGraw-Hill, 1984), p. 29.

7. Milbrey W. McLaughlin and Joan E. Talbert, "The Contexts in Question: The Secondary School Workplace," in *The Contexts of Teaching in Secondary Schools: Teachers' Realities*, edited by Milbrey W. McLaughlin, Joan E. Talbert, and Nina Bascia (New York: Teachers College Press, 1990), p. 1.

8. Tikunoff et al., *Final Report: A Descriptive Study of Significant Features of Exemplary Special Alternative Instructional Programs*, p. 9.

9. Goodlad, *A Place Called School*, p. 19.

10. Gretchen B. Rossman, H. Dickson Corbett, and William A. Firestone, *Culture, Change, and Effectiveness* (Albany: State University of New York Press, 1988), p. 141.

11. Minicucci and Olsen, *Meeting the Challenge of Diversity*, p. 12.

12. Tikunoff et al., *Final Report: A Descriptive Study of Significant Features of Exemplary Special Alternative Instructional Programs*; idem, *Final Report*, vol. 2, *Report for Practitioners*.

13. See Lucas, Henze, and Donato, "Promoting the Success of Latino Language-Minority Students" for a more complete discussion of this point.

14. Goodlad, *A Place Called School*, p. 31.

15. Minicucci and Olsen, *Meeting the Challenge of Diversity*, p. 43.

16. Theodore Sizer, *Horace's Compromise: The Dilemma of the American High School* (Boston: Houghton-Mifflin, 1985).

17. See, for example, Minicucci and Olsen, *Meeting the Challenge of Diversity*.

18. Robert B. Stevenson, "Staff Development for Effective Secondary Schools: A Synthesis of Research," *Teaching and Teacher Education* 3 (1987): 243. See also, Susan M. Johnson, "The Primacy and Potential of High School Departments," in *The Contexts of Teaching in Secondary Schools: Teachers' Realities*, edited by Milbrey W. McLaughlin, Joan E. Talbert, and Nina Bascia (New York: Teachers College Press, 1990), pp. 167-184.

19. Carlos García, "Restructuring Education to Meet the Needs of All Students" (Address at the Multifunctional Resource Center/Northern California Institute on Latino and Other Newcomer Students, Napa, CA, October 28, 1991).

20. I use the term "ESL content classes" to refer to content classes taught in English with modified instructional approaches to make the content accessible to LM students. Characteristics of this approach include: use of extralinguistic cues; adaptation of language used (for example, slower rate, repetition, elaboration); emphasis on key concepts; active participation of students, including use of interaction among students and between teacher and students.

21. See Minicucci and Olsen, *Meeting the Challenge of Diversity.*

22. For more information on Newcomer Centers, see Hedy N. Chang, *Newcomer Programs: Innovative Efforts to Meet the Educational Challenges of Immigrant Students* (San Francisco: California Tomorrow, 1990); Monica Friedlander, *The Newcomer Program: Helping Immigrant Students Succeed in U.S. Schools* (Washington, DC: National Clearinghouse for Bilingual Education, 1991); Multifunctional Resource Center/ Northern California, *Resource Guide: Bilingual Education for New Immigrant and Refugee LEP Students* (Oakland, CA: ARC Associates, 1991).

23. Timothy Beard, of ARC Associates, Oakland, CA, provided descriptions of these two schools.

24. Ernest L. Boyer, *High School: A Report on Secondary Education in America* (New York: Harper and Row, 1983); Goodlad, *A Place Called School*; National Center on Effective Secondary Schools, *Final Report: National Center on Effective Secondary Schools* (Madison, WI: Wisconsin Center for Education Research, University of Wisconsin, Madison, 1991); Arthur G. Powell, Eleanor Farrar, and David K. Cohen, *The Shopping Mall High School: Winners and Losers in the Educational Marketplace* (Boston: Houghton-Mifflin, 1985); Sizer, *Horace's Compromise*, 1985.

25. See Minicucci and Olsen, *Meeting the Challenge of Diversity.*

26. Ibid., pp. 27-30, 46.

27. Lily Wong Fillmore, "The Language Learner as an Individual: Implications of Research on Individual Differences for the ESL Teacher," in *Pacific Perspectives on Language Learning and Teaching*, edited by Mark A. Clarke and Jean Handscombe (Washington, DC: TESOL, 1983).

28. Goodlad, *A Place Called School*, pp. 246-247.

29. J. David Ramírez, Sandra D. Yuen, and Dena R. Ramey, *Final Report: Longitudinal Study of Structured English Immersion Strategy, Early-exit and Late-exit Transitional Bilingual Education Programs for Language-minority Students*, Executive Summary (San Mateo, CA: Aguirre International, 1991), p. 8.

30. Michael G. Fullan, "Change Processes in Secondary Schools: Toward a More Fundamental Agenda," in *The Contexts of Teaching in Secondary Schools: Teachers' Realities*, edited by Milbrey McLaughlin, Joan E. Talbert, and Nina Bascia (New York: Teachers College Press, 1990), p. 230.

31. Lucas, Henze, and Donato, "Promoting the Success of Latino Language-minority Students."

32. Frederick Erickson and Jeffrey Schultz, *The Counselor as Gatekeeper: Social Interaction in Interviews* (New York: Academic Press, 1982).

33. Bruce L. Wilson and Thomas B. Corcoran, *Successful Secondary Schools: Visions of Excellence in American Public Education* (London: Falmer Press, 1988), p. xi.

34. Sara Lawrence Lightfoot, *The Good High School: Portraits of Character and Culture* (New York: Basic Books, 1983).

35. Jim Cummins, *Empowering Minority Students* (Sacramento, CA: California Association for Bilingual Education, 1989), p. 6.

36. Lucas, Henze, and Donato, "Promoting the Success of Latino Language-minority Students."

37. Ibid., pp. 328-329.

38. Erwin Flaxman and Morton Inger, "Parents and Schooling in the 1990s," *ERIC Review* 1, no. 3 (1991): pp. 2-6.

39. Following Violand-Sánchez et al., I am using the term *family involvement* rather than the more usual *parent involvement* in recognition of the fact that people with various types of relationships to students may provide support through involvement with the schools. See Emma Violand-Sánchez, Christine P. Sutton, and Herbert W. Ware, *Fostering Home-School Cooperation: Involving Language Minority Families as Partners in Education* (Washington, DC: National Clearinghouse for Bilingual Education, 1991).

40. See Lucas, Henze, and Donato, "Promoting the Success of Latino Language-minority Students"; Violand-Sánchez et al., *Fostering Home-School Cooperation*.

41. Wilson and Corcoran, *Successful Secondary Schools*, p. 146.

CHAPTER VI

Assessment of Students in Bilingual Education

CARMEN MERCADO AND MIGDALIA ROMERO

Testing has served two contradictory purposes in bilingual education. On the one hand, it has served to safeguard the rights of students; on the other, it has served to violate them. The reasons for this become obvious when we consider that bilingual education is one approach to educating youngsters who, for reasons of language, are at a disadvantage in English-speaking classrooms. These students are entitled by law to receive a specialized form of instruction that takes into account their language differences. The intent is to enable them to learn academic content in their native language as they acquire sufficient language skills to enter the English-speaking classroom. The fact that most of these students are Spanish-speaking and of Mexican or Puerto Rican ancestry is significant given their historical relations to the United States.

To comply with federal regulations, school districts are required to determine who is entitled to receive special instructional services. Although bilingual education is an educational alternative that has tremendous potential for preserving the linguistic capital of our nation, participation in these programs is largely limited to students with a demonstrated need.[1] For the most part this need has been established through a score at a predetermined level on "approved measures" in English. In this manner testing has played a role in protecting the rights of bilingual students[2] to have access to an educational opportunity which is, in principle, "equal." However, because bilingual education has been mired in political controversy, concerns over funding, justification, and compliance have resulted in additional testing for students in these programs. School districts receiving funding from federal and state governments must demonstrate that students are learning English and that they are

Carmen Mercado is Associate Professor in the Department of Curriculum and Teaching, Hunter College, City University of New York. Migdalia Romero is Professor and Chair of the Department of Curriculum and Teaching at Hunter College, City University of New York.

performing competently on tests (in English) of academic achievement in other subjects. When these particular demands for testing are added to the demands that state and local policies impose, it is not difficult to see why bilingual students are subjected to more tests and with greater frequency than their monolingual counterparts.

The reasons why bilingual students have tended to perform poorly on such measures are complex and multiple, involving the interaction between the characteristics of tests and the characteristics of students. Tests that rely heavily on the comprehension of academic English are problematic for students who are in the process of acquiring English as a second language. When students' weaker language is used to measure knowledge of content, their linguistic competence contaminates the results. Tests are also biased by their allusion to information which is skewed toward the dominant culture.[3] In addition, performance is strongly influenced by such student characteristics as their length of time in the United States, their previous exposure to English, the extent of schooling in their native language, their level of literacy in the native language, and their socioeconomic status both in their country of origin and in the United States.[4] Consequently, students in bilingual programs may not appear to be competent in any language, sometimes scoring at the zero percentile or below the cut-off point in both languages, an important issue to which we give attention in this chapter.

Nevertheless, acknowledging the complexities and limitations of testing does not justify the devastating effects that these practices have on the lives of children. Because performance on standardized tests has been tied to promotional policies, many bilingual students have been retained, some as many as two and three times. Those who are not retained are typically subjected to the type of curriculum that mirrors the content, format, and language of tests.[5] Worse yet, many students are tested and placed inappropriately in remedial or special education programs on the basis of such measures.[6] More specifically, as Ortiz and Maldonado-Colón argue: "Behaviors directly or indirectly related to linguistic proficiency constitute the most frequent reason for referral of language minority students."[7]

It is for these reasons that some maintain that assessment "has played a role in legitimizing the disabling of minority students."[8] The dilemma is that testing has also served to protect their rights to alternative forms of instruction that otherwise may not be made available to them. Testing has been a powerful force in assuring that school districts respond to the special instructional needs of these students while simultaneously complying with legislative mandates. The challenge educators face is that of understanding the politics of testing, of minimizing unnecessary testing, of gaining the most from tests that are absolutely necessary, and of exploring other possibilities for assessment that are inherent in the teaching-learning process. Coming at a time when President Bush has issued a long-range plan—*America 2000*—that seeks to improve the achievement of all students, particularly in English literacy, science, and mathematics, and to measure progress through national standardized testing,[9] the challenge is daunting. It is all the more so because this plan ignores the needs of culturally and linguistically diverse students.

In this chapter, we trace the developments in assessment in bilingual education and the legislation that has driven it. We move from the more traditional forms of testing which dominated the field in its early history to the nontraditional forms which have developed and continue to evolve. We then explore the potential that these nontraditional forms of assessment have for transforming both the teaching-learning process and the assessment process to the benefit of students and teachers alike.

Throughout we shall be using the terms testing and assessment to refer to two distinct but interrelated notions. We agree with Chittenden that testing refers to a range of devices—from commercial instruments and standardized tests to teachers' formal and informal measures that rely primarily on student responses to questions or problems presented at one point in time.[10] In contrast, assessment is a process that is inclusive of, but more comprehensive than, testing. Accordingly, assessment is ongoing, employs multiple measures, and seeks out multiple perspectives including that of the learner.

Historical Context for Assessment in Bilingual Education

The original impetus for bilingual programs in the 1960s came from two actions on the part of the federal government. The first was concerned with equal and meaningful access and educational opportunity for all students. Title VI of the Civil Rights Act of 1964, prohibited discrimination on the grounds of race, color, or national origin in programs or activities that receive federal financial assistance. More specifically, with reference to students whose native language is not English it mandated that "districts take affirmative steps to rectify the language deficiency in order to open [their] instructional program to these students."[11] According to the Office of Civil Rights this meant that "recipients [of federal funds] need to have procedures in place for identifying and assessing LEP students."

The second action was the Supreme Court decision in *Lau v. Nichols* in January, 1974. The critical question was whether non-English-speaking students received equal access and equal educational opportunity as stipulated by the Civil Rights Act of 1964 when instruction was in a language they could not understand.[12] The *Lau* decision, while not mandating a specific approach to educating non-English-speaking students, upheld their right to special services and programs designed to meet their English language and academic needs.

Both legal actions had a direct impact on funding and, by extension, on testing. In mandating specialized services for language minority students, the federal government was faced with the responsibility of making some form of funding available to districts and schools to help them establish the required services and programs. Federal funding was made available through Title VII of the Elementary and Secondary Education Act, also known as the Bilingual Education Act. Schools, on the other hand, were faced with the responsibility of complying with the legislation by identifying eligible students and by providing special services for them. In addition, schools had to demonstrate that the programs were educationally sound and were achieving the desired results. In terms of testing this meant that students whose native language was other than English had to have their English language proficiency assessed to determine entitlement and schools had to test students in the program to determine the program's effectiveness.

On the heels of the *Lau* decision, individual states drew up legislation which had additional impact on pupil assessment. As a way of safeguarding against discrimination and especially against inappropriate placement of non-native English speakers in special education and in classes for students with learning disabilities, some states also mandated the testing or linguistic assessment of bilingual students in their dominant language. The net effect was the extension of testing to include the assessment of students' language proficiency in two languages, whenever possible. For example, New York's court-mandated Aspira consent decree required the Board of Education to "design and implement an improved method for assessing Hispanic students' skills in English and Spanish in order to identify those students with English-language difficulties who, accordingly, have rights under *Lau*."[13]

In theory, dual language testing was to be used to determine the relative proficiency of ESL students in two languages.[14] It could not be assumed, just because students had been born in this country or lived here for some time, that they were sufficiently proficient in English and did not require special language services, particularly because of the circular migration which characterizes some of the language minority groups. In practice, however, very little dual language testing was possible, since there were few instruments available. Many were inadequate for use with second language learners or for "urban and minority group pupils"[15] for many reasons, not the least of which was their reliance on translation of existing tests and the inclusion of content that was culturally foreign to these students.

A second level of assessment built into the legislation was the testing of students' linguistic and academic progress to determine simultaneously a program's effectiveness and a student's readiness for transition into the mainstream where only English would be used for instruction. Both achievement data and linguistic proficiency data were collected for these purposes. In the absence of research data, arbitrary cut-off points were often established on standardized achievement tests and/or on linguistic proficiency tests. They ranged from the 20th to the 40th percentile and were used as indicators of readiness for mainstreaming.[16] An assumption was made, often prematurely, that satisfactory performance on an English language proficiency test, that is, scoring above the minimum cut-off point, meant that students were ready to handle academic content taught exclusively through English. However, poor performance in academic content classes by many mainstreamed students did not support this assumption and deficiencies attributed to students were not always warranted.[17]

Clearly, federal, state, and local legislation has served as the impetus for testing in bilingual education and in programs designed to serve the linguistic and academic needs of English language learners. To comply with legislation, schools had the responsibility to determine entitlement of students for special language services and then to document student progress within those programs as a way of establishing accountability.

TRADITIONAL ASSESSMENT PRACTICES IN BILINGUAL EDUCATION

Assessment in bilingual education traditionally serves both administrative and instructional functions. Included among the administrative functions are (1) determining students' entitlement to services, (2) placing students in appropriate classes within existing programs, and (3) evaluating program effectiveness. Once students are identified and placed, assessment moves into the realm of instruction. At the classroom level, bilingual and ESL teachers are encouraged to use assessment instruments to plan instruction and, in some programs, to group students based on their linguistic proficiency, whether or not this is in their best interest. The assessment data used to place students and to plan instruction are often also used to evaluate the effectiveness of a program.

Administrative functions. The most basic and global administrative function of assessment in bilingual education, as noted, is to determine a student's eligibility for special services. The task is to identify a student's dominant language, that is, the language a student understands best, and uses most comfortably to process new information and to participate in and contribute to classroom discussion. This is usually done by evaluating students' proficiency in English or their relative proficiency in two languages. In turn, this information is used to determine whether a student can profit from instruction delivered exclusively in English. While the questions which dominance testing are meant to answer may be critical to students' success in schools, the methods used to establish dominance are rudimentary and superficial.[18]

The *home language survey* is a self-report instrument used in the initial screening of students entering school. The survey gives students and/or parents the opportunity to describe the extent to which one language is used over another at home and in the community. However, the information it yields is only as accurate and useful as the self-awareness[19] and truthfulness[20] of the respondents. Parents or guardians who are asked to report on their use of language at home and with their children may feel a need to misrepresent the language most frequently spoken in the home for a number of reasons. They may not want their child to participate in the bilingual program, not fully understanding the instructional approach or doubting its effectiveness. Some may have fears and suspicions related to their status as citizens.

A second form of dominance assessment is the *language rating scale.* Scales are subjective judgments, usually by teachers, of a student's ability to use one or two languages on a variety of continua. Self-report rating scales give speakers the opportunity to assess their own linguistic skills. Either type of scale can be used to describe proficiency in one language or relative proficiency in two languages. A prototype of the most global scale is the OCR five-point scale.[21] It forces the rater to categorize a student's proficiency in two languages along a five-point continuum from (A) to (E): (A) Speaks a language other than English exclusively; (B) Predominantly speaks a language other than English, but also some English; (C) Bilingual (speaks both languages with equal ease); (D) Predominantly speaks English but speaks some of the language other than English; (E) Monolingual speaker of English (speaks English exclusively).

Other scales focus on describing a student's proficiency in L1 and/or L2, independently of each other. Raters evaluate language skills on a number of dimensions, using a rating from 1 to 5 to try to capture the degree of proficiency a student has over them. Some dimensions included are the following: (1) phonology or pronunciation (control over a language's sound system); (2) morphology (control over the structure of words and word parts); (3) vocabulary; (4) syntax or grammar (control over the structure of sentences); (5) semantics (control over the meaning system); (6) comprehension; and (7) overall communication.

A major problem with scales is that they are limited by their subjectivity and reliability.[22] Raters do not always concur on their ratings. In addition, outside raters have not usually had the opportunity to hear and observe students use both languages in a variety of academic and social contexts. Therefore, the sample on which they are forced to make a judgment is limited and may not be representative of the students' true proficiency. Students who rate themselves may overrepresent or underrepresent their ability for social reasons.

The two formal ways in which dominance testing is conducted is through the *oral language proficiency (OLP) test* and, more comprehensively, through *language assessment batteries*. The former focuses on speaking only, whereas test batteries focus on listening, speaking, reading, and writing, often as four independent skills. Both measures provide standardized baseline data regarding a student's linguistic ability in one or two languages. When a student is tested in two languages, an assumption is made that the language in which the higher score is achieved is the student's dominant language. When only one language is tested, and sometimes even when both are, a minimal cutoff score is established to indicate that special services are needed if performance falls below that level. On the other hand, performance above a predetermined level may be used at best to place students at their assigned level of language competence and at worst to limit their accessibility to programs or to exit them prematurely.

Sometimes, however, students score below the cut-off in both languages. Part of the problem may be a student's lack of test-taking sophistication and/or the emphasis on print and literacy in the formal testing process. It may also reflect the complexity of assessment and the interactive relationship between the characteristics of the test and those of the test-taker. What is ignored is that poor performance in two languages may not be a reflection of a student's communicative ability exclusively. Consequently, dominance testing may result in the inappropriate labeling of students, to their detriment. While sounding harmless, labels such as "comparably limited" may have a profound influence on teachers' expectations and perceptions of students which, in turn, influences how they treat students and how students respond to this treatment.

Overall, dominance testing for entitlement tells educators very little about the specific linguistic or instructional needs of individual students. While formal measures provide more standardized and reliable information than home language surveys and scales, all focus heavily on linguistic competence and knowledge of language in isolation rather than on competence in the context of learning academic content. The focus on linguistic competence to the exclusion of sociolinguistic competence gives one information on what students know about a language or what they can do with language in an artificial context. Oral language proficiency tests and language assessment batteries usually cannot tell us what students are able to do with language in face-to-face communication or in classrooms when academic content is the focus of instruction. Although there may be a battery of tests designed to be context-sensitive, such tests cannot fully replicate a natural communicative context.

Instructional functions. While assessment data are used to place students in appropriate programs of instruction, teachers may also be encouraged to use these data to plan instruction. Specifically, data from *language proficiency tests, standardized achievement tests, criterion-referenced tests*, as well as from performance on informal tests and tasks in class, are often used in profiling students' linguistic and academic progress. In theory, results from tests should reveal how much English to use, which subjects can effectively be taught in English, and when students are ready to be mainstreamed. However, evaluation of students' readiness to be exited from a program is most often based on their performance on approved and formal measures of language assessment.

Historically, language proficiency testing (in contrast to language dominance testing) has focused on the discrete language skills students have or need to develop in order to communicate and perform competently in school. Tests of language skills, however, have their limitations. Their focus on language as a composite of discrete skills does not take into account that language is more than the sum of its parts and that control over its parts does not necessarily mean control over the whole. Responding to language items on a test is no assurance that one is able to handle communication in a face-to-face context or handle academic content taught through that language.[23]

Standardized achievement tests administered in English tell us even less about bilingual students as learners. Once the weaker language is used to measure knowledge of content, a learner's linguistic competence contaminates results. One cannot be sure if an incorrect response is the result of misunderstanding because of language or because of a lack of knowledge of content.

Both language and achievement tests are also often biased by their allusion to information which is skewed toward the dominant culture, making them culturally loaded. Both linguistic and cultural load are factors which impact adversely on students who do not share the same linguistic or cultural knowledge as their monolingual counterparts.[24] Students may understand the questions literally, but have difficulty with cultural innuendos or with expressing their understanding in writing or in connected spoken discourse, placing them at a disadvantage. *The larger question is whether tests of academic achievement are truly tests of content knowledge, or tests of literacy, or tests of cultural adaptation.*

ASSESSMENT TRENDS IN BILINGUAL EDUCATION

As is evident from the extensive use of testing at both the administrative and instructional levels, a dominant focus of assessment in bilingual programs has been on language, particularly a student's control over and knowledge of English, the second language. The field however is evolving, particularly in response to the misuse and the limited utility of testing as it has traditionally been practiced and to the negative impact of testing on bilingual students.

One movement is from *discrete point testing* of language skills with a reliance on multiple-choice questions and single-word responses to *open-ended assessment* where responses require connected discourse. There are problems with both types of responses. One problem with the more open-ended assessment measures when used only in English is that they may be more difficult for ESL students who lack the necessary vocabulary and fluency which are used to evaluate progress. On the other hand, multiple-choice responses require limited production and attempt to isolate a student's control over specific elements of language out of context.

A related movement is from a focus on the *assessment of linguistic competence* or control over the elements of language to a focus on *sociolinguistic competence*. At least in theory, the latter focuses on control over the use of language in more natural contexts where face-to-face communication is stressed and/or where language is used for interaction and the negotiation of meaning. With such a focus, individuals use the various elements of language integratively to engage in meaningful discourse. Thus, the assessment of sociolinguistic competence also requires that the individual be engaged in the integrative use of language during meaningful speech events.[25]

An extension of this movement to look at social competence is the evaluation of *academic competence*. While assessment of social or sociolinguistic competence is a step up from testing only linguistic competence, it alone does not provide information on what students can or cannot do with language in an academic context. Students who successfully negotiate their social environment and needs may not be able to negotiate the academic content of their classes and textbooks.

Another movement is from the use of *single standardized summative (formal) measures* to place students and evaluate their performance to the use of *multiple formative measures* gathered over time to assess the growth of students both in their native and their second language. This approach to assessment is clearly the most comprehensive and makes use of formal standardized measures in conjunction with more informal measures. More important, it views every act of learning and every task completed by the student as a potential and powerful source of information on the student's development. We explore this movement in depth in the next section.

In summary, the major problem with assessment as it has evolved in bilingual education is that it has responded to legal concerns and political pressures rather than to the real needs of students. Because of the emphasis on the acquisition of English, summative forms of assessment of English language skills have dominated the field. In addition, traditional testing of both language proficiency and academic achievement has yielded very little information about bilingual students as learners. One possible course of action is to bring together tests, test results, and instruction so that they inform each other for the benefit of students who by law are entitled to meaningful and equal access to education. In so doing, assessment becomes a comprehensive and ongoing process of which testing is only a small part. Another possibility is to explore alternative forms of assessment. Both of these possibilities are discussed in the next section.

Toward a More Expansive View of Assessment for Bilingual Students

We have already alluded to the poor pattern of performance of bilingual students on standardized tests of language proficiency and academic achievement as well as the overrepresentation of these same students in remedial and special education programs. We have also called attention to the increased number of grade retentions that are found among these students.

While it is difficult to argue with the belief that it is important to determine what students are capable of doing or what they have learned in order to meet their instructional needs more effectively, it is apparent that traditional assessment practices have had an entirely different effect. These practices have led both to an underestimation of the cognitive abilities of bilingual students,[26] and to an overestimation of their knowledge of the English language,[27] thereby subjecting them to instruction that is unchallenging and unstimulating or forcing them to learn in a language in which they have minimal proficiency.

Admittedly, standardized tests are currently used to satisfy an assortment of requirements for legal and funding purposes. However, whether they are necessary is a critical question and whether they are the most appropriate means of assessment is subject to interpretation. Yet these and other forms of snapshot assessments that gauge learning or knowledge at one moment in time have serious limitations for purposes of making instructional decisions that are in the best interest of bilingual students. Recent developments in alternative forms of assessment may provide a way to deal with this dilemma and to assure that these students are treated fairly, receive appropriate programs of instruction, and experience school success, at least at a rate that is not disproportionately different from that of other groups. O'Malley and Valdez Pierce report that the federally funded centers which provide assistance to bilingual and ESL programs in the areas of assessment and evaluation have received an increasing number of requests over the past few years for workshops on alternative assessment and portfolio development.[28]

What is seemingly different about these "new" assessment practices is that they challenge teachers to find ways that are not merely impressionistic for documenting what and how students are learning in the classroom. According to Zessoules and Gardner, assessment occurs at a moment in the educational process which captures the peaks and valleys of development.[29] More important, they argue that assessment must be used as an opportunity to develop complex understandings. Therefore, beyond capturing what and how students learn, alternative forms of assessment, if used appropriately, have the potential to transform the very character of classroom learning and teaching.

Perrone reminds us that these approaches are not new:

The kind of record keeping that makes up what is currently called *documentation*, the types of work that fill a *portfolio*, and the projects that are the basis for what we now call *performance assessment* or *exhibits of learning* were common in most 19th century schools and were basic to practices in numerous early progressive schools influenced by the work of John Dewey, William Kilpatrick, Marietta Johnson, and Caroline Pratt, among others.[30]

These approaches continue to be used in the alternative school movement, as is evident in the work of Pat Carini at the Prospect School in Vermont, of Deborah Meier at Central Park East School in New York City, and of the Coalition of Essential Schools.[31] Recently, however, these approaches have begun to take root in traditional public school settings having high concentrations of second language learners, whether or not these are bilingual programs or English as a second language (ESL) programs. This is evident in individual districtwide and statewide efforts such as those of Bárbara Flores, who has been working on whole language literacy at the primary school level in Arizona and California; Carmen Mercado, who has been working on alternative assessments with preservice and in-service teachers and with a middle school collaborative project in New York City; and Michael O'Malley, who has developed a portfolio assessment model for ESL students.[32]

Freeman and Freeman suggest that the impact of these practices is especially strong in California and in Florida, where more than 2,000 elementary teachers are reportedly using portfolio assessment with over 45,000 students.[33] Although there may be differences in the way particular practices have developed across individual projects, the view that assessment should be an integral part of instruction for bilingual students is the common focus.

CONSIDERATIONS IN THE USE OF NONTRADITIONAL FORMS
OF ASSESSMENT WITH BILINGUAL STUDENTS

Nontraditional forms of assessment blur the distinction between assessment and instruction. Every opportunity to teach becomes an opportunity to learn and similarly every opportunity to assess becomes an opportunity to teach and learn. Therefore, reconceptualizing assessment as a form of learning that is an ongoing part of instruction means reconceptualizing teaching. For bilingual students, the implications are great. It is only when assessment is an integral part of instruction that teachers of bilingual students are able to create learning environments that have the potential for stimulating learning and development. Structured and unstructured activities in the classroom and careful observation are the only means to determine the point at which activities are appropriately difficult for these or any other students. Vygotsky referred to this point as the "zone of proximal development,"[34] a construct that, not surprisingly, is having a growing influence on research and theory on instruction for bilingual students. Instruction that aims at the zone of proximal development looks very different from traditional instruction and assessment. It requires teachers to assume a different stance toward the learner and toward the content and processes of instruction.

Capturing and documenting what bilingual students are learning— their academic progress, their growing confidence and independence in using English, as well as their vulnerabilities—requires actual examination of what they say and do during learning activities, over a period of time. For teachers of bilingual students this means observing the way the language of the activities influences the construction of knowledge, being sensitive to the way linguistic responses and productions in English serve to conceal as well as reveal not only students' capabilities and understandings but also their vulnerabilities. Through this reciprocal process of teaching and learning together, students and teachers learn a great deal about each other—information that will help them to make better sense of one another during classroom interaction. Chronicling growth in this manner acknowledges that learning is constantly evolving, growing, and changing;[35] that it is not a linear, monolithic process; and that sudden shifts in development are not unusual and are to be expected.

This approach to assessment helps us to document and understand such variability in the context of instruction for bilingual students. Variability is an aspect that merits careful consideration as it occurs on several different levels simultaneously. Though often overlooked, there is variability across groups speaking the same language, as is evident among Mexican-Americans, Puerto Ricans, and Cubans—the three largest Spanish-speaking groups in American schools. Ogbu and Matute-Bianchi's insightful analysis reminds us of the socio-historical forces that are at play in these differences.[36] There is also variability within these groups and oftentimes the differences within groups are greater than the differences across groups speaking the same language.

All students bring unique gifts to the classroom and bilingual students are no different. It is the purpose of assessment to discover what these gifts are. Accomplishing this requires a great deal of observation and personal contact with students in order to learn who they are and what they bring to the classroom, as one future teacher realized:

Children who are entering school and the country as new arrivals look at things differently, the language is new and foreign, everything is new and different. They bring many treasures with them to this country, but unfortunately most of us never delve deep enough into their lives to discover them and they lay hidden.[37]

Bilingual students are an important source of information on what they are learning and on the type of help they may need to progress academically, linguistically, and socially. Enabling bilingual students to explain or clarify what they mean and to tell us what their specific needs are, in whatever language they choose, is especially important for intermediate and high school students who are able to articulate these needs. Moreover, by reflecting on the strategies they use to learn language and to learn instructional content, bilingual students may be able to assume a more active role in their own development. Assessment can play an important role in empowering bilingual students to assume greater control of their own learning. However, teachers need to create opportunities for discussing these issues with the students, individually as well as collectively.

Through ongoing assessment teachers gain understandings in a timely manner of how their actions influence students. Communicating across language and cultural differences creates too many possibilities for misunderstandings and misinterpretations. Teachers may use this knowledge to understand the reactions of students better, and also to modify their own behaviors and to plan instruction that is responsive to evolving needs and interests. This is important as no one can possibly anticipate how individual students will respond to particular activities, nor how their interests and needs will change over time, sometimes dramatically. By being sensitive to the potential consequences of their actions teachers are better able to respond to the needs of their bilingual students.

In effect, in the context of instruction for bilingual students more than in any other context, assessment must be viewed as an ongoing, dynamic, collaborative, and reciprocal process which is inseparable from teaching and learning. In this process teachers are able to create learning environments that respond to the needs of bilingual students' and that challenge them to grow. Rather than being a race to "cover content," to "catch up," and to "perform" in English,[38] as is often the case, teaching becomes a form of research—a journey into discovering how and what the students are learning and the type of support they may require at a particular time.

It is precisely because of the strong connection between assessment and instruction that alternative assessment approaches cannot be appended to existing instructional practices. They represent a distinct view of learning and teaching. This may be why whole language approaches, which seek to preserve the integrity of language and its authentic use, usually involve portfolio assessment. Perhaps most important, activities in a whole language approach and in portfolio assessment both reflect the belief that language and literacy are at the service of learning and that learning occurs when students are engaged in challenging and interesting activities, in collaboration with others. By making assessment an integral part of instruction, it is possible to create learning environments that challenge bilingual students to learn forms of language that are important to academic progress *while* they are learning academic content. Ideally this should occur in the native language of the students, but it is more likely to occur in English and in mainstream classrooms given what we know about the relatively small percentage of students who actually receive instruction through the medium of their native language.

ALTERNATIVE ASSESSMENT PRACTICES IN CURRENT USE

There are a number of procedures and practices that are being used to gain an understanding of how and what students are learning, yielding data which are neither impressionistic nor unreliable and that meet the requirements of the state and federal governments. Unlike traditional standardized tests, these procedures form a natural part of instruction, and as such do not disrupt the school day nor provoke unnecessary anxiety on the part of students.

Combining existing data sources with new sources of information results in a more complete profile of individual learners. Compiling and carefully analyzing information from a variety of sources and perspectives allows for the detection of learning patterns. Inconsistencies that surface or that are sought are instructive and should be carefully examined, recorded, and reported. In so doing, teachers play an important role as advocates for the bilingual students entrusted to their care, assuring that instruction is appropriately challenging and that it works in the best interest of these students. This was also evident, as noted earlier, when classroom teachers in New York City helped to redefine the cut-off score for exiting students from bilingual programs.

Observations of bilingual students. Observation, which includes listening, is possibly the most powerful way to gain insights about the verbal (oral and written) *and* nonverbal (postural, gestural) ways that bilingual students use language to learn and to demonstrate what they know. Untestable through traditional assessment measures, nonverbal communication is often overlooked as a source of information. Yet, it is the first stage in the development of a second language, commonly referred to as the "silent period,"[39] when ability to comprehend usually exceeds one's ability to produce in a second language.

Observing how bilingual students communicate during classroom activities, teachers gain an understanding of students' developing competence in understanding and using academic English and also in using English for social purposes.[40] Both are important because social competence influences the acquisition of academic competence, as is evident when students attempt to negotiate their understanding of academic content or to seek assistance from peers. However, social competence should not be confused with academic competence, a common error that results in teachers assuming that students possess greater competence than they actually have.

It is inherent in the role of teacher to observe students during the school day as they engage in a variety of activities, in and out of the classroom. However, to be used as a source of data, systematic records must be kept of what students *say* and *do* over time, much like the keeping of anecdotal records in which behaviors are carefully documented in a journal or composition notebook for official purposes.

Getting a sense of students' sociolinguistic competence requires that students be observed in a variety of contexts and situations; it is not unusual for students to look and act differently with different people, during different activities, and when using different languages. In particular, students' reactions and behaviors may differ during whole-class activities, during independent activities, and during play time. Not surprisingly, students may also act differently with Spanish-speaking teachers and peers and with English-speaking teachers and peers.[41] Observing students over time, in real contexts of use, is the only means of getting a fair reading of how students are learning language and content in English and of the fundamental role that native language development plays in this process.

Students' voluntary efforts to communicate with their peers and with adults, to read and to write in English or in any combination of English and Spanish are significant, as is students' use of Spanish to understand academic content presented in English. Teachers may need to look closely to examine the uses of English and Spanish for learning and for social purposes as the tendency has been to make students feel that dependence on the native language is a deficiency rather than a strength. It bears repeating that even when instruction occurs in English, the students' native language plays a critical role in their learning. Its use for this purpose should be acknowledged and encouraged.

Much occurs below a teacher's level of awareness because of the sheer impossibility of knowing everything that occurs in classrooms,[42] as was dramatically documented in a case study of a bilingual Spanish-dominant first-grade holdover who was said to have "weak" English language skills.[43] Videotaping classroom activities enabled the researchers in this study to capture the students' "out of sight" behaviors, which revealed intellectual and interactional competencies that exceeded the assessments made by the classroom teacher. Recording devices or the assistance of another adult may be necessary to help teachers document the behaviors of bilingual students in the classroom.

Analysis of students' work over time. Another important source of information on student growth and development is the analysis of the products of their learning over time. Students' writing efforts, especially art work for younger learners, are particularly revealing of their social, cognitive, and linguistic development. Because reading, writing, and oral language develop concurrently, there is no prerequisite age or stage of readiness for English language development before writing activities can commence. Edelsky, Flores, and Hudelson have each chronicled the biliterate development of early childhood bilingual students,[44] providing dramatic documentation of growth in English language development even before formal instruction in English has begun and even when the students score below the 20th percentile on standardized tests. For intermediate and high school students, writing provides an important means of self-expression, circumventing concerns over pronunciation to which students are especially sensitive at this age.[45]

It is evident that writing is an especially powerful medium for examining the bilingual students' developing proficiency in using English to learn academic content, but it also has the potential to reveal other important influences on learning, as the following two examples illustrate:

From reading their writings, I got a sense of who the students are . . . what it's like for them walking to school and using this information to help the kids learn what they want to learn about.[46]

My most insightful assignment so far has been my "How I Read" piece. I didn't expect them to have such a low estimation of their reading ability as shown in their critique of their skills. I felt I praised them a lot, but I realize I must do more.[47]

As varieties of literacies are the norm in and out of school, it is necessary to examine writing samples that represent a range of purposes, styles, and writing contexts. During the course of a routine day, students engage in a number of learning activities involving writing. These may include (1) writing that responds to specific questions or situations under study, resulting in texts such as summaries, stories, friendly letters, and business letters; (2) assignments in which students report on topics they have chosen to study in depth; and (3) interactive journal writing in which teacher and student sustain a written conversation about the progress and concerns of the students. In addition, self-initiated writing and personal notes to the teacher are important sources of information that should be included.

Valencia cautions that written products should be obtained from authentic learning activities,[48] that is, activities that students view as important for their learning. Otherwise, the students' responses may not accurately represent what they are capable of doing. Writing products should also be obtained from activities across the curriculum—not only from activities in classes in English language arts or English as a second language—to provide a broader indicator of what students are able to do on a variety of tasks across the major areas of the curriculum. When sorted according to purpose and context, these documents yield a base from which to select representative samples for intensive examination. These procedures are important as they add to the validity and reliability of this assessment approach, as does consulting with students to ascertain what they feel best represents them and what they are able to do. When examined at regular intervals, these documents provide dramatic evidence for the peaks and valleys of development. Specifically, they provide evidence for the progress students are making in (1) English language development, (2) learning academic content, and (3) their social and emotional development. This third aspect, which is a significant influence on school learning, is typically overlooked in traditional assessment measures.

Conferences with students and caretakers. Conferences provide an opportunity to converse with students about their work, about their progress in learning English and learning through English, about their background and interests, and about problems getting in the way of this learning. Conferences with a bilingual student may require the assistance of a peer, a sibling, or adult who speaks the student's language and who may serve to mediate the exchange. Giving students a language choice is instructive to teachers. It also lessens the anxiety that students are likely to experience.

For bilingual students in particular, conferences serve multiple and important purposes. They enable students and teachers to review the products of learning periodically, thus helping students to understand more concretely the progress they are making in specific areas. Conferences also enable teachers to probe and learn about the thinking processes and strategies individual students use to learn academic content in English. Teachers thus have opportunities to provide timely assistance, and bilingual students are helped to become more deliberate and self-directed learners.

Conferences are important teaching opportunities that enable teachers to probe and develop complex understandings about the processes and content of learning in a way that is not possible during whole-class activities. In this relatively unthreatening and relaxed atmosphere, teachers may also provide the moral support and encouragement needed to deal with attendant stresses of learning in a second language. A third-grade teacher reflects on the way student-teacher conferences strengthened the relationship that she had with her multiethnic class:

My most useful tool for guiding student's work has been meeting with them one-on-one to help them get started on an assignment or to discuss first drafts and the direction they could go in. It makes the student feel their work is *important* to you and so makes it even more important to them. I wish there was more time to sit with them and to get into more depth.[49]

Working with middle school students in a different instructional context, a preservice graduate student brings to light another aspect of teacher-student conferences with bilingual students:

During the one-on-one conversation that I had with E. on April 20th, I asked him about his speaking Spanish. He told me that he speaks Spanish at home because his mom speaks Spanish and doesn't speak very much English. At this point, there is a note in my journal which says "Instinct tells me that E. is the man of the house and his mother is dependent on him for everything including translation." He writes words on a blackboard he has at home. I asked him about his being held back in the first grade because of language barriers (something I had discovered through his teacher). He said that it made him mad because "it was just 'cause I was Spanish." I told him that I felt that being bilingual was no easy feat, that he had two complete languages. I felt that functioning in two languages was something to be commended.[50]

These examples demonstrate the potential value of conferences with bilingual students that goes beyond the domain of traditional assessment measures. Most important, the act of sitting and talking individually with students conveys the message that teachers are available to help students with academic content, but also to deal with negative experiences that are related to the condition of being bilingual in this society.

Conferences with parents enable teachers to view their students through the eyes of their parents and to tap yet another important source of data that usually is not included as part of students' assessments. Although conferences are held regularly for purposes of reporting on the academic progress of students, relatively less attention has been given to inquiring about important influences on learning such as the students' medical histories, their background experiences, their home responsibilities, and about significant learning opportunities that are provided in the home. Indeed, Moll and his associates have found that the homes of poor and working-class families contain cognitive resources useful for instruction, even though schools do not usually take full advantage of these resources.[51]

Parents may also play an important role in interpreting their children's performance on particular assignments and in verifying teachers' assessments in those areas where parents are knowledgeable. However, to obtain these types of insights, teachers need to assume the stance of learners, seeking out rather than putting forth explanations. This approach needs to be explained to parents who tend to view teachers as the authorities. Arranging for the presence of a translator communicates a genuine interest in understanding what parents have to say, but it also increases the likelihood that parents or caretakers relate detailed and accurate information about their children. In this manner, teachers may come to understand the bilingual students in their classes.

It should be clear by now that alternative assessments are highly dependent on the relationships that teachers have with students, with caretakers, and with other individuals who have knowledge of the bilingual students' social, linguistic, and academic development. The extent to which information is forthcoming and accurate is a function of the strength of this relationship.

Alternative forms of assessment we have described carry with them a redefinition of the role of teachers. These practices emphasize the role of teachers as researchers and learners. Teachers are challenged to: (1) create opportunities to observe and describe the learning activities of their students; (2) find ways of probing more intensively their students' understandings in two languages; (3) analyze students' performance and interpret their progress over time; and (4) seek out multiple sources of information and multiple perspectives on their students.

Implications for Teacher Education

Alternative assessment practices are clearly far more demanding on teachers than traditional assessment measures, especially in the case of assessment in bilingual education. Organizing the documentary evidence obtained over time from a number of sources, selecting representative samples in an objective manner, and synthesizing interpretations for what is to become an official record of progress can be an intimidating process. Yet the promise it holds for achieving educational equity and excellence for bilingual students is great.

Although the approach should not be dismissed as just another educational fad, it should be entered into carefully and with a great deal of support. Teachers have acknowledged the need for assistance in (1) learning to become careful observers and listeners; (2)

interpreting students' responses; (3) selecting and organizing the evidence of learning, and (4) becoming reflective and analytical practitioners.

Specifically, teachers require assistance in capturing or recording classroom observations during the school day. While there are no standard procedures for recording observations, it is important that this type of evidence is sufficiently precise and that it documents the range of interactional and learning situations and activities that are typical in a given classroom. Because teachers have a tendency to evaluate rather than to describe behaviors, they need to be made aware of the way in which their language tends to evaluate even when they believe they are describing, as is evident in the use of such terms as "bright," "lazy," and "moody." In contrast, the example which follows illustrates the power of an astute observation/description to capture the silent period of a young second language learner in a mainstream English speaking setting:

The first thing that I noticed about G. were her eyes. Large, brown, and questioning, they seem extremely alert and aware. Not yet able to speak in English and seeming reticent to use her Spanish, most of her communication is accomplished through the use of her eyes. If she is feeling confident and involved in an activity, they sparkle, illuminating her entire face. If she is unsure, they become round with wondering. If she is unhappy, their focus is down and inward and she will turn her head away.[52]

In order to serve bilingual students better, teachers also need to understand some common reactions that these students may have to instruction in English. Bilingual students may be quiet, slow to respond, reluctant to try, or they may require constant reassurances and directions. These reactions may reflect the condition of being a second language learner, but they may also reflect ways of behaving that are valued among certain groups of people. They may also indicate difficult past experiences related to the migrant/immigrant experience or to the condition of being poor in the United States today. The point is that there are a broad range of possible factors which explain students' reactions to instruction in English.

Responses and reactions are not easy to interpret and what may be an indicator of giftedness to one person may appear to be dysfunctional to another. Admittedly, establishing criteria for judging the appropriateness of a student's work is difficult as we are just beginning to understand the uneven line of development that characterizes growth, not just for bilingual students, but for all students. Through her work in portfolio assessment one future teacher came to this realization on her own:

My impressions of how the students were learning information was very different when I viewed their oral explanations and their written work separately. Some students were able to tell me a lot about what they had learned, but when they put it down on paper most of the information was lost, while other students who appeared to lack motivation during class discussions surprised me with the amount of detail that they remembered from these same discussions. Two examples are E. and D. Student E. was an active participant in group discussions and was able to speak authoritatively on his topic, while student D. rarely uttered two words. However, if you were to compare the writing of these two students, D. would appear far superior in his ability to express different ideas and thoughts about his topic.[53]

Clearly, teachers are challenged to suspend judgment, to seek out counterevidence, and to verify their tentative conclusions with students, their parents, and with colleagues who bring distinct perspectives to the interpretive process.

Because classroom learning is an interactive social process, engaging in these observations also requires that teachers take a closer look at their own behaviors and their expectations of what students will or will not be able to accomplish, especially on the basis of racial, ethnic, and linguistic characteristics. Teachers also have to be willing to subject their practice to careful examination in order to see how they may be contributing to what they observe in their students.

Having an awareness of the reciprocal influence students and teachers have on one another is essential if teachers are to understand the behaviors of the bilingual students in their classrooms and of the students they are allowed to become.

Conclusion

In this chapter, we have sought to describe the role that assessment has played within the context of instruction for students who are learning English as a second language, and in particular those who are native speakers of Spanish. Our goal has been to emphasize the significance of assessment in ensuring equity and excellence in education. These are not synonymous, nor should we settle for one at the expense of the other. Both are essential, and both make distinct demands on assessment. It cannot be denied that the courts have played a central role in monitoring the efforts of school districts to meet the educational needs of bilingual students through required assessments. Without this involvement, it is doubtful that these students would have been given the equal educational opportunity which is their right particularly in times of budgetary constraints and cutbacks. However, it is questionable whether much headway would have been made toward achieving educational excellence had there not been a similar effort on the part of concerned educators and researchers. Their desire to create challenging learning environments for these students has broadened our understanding of the relationship between assessment, instruction, and research.

By focusing on the traditional forms of assessment that evolved during the early stages of the bilingual education movement and then moving into the nontraditional forms that have developed subsequently, we have tried to demonstrate the concerns of the field. While assessment serves to inform educators about the academic needs of students, it has the equally important function of chronicling their progress. Both aspects are essential as guides for teachers in helping all their students reach their full potential.

NOTES

1. There are a number of local- and state-funded initiatives, as are the two-way programs emerging throughout the country, in which bilingual education is available as an educational option to students whose caretakers view it as an opportunity to become bilingual. Students in these "enrichment" programs are subjected to the same type of intensive testing associated with any innovative educational program, but this testing is fundamentally different from the use of tests for purposes of establishing entitlement.

2. "Bilingual" is defined by Webster as "capable of using two languages, often with equal facility" (*Webster's New World Dictionary of the American Language*, concise edition [New York: World Publishing Co., 1966], p. 74). However, the term is used in U.S. education circles as a euphemism for children who speak a language other than English natively and who are learning to speak English as their second language. For many the term is used to focus on the limitations of these students (limited English proficient) rather than on their strengths, such as their ability to speak one or more non-English languages. The proof of this attitude is that many of these students enter school speaking a non-English language and have lost that ability by the time they finish school.

3. Joseph Woo, *Handbook for the Assessment of East Asian Students*, written for the Training Program for Teachers of Handicapped Children of Asian Origin (New York: Department of Special Education, Hunter College of the City University of New York, 1988).

4. John U. Ogbu and María Eugenia Matute-Bianchi, "Understanding Sociocultural Factors: Knowledge, Identity, and School Adjustment," in *Beyond Language: Social and Cultural Factors in Schooling Language Minority Students* (Los Angeles: Evaluation, Dissemination, and Assessment Center, California State University, 1986).

5. Carmen I. Mercado, "An Ethnographic Study of Classroom Help with Language Minority Students" (Doctoral dissertation, Fordham University at Lincoln Center, New York, 1988).

6. Alba A. Ortiz, Cheryl Y. Wilkinson, and Charlene Rivera, *AIM for the BESt: Assessment and Intervention Model for the Bilingual Exceptional Student*, Technical Report (Washington, DC: Office of Bilingual Education and Minority Languages Affairs, U.S. Department of Education, 1991); Jim Cummins, "Tests, Achievement, and Bilingual Students," *Focus*, no. 9 (Rosslyn, VA: National Clearinghouse for Bilingual Education, February, 1982); Minerva Mendoza-Friedman, "Spanish Bilingual Students and Intelligence Testing," *Changing Education* (Spring, 1973): 25-28.

7. Alba A. Ortiz and Elba Maldonado-Colón, "Reducing Inappropriate Referrals of Language Minority Students in Special Education," in *Bilingualism and Learning Disabilities*, edited by Ann C. Willig and Hinda F. Greenberg (New York: American Library Publishing Co., 1986), p. 39.

8. Jim Cummins, as quoted in John W. Oller, "Language Testing Research: Lessons Applied to LEP Students and Programs," in *Proceedings of the Second National Research Symposium on Limited English Proficient Student Issues: Focus on Evaluation and Measurement*, vol. 1 (Washington, DC: Office of Bilingual Education and Minority Languages Affairs, U.S. Department of Education, 1992), p. 94.

9. U.S. Department of Education, *America 2000: An Education Strategy* (Washington, DC: U.S. Department of Education, 1991).

10. Edward Chittenden, "Authentic Assessment, Evaluation, and Documentation," in *Expanding Student Assessment*, edited by Vito Perrone (Alexandria, VA: Association for Supervision and Curriculum Development, 1991), pp. 22-31.

11. Office of Civil Rights, "Memorandum, May 25, 1970" (Washington, DC: Office of Civil Rights, U.S. Department of Education, 1970).

12. Herbert Teitelbaum and Richard Hiller, "Bilingual Education: The Legal Mandate," in *Bilingual Multicultural Education and the Professional*, edited by Henry Trueba and Carol Barnett-Mizrahi (Rowley, MA: Newbury House, 1979), pp. 20-53.

13. Ibid., p. 27.

14. Perry Zirkel, "The Whys and Ways of Testing Bilinguality before Teaching Bilinguality," in *Bilingual Multicultural Education and the Professional*, edited by Henry Trueba and Carol Barnett-Mizrahi (Rowley, MA: Newbury House, 1979), pp. 391-396.

15. Thomas Fitzgibbon, *The Use of Standardized Instruments with Urban and Minority Group Pupils* (New York: Harcourt Brace Jovanovich, 1972).

16. JoAnn Canales, "Innovative Practices in the Identification of LEP Students" (Paper presented at the National Research Symposium on Limited English Proficient [LEP] Students' Issues: Focus on Evaluation and Measurement, September 5, 1991).

17. In New York State, for example, the initial cut-off point on the Language Assessment Battery was set at the 20th percentile, reconciling the demands of the plaintiffs and the defendants in Aspira's class action suit against the New York City Board of Education (NYC BOE). Recently the cut-off was raised to the 40th percentile as a result of three interrelated developments. First, classroom teachers perceived that students exiting bilingual programs at the 20th percentile were unprepared for instruction in mainstream classes, and that consequently they needed additional support during a transitional period when such support is not usually made available. Second, a study conducted by the NYC BOE Office of Educational Assessment/Evaluation found that the scores of students above the 40th percentile tended to remain more stable over a long school recess than those of students scoring between the 20th and 40th percentile, suggesting the predictive validity of the higher cutoff. Third, a study conducted by the New York State Education Department to review cutoff scores across the nation found that few states actually used anything below the 40th percentile. Personal communication with Judith Torres, Director of Institutional Research of Hostos Community College, 1992.

18. Roger Shuy, "Problems in Assessing Language Ability in Bilingual Education Programs," in *Bilingual Education*, edited by Hernán La Fontaine, H. Persky, and L. Golubchick (Wayne, NJ: Avery, 1978), pp. 376-380; Oller, "Language Testing Research."

19. Joshua A. Fishman, *Language Loyalty in the United States* (The Hague: Mouton, 1966).

20. Canales, "Innovative Practices in the Identification of LEP Students."

21. Edward A. DeAvila and Sharon Duncan, "A Few Thoughts about Language Assessment: The *Lau* Decision Reconsidered," in *Bilingual Multicultural Education and the Professional*, edited by Henry Trueba and Carol Barnett-Mizrahi (Rowley, MA: Newbury House, 1979), pp. 441-453.

22. Shuy, "Problems in Assessing Language Ability in Bilingual Education Programs."

23. Carmen I. Mercado, Migdalia Romero, and José A. Vázquez, *Conceptual Framework for a Comprehensive Assessment Program* (Arlington, VA: National Clearinghouse for Bilingual Education, 1979).

24. Woo, *Handbook for the Assessment of East Asian Students*.

25. Canales, "Innovative Practices in the Identification of LEP Students."

26. Stephen Díaz, Luis C. Moll, and Hugh Mehan, "Sociocultural Contexts of Language Development," in *Beyond Language: Social and Cultural Factors in Schooling Minority Students* (Los Angeles: Evaluation, Dissemination, and Assessment Center, California State University, 1986), pp. 187-230; Robert L. Carrasco, Arthur Vera, and Courtney B. Cazden, "Aspects of Bilingual Students' Communicative Competence in the Classroom: A Case Study," in *Latino Language and Communicative Behavior*, edited by Richard P. Duran (Norwood, NJ: Ablex, 1981).

27. Cecilia Navarrete, Judith Wilde, Chris Nelson, Robert Martínez, and Gary Hargett, *Informal Assessment in Educational Evaluation: Implications for Bilingual Education* (Arlington, VA: National Clearinghouse for Bilingual Education, 1990).

28. J. Michael O'Malley and Lorraine Valdez Pierce, "Portfolio Assessment: Using Portfolio and Alternative Assessment with LEP Students," *Forum* 15, no. 1 (1991): 1.

29. Rieneke Zessoules and Howard Gardner, "Authentic Assessment: Beyond the Buzzword and into the Classroom," in *Expanding Student Assessment*, edited by Vito Perrone (Alexandria, VA: Association for Supervision and Curriculum Development, 1991), pp. 47-71.

30. Vito Perrone, "Introduction," in *Expanding Student Assessment*, edited by Vito Perrone (Alexandria, VA: Association for Supervision and Curriculum Development, 1991), p. viii.

31. David Carroll and Patricia Carini, "Tapping Teachers' Knowledge," in *Expanding Student Assessment*, edited by Vito Perrone (Alexandria, VA: Association for Supervision and Curriculum Development, 1991), pp. 40-46; *HORACE* 6, no. 3 (1990): 1-12.

32. O'Malley and Valdez Pierce, "Portfolio Assessment."

33. Yvonne Freeman and David Freeman, "Portfolio Assessment: An Exciting View of What Bilingual Children Can Do," *BE Outreach* 2, no. 1 (1919): 6-7.

34. Lev S. Vygotsky, *Mind in Society*, translated and edited by Michael Cole, Vera John-Steiner, Sylvia Scribner, and Ellen Souberman (Cambridge, MA: Harvard University Press, 1978).

35. Sheila Valencia, "A Portfolio Approach to Classroom Reading Assessment: The Whys, Whats, and Hows," *Reading Teacher* 43 (January 1990): 338-340.

36. Ogbu and Matute-Bianchi, "Understanding Sociocultural Factors."

37. Lori Weiser, unpublished notes, 1991. This and other examples cited on the following pages represent the views and experiences of nontraditional teacher education students—preservice and in-service teachers who learned about using alternative assessment practices with culturally and linguistically diverse students through a graduate reading course. We wish to express our appreciation to each of these students (Patricia Drudy, Sue Hunter, Diane Kane, Pamela Siegel, and Lori Weiser) for allowing us to use excerpts from their notes.

38. Mercado, "An Ethnographic Study of Classroom Help with Language Minority Students."

39. Stephen D. Krashen and Tracy D. Terrell, *The Natural Approach* (New York: Pergamon, 1983).

40. Jack S. Damico, "Performance Assessment of Language Minority Students," in *Proceedings of the Second National Research Symposium on Limited English Proficient Students' Issues: Focus on Evaluation and Measurement* (Washington, DC: Office of Bilingual Education and Minority Languages Affairs, U.S. Department of Education, 1992).

41. Díaz, Moll, and Mehan, "Social Contexts of Language Development."

42. Mercado, "An Ethnographic Study of Classroom Help with Language Minority Students."

43. Carrasco, Vera, and Cazden, "Aspects of Bilingual Students' Communicative Competence in the Classroom."

44. Carole Edelsky, *Writing in a Bilingual Program* (Norwood, NJ: Ablex, 1986); Bárbara M. Flores, "Children's Psychogenesis of Literacy and Biliteracy," in *Proceedings of the First Research Symposium on Limited English Proficient Students' Issues* (Washington, DC: Office of Bilingual Education and Minority Languages Affairs, U.S. Department of Education, 1990), pp. 281-320; Sarah Hudelson, "Kan Yu Ret and Rayt en Ingles? Children Become Literate in English as a Second Language," *TESOL Quarterly* 18 (1984): 221-238.

45. Carmen I. Mercado, "Native and Second Language Development: The Promise of a New Decade," in *Bilingual Education and English as a Second Language: A Research Handbook 1988-1990,* edited by Alba Ambert and María Alvarez (New York: Garland, 1991), pp. 171-195.

46. Patricia Drudy, unpublished notes, 1991.

47. Diane Kane, unpublished notes, 1991.

48. Valencia, "A Portfolio Approach to Classroom Reading Assessment."

49. Diane Kane, unpublished notes, 1991.

50. Pamela Siegel, unpublished notes, 1991.

51. Luis C. Moll, Carlos Velez-Ibáñez, and James Greenberg, *Community Knowledge and Classroom Practice: Combining Resources for Literacy Instruction*, Final Technical Report, Innovative Approaches Research Project (Arlington, VA: Development Associates, 1990).

52. Sue Hunter, unpublished notes, 1991.

53. Patricia Drudy, unpublished notes, 1991.

CHAPTER VII

Language and Culture in the Preparation of Bilingual Teachers

BÁRBARA J. MERINO AND CHRISTIAN J. FALTIS

In this chapter we describe and examine the education of prospective teachers who are expected to work in culturally and linguistically diverse settings. In many cases such teachers will work in bilingual education programs but they may also work in English as a second language (ESL) programs, structured immersion, two-way immersion, or sheltered English programs and at the secondary level even in foreign language programs in courses such as Spanish for native speakers. A unifying characteristic of all these programs is that they are designed to serve students who are in the process of acquiring a second language and a second culture. These programs vary in the degree to which development of the primary language continues to be a focus. In this chapter we center our attention on the preparation of teachers for positions in bilingual education but will make reference as appropriate to the preparation of foreign language and ESL teachers as well.

Preparing Bilingual Teachers: The Current Context

The need for bilingual teachers. The population of limited English proficient students aged five to fourteen in the United States reached 2,092,700 in 1990. In California the number of language minority students (K-12) that same year was 861,551. Also in that year there were 22,365 positions in California K-12 schools for teachers with bilingual cross-cultural credentials, while only 8,033 teachers with appropriate credentials were employed at local public schools. Thus the demand for bilingual teachers in California exceeded the supply in 1990 by 178 percent.[1] See table 1 for an overview of teacher need and supply by language group in California.

Bárbara J. Merino is Associate Professor and Director of Teacher Education at the University of California at Davis. Christian J. Faltis is Associate Professor of Multicultural Education in the Division of Curriculum and Instruction, College of Education, Arizona State University, Tempe.

TABLE 1

LIMITED ENGLISH PROFICIENT STUDENTS AND TEACHER
SUPPLY IN CALIFORNIA (1990) BY LINGUISTIC GROUP

LINGUISTIC GROUP	STUDENTS IN K-12	TEACHERS NEEDED	TEACHER SUPPLY	TEACHER SHORTAGE	PERCENT OF TOTAL SHORTAGE
Spanish	655,097	17,435	7,602	9,833	69
Vietnamese	34,934	762	46	736	5
Cantonese	21,154	488	220	268	2
Cambodian (Khmer)	19,234	514	0	514	4
Filipino/Tagalog	19,092	389	56	333	2
Hmong	18,091	508	1	507	4
Korean	13,389	303	34	269	2
Lao	12,177	301	2	299	2
Mandarin (Putonghua)	7,210	156	13	143	1
Armenian	9,046	208	17	191	1
Japanese	5,505	132	11	121	1
Farsi (Persian)	4,875	114	2	112	1
Other Chinese	3,313	70	1	69	0
Mien (Yao)	2,834	78	0	78	1
Portuguese	2,830	72	20	52	0
Arabic	2,771	73	0	73	1
Punjabi	2,093	51	3	48	0
Hindi	1,754	45	0	45	0
Samoan	1,490	41	0	41	0
Ilocano	1,031	22	0	22	0
All Others	23,640	583	5	578	4
Totals	861,551	22,365	8,033	14,332	100

Source: California State Department of Education

Accounts of the national need for bilingual teachers indicate a similar pattern of growth and need particularly in heavily impacted states.[2] National estimates indicate that only 46 percent of first-grade language minority students not fluent in English have regular classroom teachers with credentials in either bilingual education or teaching English as a second language.[3] Approximately 5.8 million students come from homes in which the primary language is not English. Nine states have at least 25,000 students with limited English proficiency. New York has approximately a quarter of a million such students and Texas has at least half a million.[4]

Historical antecedents. Teacher preparation in bilingual education owes much of its beginnings to foreign language education and has been influenced concurrently by ESL philosophies and methods. Over the past forty years the education of second language teachers has shifted dramatically from a view that such teachers must be trained in the skills of a particular method, namely, the audiolingual method,[5] toward a view that teachers must know an array of methods and techniques from which to choose as the needs of their students dictate.[6] Lesson design has moved from the prescriptivism of audiolingual methodology, where even the place of a grammatical explanation was the object of intense debate, toward a more open teacher- and student-centered approach where teachers decide how to design lessons, often incorporating their students' ideas in the design process.[7] And, whereas researchers formerly investigated the relative effectiveness of particular methods in search of the one way to teach a second language, current research explores variable paths to success depending on the interactions among context, the school, the community, and the learner.[8]

The content of teacher education for second language teachers has been influenced in varying degrees by professional organizations and state legislation.[9] Guidelines for preparing teachers were established by TESOL (Teachers of English to Speakers of Other Languages) in 1976 and by ACTFL (American Council on the Teaching of Foreign Languages) in 1988. The Center for Applied Linguistics published competencies for teachers in bilingual education in 1974.[10] More recently, Riojas Clark and Thonis each provided overviews of the competencies deemed necessary for teaching in bilingual classroom settings.[11]

In spite of all this specification of competencies, what actually goes on in teacher education for second language teachers remains a "black box."[12] It should be remembered, however, that the content of teacher education for mainstream teachers remains similarly undefined.[13] Nonetheless, attempts have been made to define major aspects of teacher education for second language teachers. In this chapter we focus on some of these aspects: the research on teacher effectiveness in culturally and linguistically diverse contexts, methods of teaching a second language, models of supervision, research on second language acquisition, the use and distribution of language in bilingual classrooms for literacy and content instruction, and effective approaches for infusing knowledge of cultures in an educational context. Most of these issues relate to two central themes: language and culture. In most bilingual teacher education programs these issues and themes are addressed through coursework and in field experience (practica or student teaching).

In the following sections, we turn our attention to these issues and the themes of language and culture in bilingual teacher education. We preface these sections with a brief overview of the reform movement in teacher education. This movement has directly impacted bilingual teacher education by focusing attention on key components of the teacher preparation process, in particular on the need for changing the nature of the knowledge base required for teaching and on the role of student teaching in developing teachers to work effectively in linguistically and culturally diverse schools.

A call for reforms in teacher education. In the early 1980s the federal government commissioned *A Nation at Risk*,[14] a report in which American public schools were depicted as declining in quality primarily because of a widespread acceptance of mediocrity over excellence. That same year, no fewer than four other reports were published, all of which reaffirmed the government's concern over the deterioration of the nation's schools. Almost immediately following the publication of these national reports came a thunderous call for reforms such as a return to the basics, higher standards in schools, and accountability through increased use of testing. The reports also indirectly placed major responsibility for implementing new reforms in the hands of teacher educators. Moreover, teacher education itself became a target of reform, with calls for changes in the professional education of teachers, for upgrading their preparation in the subject matter of the liberal arts, and for testing their general, professional, and subject-matter knowledge.

The impact of these largely top-down calls for reform in teacher education has been sporadic and uneven at best. A nationwide study by Goodlad of twenty-nine institutions representing six types of teacher education schools and departments revealed that teacher education practices have changed little since the early 1960s.[15] Today, the components found in a majority of teacher education schools and departments differ little from the three components comprising the programs James Conant described in 1963: some sort of a social foundations component, a component dealing with how children develop and learn as they grow, and a component on principles of teaching.[16] Presently, as before, most teacher education majors are taught to teach using research-based teaching competencies frequently generated by state departments of education or commissions. Cooperating teachers and their university supervisors are trained to provide systematic feedback and instruction in those same competencies.

Although the Goodlad study did not specifically mention bilingual, ESL, or foreign language teacher education programs, it is fairly safe to assume that the same components also appear in these teacher education programs, which are most often specializations within elementary and secondary teacher education. Bilingual education majors usually take a special set of methods courses organized to incorporate language and cultural competencies and proficiency in a non-English language.[17] Students working toward an ESL endorsement take between twelve and twenty-one additional credits for coursework in ESL methods, second language acquisition, ESL assessment, and ESL curriculum and materials in addition to their regular program requirements.[18]

Toward improving teacher education. Despite the relatively limited impact the reform-minded reports have had on how teachers are prepared to teach in general, they have encouraged significant research in teacher education, which in turn has led to reforms in teacher education programs at individual institutions. In particular, two major research findings have influenced improvements in teacher education. First, some of what was once presumed to be effective teaching practice is not working in today's culturally and linguistically diverse schools.[19] Research in bilingual and multicultural classrooms has shown, for example, that teachers who rely almost exclusively on practices linked to research on effective teaching can easily misjudge their students' abilities and learning potential.[20] This is partially because the research on effective teaching for the most part has disregarded language and cultural variation in the ways students interact and respond to instruction, emphasizing instead the consistent use of teaching practices found in classrooms with high-achieving English-speaking students.

A new wave of research conducted in individual bilingual and multicultural classrooms taught by expert teachers[21] has led to the study of exemplary practices which point out the ways that expert teachers facilitate learning in culturally and linguistically diverse classroom settings.[22] The goal of this research is to discover the kinds of pedagogical, language, and content knowledge expert teachers use for teaching in multicultural and bilingual classrooms. For example, we have examined four traditions of research that have contributed distinct perspectives on what makes a bilingual teacher exemplary: (a) the competency tradition, (b) the teacher effectiveness tradition, (c) the ethnographic tradition, and (d) the literary tradition.[23] This information adds to the existing knowledge base on teacher education, pointing to the kinds of abilities and understanding about teaching bilingually that prospective teachers need to attain.

A second kind of research finding that is helping to improve teacher education is concerned with the relationship of the student teaching experience to the formation of effective teachers. Cochran-Smith argues that the way teacher educators regard and work with teachers during student teaching and the way they supervise student teachers are reflections of their beliefs about the roles teachers can play in improving teaching.[24] Moreover, based on her work in a teacher education program in Pennsylvania, Cochran-Smith concludes that "students of teaching cannot learn how to reform teaching in a general sense during the student teaching period, but only how to be reformers in one specific classroom or school."[25] According to this view, the goal of student teaching is to prepare student teachers who learn from teaching by inquiring into their own practices and by collaborating with their mentor teachers for the purpose of building an understanding of teaching that supports ongoing professional growth and reform. Cochran-Smith calls this the "collaborative resonance" approach to student teaching and contrasts it with the more traditional goal of student teaching, which is to prepare student teachers who are well versed in the behaviors and the knowledge base associated with "effective" teaching and who are trained to be decision makers and solvers of common classroom management problems.[26] Students in this approach are evaluated according to competency-based performance criteria. In the collaborative resonance approach, students engage in classroom action research, maintain dialogue journals, and attend weekly seminars that are conducted collaboratively with teachers, supervisors, and teacher educators. Moreover, in contrast to the traditional model, the goal of the collaborative resonance model is the transformation of teaching. Cooperating teachers are selected because they see themselves as change agents in the school, as inquirers who question teaching and learning activities and work with other professionals to seek answers. Student teachers who work with these teachers participate in experiences and research that involve them in making changes in schools. In short, the collaborative resonance model "takes the perspective that the status quo in schools (and in society) should *not* be maintained; that teachers should be change agents working both for better schools and a more just and truly democratic society."[27]

Language Issues in Teacher Education in Bilingual Education Programs

The use and distribution of language in bilingual education. Few topics have provoked more discussion or research in bilingual education than the issue of language use. Indeed, for many educators, the language of instruction is the variable that best differentiates bilingual programs from all others. What does research say about language use in bilingual classrooms?

Merino recently reviewed the literature on language choice in bilingual classrooms and found that most studies on language distribution have been descriptive rather than experimental, focusing most often on the distribution of languages among teachers and students.[28] As in mainstream all-English classrooms, teacher talk predominates in bilingual classrooms and teachers vary a great deal in their adherence to the use of the students' primary language in the classroom.[29] At one extreme, for example, some studies have found that teachers' use of the primary language in designated bilingual classrooms ranges from zero to a high of 22 percent.[30] In well-articulated early and late exit bilingual programs, however, teachers tend to be more faithful to the use of the primary language.[31] Thus, context seems to affect language use.

What factors beside the nature of the program seem to be related to high use of the first language (L1)? Teacher language proficiency and late exit programs are two contextual factors that are related to high L1 use.[32] Other factors such as the degree of separation of the two languages within the bilingual model may also influence parity of distribution.[33] Some have suggested that models such as the preview/ review or alternate day models, where languages are separated in fixed units, are more likely to ensure equity of distribution. Others have argued that it is the approach used in training teachers that makes the difference.[34] Jacobson has advocated the use of what he terms "the new concurrent approach," which allows for switching from one language to the other (without translation) within the lesson, but which requires the teacher to reflect about the pedagogical plan being used to make decisions about language choice.[35] Very little is said in the literature about how individual teacher education programs train their student teachers in generating a plan for language use. And there is virtually no information about how expert bilingual teachers make those choices. Jacobson describes how bilingual teachers in Texas were trained to use the new concurrent approach to bilingual teaching.[36] As part of a three-year demonstration project, Jacobson used workshops, videotapes of lessons, and playbacks of teaching events to train eight teachers and four classroom aides to respond to and self-monitor the use of sixteen situational cues distributed over four areas to guide language-switching behavior during classroom instruction. Once the teachers and aides became familiar with the cue system, they designed lessons in which they anticipated switching from one language to the other, according to the cue system. The lessons were videotaped and were then used for critical discussion and for refining subsequent lessons.

Methods and techniques in teaching a second language. Preparing bilingual teachers in the use of effective second language teaching methods is considered an absolute essential in any teacher preparation program in bilingual education. Often programs make distinctions between methods that promote oral development in the second language and those that promote literacy as well as the teaching of content, particularly science and mathematics, in the second language. In many programs, particularly those influenced by the whole language school, the teaching of language is presented as an integrated system that involves speaking, listening, reading, and writing across the curriculum.[37] Most discussion on methods in bilingual education and ESL has focused on describing methods and their rationales. Blair and Richard-Amato both describe various methods that language teachers have used successfully.[38] Within whole language oriented programs, the discussion centers upon strategies and techniques for exposing students to language and literacy in many different forms. For example, prospective teachers learn to encourage authentic conversation, and to use semantic maps along with brainstorming, dialogue journals, writing folders, literature study groups for reading and writing instruction, and writing workshops. Flores et al. and Freeman and Freeman present whole language teaching strategies and supportive materials geared for use in bilingual and ESL classrooms.[39]

In a recent paper, Uber Grosse reported on a survey of 120 TESOL methods courses across the United States.[40] In reviewing fifty-five course syllabi, she found that most course objectives focus on language learning (theory and practice) and on the teaching of second language skills. To a lesser degree, methods courses focus on program design and materials and more rarely on research and technology. Assignments and classroom activities vary, but typically examinations and papers figure as the core of the grade in most cases, with almost half of the programs also requiring curriculum development and teaching demonstrations as well as classroom observation and tutoring or teaching. Teachers of methods courses identified five areas for improvement: more observation of skilled teachers, more videotaping of students for feedback, greater emphasis on solving classroom problems, separate classes for preservice and in-service teachers and improved teaching materials. Uber Grosse's study is the first to generate an empirical definition of the content of a course in methods of teaching a second language but leaves to future research two critical questions: How effective are methods courses in getting novice teachers to implement effective methods? What is it like to be in one of these methods courses?

Milk provides some insight into what students experience in a methods course.[41] He describes a Spanish course designed to prepare teachers for integrating language and content instruction in bilingual classrooms. The course incorporated cooperative learning and introduced students to subject matter lessons in Spanish through hands-on activities similar to a program described by Merino and Faltis.[42] Students also kept dialogue journals to encourage Spanish literacy development. They used only Spanish to plan and design learning activities for content areas and then presented these in Spanish to their peers in class. Learning activities were required to encourage two-way interaction, to be cognitively difficult, and to involve cooperative interaction in small groups. Students who participated in the class perceived that they had greatly increased their understanding of the second language acquisition process. A majority of students felt that their fluency in Spanish had improved significantly as a result of participating in the course.

Ortiz also provides a picture of what can go on in a methods course.[43] She studied the use of videotaping and microteaching in preparing bilingual teachers. Her description is a very rich, detailed account of the cycle of presenting a prototype model for a lesson and what happens when three student teachers sought to implement the models in their classrooms. Unfortunately, the direction of the training was very prescriptive. Student teachers were told to set up their lessons in a certain way and to focus on pattern drills, although these were made somewhat meaningful by using the teacher as a model for teaching commands. Research of this type, however, which actually charts what happens as student teachers are taught certain behaviors or learn to use specific strategies of inquiry, needs to be a part of the agenda of future research efforts. A critical question is whether behaviors practiced in microteaching settings transfer to classroom settings.[44]

Literacy and biliteracy. Preparing teachers of literacy is one component that is common to all programs within teacher education. Students typically take one or more courses in methods of teaching reading and language arts, although it has become increasingly common to take coursework in literacy instruction, where the teaching of reading and writing are considered together. There is little consensus across teacher education programs, however, about what reading or literacy is and therefore what it is that children need to learn to do.

Instructionally as well as philosophically, there are two diametrically opposed approaches to methods of teaching reading and literacy. At one end is a phonics-based skills approach in which teacher education students are taught to present reading and writing as a set of skills that begins with decoding and letter-sound correspondence exercises for spelling words in isolation and progresses to comprehension exercises and structured activities for writing sentences and paragraphs.[45] At the other end, reading and writing are presented holistically as inseparably tied to language use for meaningful and purposeful reasons in general.[46] Teacher education students who learn about literacy from such a whole language perspective view literacy as integrated with the acquisition of listening and speaking. Schooled from this perspective, they learn how to create classroom environments that enable children to explore topics of interest and thus to engage naturally in reading and writing about these topics.[47]

The way that students in bilingual teacher education are taught about reading and literacy strongly affects their understanding of critical issues in bilingual education.[48] For example, it is axiomatic in bilingual education that literacy skills transfer from the native to the second language, provided that the skills are solidly mastered in the native language.[49] From a phonics-skills perspective, learned skills may transfer across major skills areas, but such transfer does not occur globally.[50] In contrast, from the whole language perspective, children transfer entire cognitive processes and strategies and apply these in a global way to literacy events in the second language.[51]

Very little is known about the ways that students are prepared for teaching reading and literacy in bilingual teacher education programs. One indirect indication of how student teachers are prepared for teaching reading and literacy may be obtained by considering the types of literacy materials and methods used by most teachers in bilingual programs. Barrera and Goldenberg both intimate that most Spanish-English bilingual programs rely almost exclusively on phonics taught via the syllabic method.[52] In this method, children are introduced to beginning reading through vowels, which are then immediately paired with consonants to make syllables and words, which are practiced in isolation.[53] Reading materials are comprised of controlled vocabulary and rarely is the reader allowed to engage in literacy activities that involve language beyond the sentence level. Goldenberg reports that the Spanish basal series adopted for use in California bilingual programs in 1987 focuses almost entirely at the kindergarten level on reading readiness, syllable-sound correspondence, and sounding-out skills.[54]

Another indication of the kinds of methods that students learn for teaching reading in bilingual programs is suggested by the availability of books on reading methods and materials designed specifically for bilingual programs. Until the mid-1980s, only two such methods books written for U.S. bilingual teacher education audiences were available and both were authored by reading specialist Eleanor Thonis.[55] These books, *Literacy for America's Spanish Speaking Children* and *Teaching Reading to Non-English Speakers* introduce reading instruction as a combination of decoding and comprehension activities with the goal being the transfer of native language literacy skills to English.

Beginning in the 1980s, several new literacy methods books became available for bilingual teacher education programs. In 1986, Flores et al. published *Bilingual Holistic Instructional Strategies*,[56] a whole language teaching resource book put together by, as well as for, teachers preparing to work in bilingual classrooms. Hudelson's *Write On: Children Writing in ESL*, which relates native language literacy to ESL writing and provides strategies to promote both, followed in 1989.[57] And in 1992, Pérez and Torres-Guzmán published *Learning in Two Worlds: An Integrated Spanish/English Biliteracy Approach*, a methods book that presents instructional strategies for literacy in Spanish as well as in English.[58] These books reflect a shift in the instructional and philosophical bases from a skills to a more whole language approach to literacy instruction.

Moreover, all three of these newer literacy methods books focus on ways to promote *biliteracy*, the acquisition of literacy in two languages in order to understand and convey messages in a variety of contexts.[59] Thus, whereas the previous methods books concentrated on preparing teachers of reading in a non-English language while at the same time emphasizing ways to facilitate the transfer of skills to English, the more recent methods books cover literacy development in both languages and stress the importance of preparing meaningful contexts for reading and writing.

A third indication of the ways that students in bilingual teacher programs learn about literacy and biliteracy comes from case studies of what goes on in literacy methods courses. Mercado and Oest present a description of Mercado's reading course for bilingual and all-English teachers who are preparing to teach in linguistically diverse urban school settings.[60] The course covers topics such as reading and cognition, second language acquisition, biliteracy instruction, and multicultural education. Student portfolios and the development of thematic units serve as the two major organizing projects students are expected to complete. Based on student input about the value of the course, Mercado and Oest conclude that experiences in the course enabled students to gain an understanding of literacy instruction and to accomplish projects many believed were beyond their capabilities.

Armbruster, Anderson, and Mall describe how prospective teachers of literacy learn whole language strategies in authentic settings.[61] In this program, students spend their entire senior year in classrooms in local schools engaging in a variety of field experiences and practicing strategies taught in a "Language and Literacy" methods block. The block combines reading methods, language arts methods, and children's literature. Topics covered include emerging literacy, beginning reading instruction, reading comprehension and reading-to-learn, the process approach to writing, reading and writing across the curriculum, children's literature, and literature-based instruction. Students complete a number of projects throughout their field experiences, including classroom observation, dialogue journals, and planning and implementing lessons. Students' lessons are also videotaped. These are self-evaluated as well as critiqued by the cooperating teacher.

Unfortunately, this Language and Literacy methods block is not designed specifically for prospective bilingual teachers, and thus, some of the knowledge and content would need to be expanded to include a non-English language and a focus on literacy acquisition. For example, with regard to literature-based instruction and storybook reading in general, prospective teachers might be exposed to and practice teaching literature from existing children's books in Spanish. Freeman and Cervantes provide an annotated bibliography of quality literature storybooks, poetry, and content area books in Spanish.[62] Likewise, Rosalma Zubizarreta provides a list of distributors of children's literature and computer software in Spanish, as well as an annotated bibliography of children's literature in Spanish for the primary and intermediate grades.[63]

Another topic that might be added to such a language and literacy methods course would be the development of writing abilities in the non-English language and in English as a second language. For example, prospective teachers could be asked to study how bilingual children learn in a schooling context to read and write the alphabetic languages of Spanish and English as a second language. Numerous examples of the kinds of attempts at communication that bilingual children make as they acquire literacy and biliteracy in school are provided by Edelsky, by Flores, and by Hudelson.[64]

Science and mathematics. There is widespread recognition that students who are not native speakers of English face linguistic barriers to acquiring science and mathematics skills and knowledge in regular classes. The debate over whether to teach these subjects in English or in the students' native language[65] has shifted to a discussion of the ways in which science instruction can be a vehicle for language development and for meeting the specific challenges that vocabulary and syntax in science texts and discourse present to second language speakers.[66] Programs such as *Finding Out/Descubrimiento* (FO/D) have shown that bilingual science curriculum that is contextualized and builds on cooperative learning can have positive effects on math/science gains compared to national norms.[67] Moreover, interdisciplinary and thematic curricula such as BICOMP (Bilingual Interdisciplinary Computer-Assisted Curricula) have been shown to be effective in promoting achievement not only in mathematics and science but also in reading comprehension in comparison to a baseline comparison group from the same community.[68] An intrinsic advantage of the BICOMP curriculum is that it allows students to explore science concepts in both guided and open experiments in which students can confront their previous knowledge with the insights gained through their own discovery in learner-driven activities.

Cognitive barriers to science and mathematics achievement arise from the traditional conception of these subjects as fixed bodies of knowledge. Over the past fifteen years, new constructivist/generative models of science education have emphasized the cognitive development of the learner through exploration and reflection.[69] Instruction that relies on the recitation script and focuses on the mastery of isolated skills inhibits students' ability to understand and apply science and mathematics concepts beyond a classroom context.[70]

In science education, this learner-focused approach has been labeled "constructivist," drawing from Piaget's theories of children's thinking and learning. Constructivism operates from two basic principles: (1) the fundamental intellectual ideas of a discipline must be taught so that the essential beauty of the discipline can be appreciated by all learners; and (2) the functional skills of the discipline alone are not enough to enable learners (teachers and students alike) to use their understanding effectively and confidently. Constructivist teaching emphasizes: (1) active learning in activities that fit logically into a sequential plan and are integrated through meaningful connections; (2) a student-centered approach where the student is given control over learning, although the teacher shapes the learning objectives while following up on the needs of the learner; (3) contextualized instruction that integrates the learners' previous knowledge and connects learning to their world and experience; and (4) integrated assessment that occurs as part of every learning cycle and gives students opportunities to think about their thinking and learning as the lesson progresses in negotiation with other learners and the teacher.

The constructivist approach echoes the practices that have been advocated by second language acquisition theorists under the rubric of a "communicative approach." Thus, Krashen has advocated the use of "comprehensible input" that is interesting to the learner and understandable from the contextual cues provided by the teacher.[71] Swain has advocated a focus on what she labels "comprehensible output" not only as an indicator of what the students comprehend but also as a means to push from semantic processing to grammatical processing.[72] Long's focus on providing negotiation of interaction for second language speakers as the key to second language development argues for the kind of active learning and negotiated problem solving that constructivist approaches also call for.[73]

Data from the national evaluation of bilingual and immersion programs indicate that most classrooms continue to emphasize teacher-centered and controlled instruction.[74] The implementation of the communicative/constructivist approach would require a restructuring of the learning environment in many schools. The question for teacher educators is how to ensure that these approaches live beyond a few isolated settings. Both FO/D and BICOMP have received national exemplary status from the U.S. Department of Education and are being replicated in a wide variety of settings. The challenge for these efforts is to identify and cope with the obstacles that come from attempting radical changes in the traditional instructional style of many teachers.

Cultural Issues in Teacher Education in Bilingual Education Programs

One of the major issues confronting teacher educators in bilingual education is: How can student teachers learn to address the cultural diversity of their students in a meaningful way? Teacher educators need to realize that learning how to teach is a complex social and cognitive process that involves not only learning how to manipulate techniques and methods but also understanding and applying complex learning and instructional theories as well as integrating these with the value system and perspectives of individual teachers. The term *perspectives* is here defined as "a coordinated set of ideas and actions a person uses in dealing with some problematic situation."[75] As demonstrated by Gardner in her case studies of three student teachers learning how to teach in bilingual and ESL settings, the use of the construct of perspectives is helpful in understanding how novices go through the socialization process of becoming teachers and how they integrate course work and field experiences into their existing schema for viewing the teaching act.[76]

Within bilingual education over the past twenty years, the role of culture has been most substantively and consistently explored through the work of Henry Trueba and of George and Louise Spindler. Preparing bilingual teachers for cultural diversity in school was discussed early on by Trueba.[77] Trueba builds the case for using ethnography as a research tool for studying cultural diversity in bilingual programs and communities, particularly as a method for developing an understanding of the sociocultural context of learning. Forecasting current thinking on approaches to the infusion of culture in the preparation of teachers, Trueba outlines how the collection of life histories of Chicanos can help to transmit vividly the value system of ethnic minority groups as long as these histories are collected and analyzed without ethnocentrism.

The work of the Spindlers has been seminal in developing a body of literature that examines the contexts of learning in a wide variety of settings, through what has been termed the "ethnography of schooling."[78] Through their work and their students' work, critical themes such as home/school discontinuities, socialization practices in minority communities, and the transmission of culture have been explored with a breadth and depth far beyond the reach of survey research. For example, Macías explored the hidden curriculum of Tohonu O'odham (formerly Papago) teachers as he sought to understand how teachers who are members of the culture of their students can help to broker the transition to formal schooling.[79] Delgado-Gaitán analyzed the discontinuities that affected the performance, both perceived and actual, of Chicano elementary school children.[80]

Based on her experiences teaching and observing a course on cultural diversity to elementary student teachers for four years, Merino points out that individual student teachers come to the process of learning about cultural diversity with a range of experiences and readiness and that what they know about culture interacts with their training needs.[81] Figure 1 illustrates a model in which cross-cultural awareness is viewed as a continuum one end of which is the student teacher who may have never come into contact with a cultural group other than his or her own and thus views all cultures as foreign. Further along the continuum is the prospective teacher who may have had some contact, most of which has been superficial and short-term. This kind of student teacher may be classified as having a "tourist knowledge." At the other extreme, a student who has lived extensively in another culture and learned the language to a high degree of proficiency may be characterized as having insider knowledge or ethnographic knowledge if the knowledge has come from anthropological fieldwork. Gardner used an adaptation of this continuum in sampling her case studies and found that these different starting points do indeed create different kinds of tensions as well as different trajectories of development during the student teacher year.[82] She found, for example, that a course on cultural diversity which one year focused on bringing in speakers from different communities to speak about their communities was not considered helpful by student teachers who already had developed some knowledge and experiences with other cultural groups. However, student teachers with relatively no experience (tourist to novice) did find the experiences in the course

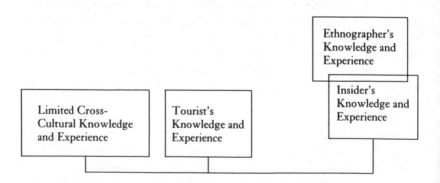

Fig. 1. A model for describing different levels of
cross-cultural awareness and readiness.

useful and productive. To our knowledge, Gardner's study is unique in exploring in depth the impact of these dimensions on student teachers as they progress through bilingual and ESL programs. More research of this sort is necessary to understand how different types of experiences may vary in their effectiveness depending on the development of the individual student teacher.

Models for preparing teachers to deal with cultural diversity in schools. How are educators training prospective teachers to deal with culturally diverse settings? Merino, Minnis, and Quintanar have identified three models used in teacher education to prepare teachers to work in culturally diverse settings.[83]

The first, labeled the *traditional course, competency model,* focuses on teaching about minority cultures in the United States with emphasis placed on learning styles, values, customs, and traditions of a few major targeted ethnic groups. Student teachers are placed for at least some of their training in culturally diverse settings and a competency-driven evaluation is used to determine if they have acquired relevant knowledge about the culture of selected groups and if they are able to demonstrate sensitivity to equity, usually through the process of classroom observation. The strengths of this model include: (a) the freedom it gives institutions to devise approaches to implement competencies identified by experts or policymakers; (b) the assurance that the student teacher will have a body of research-based knowledge about at least some communities; and (c) the belief that once competencies have been identified they are easier to verify at the conclusion of the program. The principal disadvantage of a competency-driven model focusing on a few of the largest minority groups is that individual and group variation often is ignored, resulting in the generation of new stereotypes. Furthermore, there are no guarantees that successful completion of a course and the knowledge, attitudes, and skills gained thereby will result in substantive changes in classroom practice.

To our knowledge, there are no empirically based descriptions of how such a program operates in practice. However, there are a number of textbooks which to some extent appear to represent this approach. For example, in their book entitled *Multicultural Teaching* Tiedt and Tiedt include chapters on culture, traditions, and values for major ethnic minority groups in the United States with lesson ideas suitable for use in the classroom.[84] Competency-driven models of culture, reflecting the kinds of information presented by Tiedt and Tiedt have been used at many institutions in California, where the state credentialing agency issues competency lists to give direction to universities on the content and process of their teacher education programs.

A second model, labeled the *teacher as ethnographer model*, advocates training teachers to conduct ethnographic studies. They learn how to interview informants, to be participant-observers, and to analyze ethnographic data to generate descriptions and interpretations of "cultural scenes."[85] Once the process is completed, teachers then develop curriculum materials and instructional strategies which build on the learning preferences and needs of the children in the classroom. Heath advocates this approach,[86] one of the principal advantages of which is that beginning teachers then have learned an inquiry approach that can be used to investigate any cultural group they may encounter. Student teachers can also develop cultural consciousness and empathy about their students' experiences. Some of the challenges of this approach include the time it requires to train students to learn ethnography as well as the tension between the teacher's role as an agent of the school culture and the role of the ethnographer as a scholar describing a culture from the perspective of the members of that cultural group.

There are several teacher education programs throughout the country which have incorporated aspects of this approach, most notably the University of California (San Diego) program under the direction of Hugh Mehan. The literature on how educational anthropologists have trained educators to do ethnography is another source for this approach. Spindler and Spindler sketch out how they teach credentialed teachers and administrators as well as graduate students in education how to do ethnography.[87] They begin with the report of an anthropology student who has recently returned from fieldwork outside the country. They then move to a cultural sensitization demonstration, in which education students view slides of scenes of alien cultural situations and then attempt to interpret what they see. This is followed by a demonstration-experiment, in which the students view a clip on aborigines from central Australia, and then the Spindlers role play being "difficult informants." Other techniques, such as the expressive autobiographic interview, are used as well. Unfortunately, there are no data provided on how students react to this approach, or the extent to which it may affect the development of their cultural sensitivity.

The third model assumes teachers are reflective practitioners and has been labeled by Merino, Minnis, and Quintanar as the *selective eclectic introspective model* (SEIM). This model is labeled selective because, while it draws principally from educational anthropology, it also seeks to incorporate research and methods from other disciplines. Its emphasis is on what is known about effective ways of infusing culture in the teaching process as well as on providing tools for investigating the background of students. The introspective part of the model focuses on the principle that the student teachers must assess themselves and plan how they are going to develop their cultural awareness and sensitivity.

One technique used at the University of California (Davis) to implement this model is to design a portfolio approach to the development of cultural knowledge, awareness, and sensitivity. This portfolio approach is combined with a variety of other experiences and activities provided by the program throughout the year. All elementary student teachers begin the year with an introductory course, "Teaching a Diverse Population," in which students read and discuss ethnographic research; study, critique, and develop curricula designed to address cultural diversity; read life histories from culturally diverse groups; and develop tools of inquiry, specifically interview and observation skills, to explore cultural differences. During the fall class, students write a series of short self-assessment reflective pieces designed to make them reflect about their own background and experiences with cultural diversity. At the conclusion of the fall course the students produce an action plan in consultation with the instructors on how they intend to continue their development during the year. All student teachers are placed in culturally and linguistically diverse settings. Throughout the year, supervisors and the instructors of the class meet with the students to discuss their portfolios and at year's end students present their portfolios with a final reflective piece in which they outline areas of growth, obstacles they ran into, and future plans for continued development. In the three years that we have been investigating this portfolio approach, we have found that students value the autonomy and sense of empowerment they feel from being treated as professionals who can make decisions about engineering their own development. Portfolios are evaluated on the breadth and depth of the activities the students plan and implement as well as on their willingness to reflect meaningfully about these experiences.

The Impact of Programs on Practice

What has been the impact of bilingual/ESL programs on what teachers do with regard to language and culture in their classrooms? A few studies have endeavored to explore empirically the impact of bilingual or ESL teacher education programs on practice. Clark and Milk surveyed forty-seven graduates of a bilingual education program in the Southwest to determine how the graduates implement bilingual pedagogy and to identify areas of strength and weakness.[88] A slim majority (54 percent) reported using Spanish as much as English in the classroom. Respondents felt that their training program had been helpful in their development as bilingual teachers, with 25 percent stating bilingual education coursework was most helpful, 21 percent mentioning their bilingual supervisors, and 18 percent their field experiences. A majority of the respondents (68 percent) reported science methods as their weakest area, followed by knowledge of Mexican-American history, and mathematics methods. This study is important for exploring student teachers' perceptions about the program they were trained in, suggesting areas of weakness that are probably equally problematic in other programs. However, because the method of data collection is only self-report, the reliability of the information supplied, particularly about issues related to practice, is open to question. Triangulation through observation or ethnographic research could have provided a more complete picture of the programs for student teachers.

Studies by Ortiz and by Gardner are two recent investigations that explore the impact of teacher training on classroom practice.[89] Ortiz videotaped student teachers' lessons following a training session that included modeling and microteaching. Her focus was on the implementation of an ESL lesson to teach form through drill and practice. She found a wide range of variation in implementation, much of it dictated by the student teachers' adjustments to the context in which they were teaching. Gardner's study of three student teachers, two in an ESL setting and one in a bilingual setting, found that in an inquiry-oriented teacher education program, student teachers go through a very substantive period of self-reflection and dialogue, frequently about the relevance of their experiences and coursework in their development as student teachers. The bilingual teacher engaged in frequent conversations with the cooperating teacher, the supervisor, the mentor, and other faculty about how she would decide to organize language use in her classroom, weighing the alternatives of more fixed approaches that attempt to separate the languages versus more open concurrent approaches. In this type of program, where alternative models are discussed and student teachers are pushed to make their own decisions about what they will do, the question moves from simply asking, Are the student teachers doing what they have been told is good practice? to, How do they make decisions and how do they explore the effectiveness of their decisions?

Research on In-service Programs

Another source for research on teacher education that is relevant to bilingual teacher preparation is an analysis of in-service education. In the past twenty years, school districts and policymakers have been allocating more and more money to staff development of teachers. In one of the few studies of how this money is spent, Little reports that in a representative sample of fifty California school districts, there were very few instances of long-term staff development, very few opportunities for follow up, and very little integration of staff development with other program improvements.[90] Moreover, only 27 percent of the school districts surveyed conducted systematic evaluation of the impact of staff development. The small use of coaching or follow-up is particularly disturbing, given the low transfer of skill-based staff development to classroom practice.[91] As a result of a review and meta analysis of over 200 studies of staff development, Showers, Joyce, and Bennett concluded that for training to be effectively brought back into the classroom, the following components need to be present: (a) presentation of theory supporting the strategy, (b) demonstration of the strategy, (c) initial practice in the workshop, (d) prompt feedback about the implementation of the strategy, (e) coaching/collaboration in the implementation of the strategy.[92] However, for changes that involve more than the implementation of a particular skill, there is an emerging consensus that staff development should lead to reflection about practice and collaboration in curriculum development or joint problem solving.

A few studies have attempted through in-service workshops to create a change in teachers working with culturally and linguistically diverse students. One very interesting attempt to effect change in credentialed ESL teachers at the elementary level is described in a study conducted by Politzer, Ramírez, and Hernández.[93] In this study, twenty-two ESL teachers were randomly assigned to one of three treatments provided through two weekend workshops. Treatment 1 consisted of discussion and modeling of successful teaching behaviors. Treatment 2 focused on ESL methodology, contrastive and error analysis. Treatment 3, the control group, dealt with differences in cognitive style. Teachers were videotaped teaching two ESL lessons prior to and after the treatments. The content to teach in the lessons was specified and focused on grammar, an example being the present progressive. Pupils were given pre and post tests prior to and after instruction. Teachers were given a pre and post test on ESL methodology, contrastive and error analysis. Videotapes made of all lessons taught by the teachers were analyzed to determine the degree to which teachers incorporated the behaviors emphasized in Treatment 1 as well as to determine the relationship between teacher behaviors and pupils' adjusted gains. Post testing showed almost no effect on teacher knowledge or teacher behaviors, except for teachers' use of guided questioning. There were no differences in pupils' gains, in part because the pupils were already performing at very high levels. The low impact of this kind of training may be due to the lack of coaching, the short period of training, the integration of the training within a grammar-driven curriculum, or the nature of the teaching behaviors. Nonetheless, this study is one of the few that investigate the impact of training in a classic process/product research paradigm.

Conclusions

The preparation of teachers for culturally and linguistically diverse settings primarily involves knowledge pertaining to the teaching of language and culture as well as the knowledge and abilities that teaching entails in any formal classroom setting. Teachers who wish to work in bilingual settings must be proficient in two languages and be knowledgeable about pedagogical strategies for manipulating content instruction in those languages. They must also know how to integrate students' work at various levels of linguistic and conceptual complexity, and finally they must have a working knowledge of the rules of appropriate behavior of at least two ethnic groups and be able to infuse this knowledge into the teaching process. Prospective teachers learn about teaching in culturally and linguistically diverse settings through formal coursework and field experiences under the guidance and supervision of practicing teachers and teacher educators. Teachers who are already working often rely on in-service workshops and other kinds of short-term experiences. In this chapter, we have focused our attention on what happens during the process of teacher preparation by examining how teachers learn about language and culture in bilingual education. We have pointed out the kinds of experiences that prospective teachers actually have in their training and what works with in-service education for teachers in the field. It is important to state that in preparing for this chapter, we learned that there is very little information available on what goes on in teacher education classes and during field placements and in student teaching in bilingual settings. Finally, we discovered that there is even less information on how classes and student teachers' experiences affect their practice and the development of knowledge about language, culture, and pedagogy. Much remains to be learned about the role of language and culture in the preparation of bilingual teachers.

NOTES

1. California Department of Education, *Remedying the Shortage of Teachers for Limited-English Proficient Students* (Sacramento, CA: California Department of Education, 1991).

2. Reynaldo Macías, *Bilingual Teacher Supply and Demand in the United States* (Los Angeles, CA: Tomas Rivera Center, 1989).

3. Development Associates, *National Longitudinal Evaluation of the Effectiveness of Services for Language Minority LEP Students Study* (Arlington, VA: Development Associates, 1987).

4. Laurie Olsen, *Crossing the Schoolhouse Border* (San Francisco: California Tomorrow, 1988).

5. Nelson Brooks, *Language and Language Learning* (New York: Harcourt Brace Jovanovich, 1972).

6. Jack Richards and Theodore Rogers, *Approaches and Methods in Language Teaching* (New York: Cambridge University Press, 1986).

7. Bárbara Merino and Consuelo Coughran, "Lesson Design for Teachers of Language Minority Students: Insights from a Case Study of Curriculum Development," in *Languages in School and Society: Policy and Pedagogy*, edited by Mary McGroarty and Christian Faltis (Berlin: Mouton de Gruyter, 1991), pp. 335-358.

8. Robert Politzer, "Effective Language Teaching: Insights from Research," in *The Second Language Classroom: Directions for the 1980s*, edited by James Alatis, Howard Altman, and Penelope Alatis (New York: Oxford University Press, 1981), pp. 23-35.

9. See Diane August and Eugene García, *Language Minority Education in the United States* (Springfield, IL: Charles Thomas Publishing, 1988) for information on state legislation regarding coursework required for bilingual and second language endorsements.

10. James Alatis and Kristie Twaddell, eds., *English as a Second Language and Bilingual Education* (Washington, DC: Teachers of English to Speakers of Other Languages, 1976).

11. Ellen Riojas Clark, "The State of the Art in Research on Teacher Training Models with Special Reference to Bilingual Education Teachers," in *Proceedings of the First Research Symposium on Limited English Proficient Students' Issues*, edited by the Office of Bilingual Education and Minority Languages Affairs (Washington, DC: U.S. Department of Education, 1990), pp. 361-391; Eleanor Thonis, "Competencies for Teachers of Language Minority Students," in *Languages in School and Society: Policy and Pedagogy*, edited by Mary McGroarty and Christian Faltis (Berlin: Mouton de Gruyter, 1991), pp. 281-292.

12. David Freeman, "Teacher Training Development and Decision Making: A Model of Teaching and Related Strategies for Language Teacher Edudation," *TESOL Quarterly* 23 (1989): 27-45.

13. Kenneth Zeichner, Daniel Liston, Marc Mahlois, and Mary Gómez, "The Structure and Goals of a Student Teaching Program and the Character and Quality of Supervisory Discourse," *Teaching and Teacher Education* 4 (1988): 349-362.

14. National Commission on Excellence in Education, *A Nation at Risk: The Imperative for Educational Reform* (Washington, DC: U.S. Department of Education, 1983).

15. John Goodlad, *Teachers for Our Nation's Schools* (San Francisco: Jossey-Bass, 1990).

16. James Conant, *The Education of American Teachers* (New York: McGraw-Hill, 1963).

17. S. Ana Garza, "Teaching Language Minority Students: An Overview of Competencies for Teachers," *Teacher Education Quarterly* 18 (1991): 23-36; Clark, "The State of the Art in Research on Teacher Training Models."

18. Carol Kreidler, *ESL Teacher Education* (Washington, DC: Center for Applied Linguistics, 1987).

19. Sharon Nelson-Barber, "Considerations for the Inclusion of Multicultural Competencies in Teacher Assessment," *Teacher Education Quarterly* 18 (1991): 49-58.

20. Robert Carrasco, "Expanded Awareness of Student Performance: A Case Study of Applied Ethnographic Monitoring in a Bilingual Classroom," in *Culture and the Bilingual Classroom*, edited by Henry Trueba, Grace Guthrie, and Kathryn Au (Rowley, MA: Newbury House, 1981), pp. 153-159; Luis Moll and Esteban Díaz, "Ethnographic Pedagogy: Promoting Effective Bilingual Instruction," in *Advances in Bilingual Education Research*, edited by Eugene García and Raymond Padilla (Tucson, AZ: University of Arizona Press, 1985), pp. 127-149; George Spindler, "Roger Harker and Schönhausen: From Familiar to Strange and Back Again," in *Doing the Ethnography of Schooling*, edited by George Spindler (New York: Holt, Rinehart and Winston, 1982), pp. 20-46.

21. David C. Berliner, "In Pursuit of the Expert Pedagogue," *Educational Researcher* 15, no. 7 (1986): 5-13.

22. Christian Faltis and Bárbara Merino, "Toward a Definition of Exemplary Teachers in Bilingual Multicultural School Settings," in *Critical Perspectives on Bilingual Education Research*, edited by Raymond Padilla and Alfredo Benevides (Tempe, AZ: Bilingual Review Press, 1992), pp. 279-299; Eugene García, "Education of Linguistically and Culturally Diverse Students: Effective Instructional Practices," *Educational Practice Report No. 1* (Santa Cruz, CA: National Center for Research on Cultural Diversity and Second Language Learning, 1991).

23. Faltis and Merino, "Toward a Definition of Exemplary Teachers."

24. Marilyn Cochran-Smith, "Learning to Teach against the Grain," *Harvard Educational Review* 61 (1991): 279-310; idem, "Reinventing Student Teaching," *Journal of Teacher Education* 42 (1991): 104-118.

25. Cochran-Smith, "Learning to Teach against the Grain," p. 280.

26. Cochran-Smith, "Reinventing Student Teaching."

27. Sarah Hudelson and Christian Faltis, "Redefining Basic Teacher Education: Preparing Teachers to Transform Teaching," in *Partners in Change: Developing Tomorrow's Teachers of World Languages*, edited by Gail Guntermann (Skokie, IL: National Textbook Company, forthcoming).

28. Bárbara Merino, "Promoting School Success for Chicanos: The View from Inside the Bilingual Classroom," in *Chicano School Failure and Success: Research and Policy Agendas for the 1990s*, edited by Richard R. Valencia (New York: Falmer Press, 1991), pp. 119-148.

29. J. David Ramírez and Bárbara Merino, "Classroom Talk in English Immersion, Early-Exit, and Late-Exit Transitional Bilingual Education Programs," in *Language Distribution Issues in Bilingual Schooling*, edited by Rodolfo Jacobson and Christian Faltis (Clevedon, England: Multilingual Matters, Ltd., 1990), pp. 61-103.

30. Lily Wong Fillmore, Paul Ammon, Barry McLaughlin, and Mary Ammon, *Learning Language through Bilingual Instruction*, Final Report to the National Institute of Education (Berkeley, CA: University of California, 1983).

31. Ramírez and Merino, "Classroom Talk in English Immersion."

32. J. David Ramírez, Sandra Yuen, Dena Ramey, and David Pasta, *Longitudinal Study of Structured English Immersion Strategy, Early-Exit, and Late-Exit Transitional Bilingual Education Programs for Language-Minority Children*, Final Report, vols. 1 and 2 (San Mateo, CA: Aguirre International, 1991).

33. Dorothy Legarreta, "Language Choice in Bilingual Classrooms," *TESOL Quarterly* 11 (1977): 9-16.

34. Christian Faltis, "Codeswitching and Bilingual Schooling: An Examination of Jacobson's New Concurrent Approach," *Journal of Multilingual and Multicultural Development* 10 (1989): 117-127.

35. Rodolfo Jacobson, "The Implementation of a Bilingual Instructional Model: The New Concurrent Approach," in *Ethnoperspective in Bilingual Education*, vol. 3, edited by Raymond Padilla (Ypsilanti, MI: Eastern Michigan University Press, 1982), pp. 14-29.

36. Rodolfo Jacobson, *Title VII Demonstration Program in Bilingual Methodology*, CFDA 84.003-N, Grant No. G008811025060 (Washington, DC: Office of Bilingual Education and Minority Languages Affairs, U.S. Department of Education, 1985).

37. David Freeman and Yvonne Freeman, *Whole Language for Second Language Learners* (Portsmouth, NJ: Heineman, 1992).

38. Robert Blair, *Innovative Approaches to Language Teaching* (Rowley, MA: Newbury House, 1982); Patricia Richard-Amato, *Making it Happen: Interaction in the Second Language Classroom* (New York: Longman, 1988).

39. See Bárbara Flores, Erminda García, Sharon González, Kitty Kaczmerek, and Tere Romero, *Bilingual Holistic Instructional Strategies* (Chandler, AZ: Exito, 1986), and Freeman and Freeman, *Whole Language for Second Language Learners*.

40. Christine Uber Grosse, "The TESOL Methods Course," *TESOL Quarterly* 25 (1991): 29-49.

41. Robert Milk, "Integrating Language and Context in the Preparation of Bilingual Teachers," in *Annual Conference Journal: NABE '88-'89*, edited by Lillian Malavé (Washington, DC: National Association for Bilingual Education, 1990), pp. 57-70.

42. Bárbara Merino and Christian Faltis, "Spanish for Special Purposes: Communication Strategies for Bilingual Teachers," *Foreign Language Annals* 19 (1986): 43-56.

43. Flora Ortiz, "The Use of Videotaping and Microteaching in the Preparation of Bilingual Teachers" (Paper presented at the Annual Meeting of the American Educational Research Association, Chicago, 1985).

44. See Claude Goldenberg and Ronald Gallimore, "Changing Teaching Takes More Than a One-Shot Workshop," *Educational Leadership* 49 (1991): 69-72.

45. Robert Calfee and Priscilla Drum, "Research on Teaching Reading," in *Handbook of Research on Teaching*, 3rd ed., edited by Merlin Wittrock (New York: Macmillan, 1986), pp. 804-948.

46. Sarah Hudelson, "Can yu ret an rayt en ingles?: Children Become Literate in English as a Second Language," *TESOL Quarterly* 19 (1984): 221-238.

47. Sarah Hudelson, *Write On: Children Writing in ESL* (Englewood Cliffs, NJ: Prentice-Hall Regents, 1989).

48. Carole Edelsky, *Writing in a Bilingual Program: Había Una Vez* (Norwood, NJ: Ablex, 1986); Sarah Hudelson, "The Role of Native Language Literacy in the Education of Language Minority Children," *Language Arts* 64 (1987): 227-284.

49. Eleanor Thonis, "Reading Instruction for Language Minority Students," in *Schooling and Language Minority Students: A Theoretical Framework*, edited by the Office of Bilingual Bicultural Education (Los Angeles: Evaluation, Dissemination, and Assessment Center, California State University, 1981), pp. 147-181.

50. Christian Faltis, "Initial Cross-lingual Reading Transfer in Bilingual Second Grade Classrooms," in *Language and Literacy Research in Bilingual Education*, edited by Eugene García and Bárbara Flores (Tempe, AZ: Arizona State University Press, 1986), pp. 145-157.

51. Edelsky, *Writing in a Bilingual Program*.

52. See Rosalinde Barrera, "Bilingual Reading in the Primary Grades: Some Questions about Questionable Views and Practices," in *Early Childhood Bilingual Education*, edited by Theresa Escobedo (New York: Teachers College Press, 1983), pp. 164-184, and Claude Goldenberg, "Roads to Reading: Studies of Hispanic First Graders at Risk for Reading Failure" (Doctoral dissertation, Graduate School of Education, University of California, Los Angeles, 1984).

53. Thonis, "Reading Instruction for Language Minority Students."

54. Claude Goldenberg, "Beginning Literacy Instruction for Spanish Speaking Children," *Language Arts* 67 (1990): 590-598.

55. Eleanor Thonis, *Literacy for America's Spanish Speaking Children* (Newark, DE: International Reading Association, 1976); idem, *Teaching Reading to Non-English Speakers* (New York: Collier, 1970).

56. Flores et al., *Bilingual Holistic Instructional Strategies*.

57. Hudelson, *Write On*.

58. Bertha Pérez and María Torres-Guzmán, *Learning in Two Worlds: An Integrated Spanish/English Biliteracy Approach* (New York: Longman, 1992).

59. Carmen Mercado, "Native and Second Language Literacy: The Promise of a New Decade," in *Bilingual Education and English as a Second Language: A Research Handbook 1988-1990*, edited by Alba Ambert (New York: Garland, 1991), pp. 171-196.

60. Carmen Mercado with Dawn Oest, "Through the Eyes of the Teacher and the Students: Reflective Practice and Reciprocal Teaching in a Bilingual Graduate Reading Course" (Paper presented at the National Association for Bilingual Eduation meeting, Albuquerque, NM, January 1992).

61. Bonnie Armbruster, Richard Anderson, and Cindy Mall, "Preparing Teachers of Literacy," *Educational Leadership* 49, no. 3 (1991): 21-24.

62. Yvonne Freeman and Carolina Cervantes, *Literature Books in Español for Whole Language: An Annotated Bibliography*, Occasional Papers, Program in Language and Literacy (Tucson, AZ: College of Education, University of Arizona, 1991).

63. Pérez and Torres-Guzmán, *Learning in Two Worlds*, pp. 179-194.

64. See Edelsky, *Writing in a Bilingual Program*; idem, "Bilingual Children's Writing: Fact and Fiction," in *Richness in Writing: Empowering ESL Students*, edited by Donna Johnson and Duane Roen (New York: Longman, 1989), pp. 165-176; Bárbara Flores, "Children's Sociopsychogenesis of Literacy and Biliteracy," in *Proceedings of the First Research Symposium on Limited English Proficient Students' Issues*, edited by the

Office of Bilingual Education and Minority Languages Affairs (Washington, DC: U.S. Department of Education, 1990), pp. 281-320; Hudelson, "Can you ret an rayt en ingles?"; idem, "The Role of Native Language Literacy"; idem, *Write On.*

65. Jacob Ornstein-Galicia and Joyce Penfield, *A Problem Solving Model for Integrating Science and Language in Bilingual/Bicultural Education* (Los Angeles: National Dissemination Center, California State University, 1981); Anna Chamot, "A Transfer Curriculum for Teacher Content-Based ESL in the Elementary School," in *On TESOL '83: The Question of Control,* edited by Jean Handscombe (Washington, DC: Georgetown University, 1983), pp. 125-131; Carlos Ovando, "Teaching Science to Native American Students," in *Teaching the Indian Child: A Bilingual/Multicultural Approach,* edited by Jon Reyhner (Billings, MT: Eastern Montana College, 1986), pp. 159-185.

66. George Spanos and JoAnn Crandall, "Language and Problem Solving: Some Examples from Math and Science," in *Bilingual Education: Issues and Strategies,* edited by Amado Padilla, Halford Fairchild, and Concepción Valadez (Newbury Park, CA: Sage, 1990), pp. 157-170.

67. Elizabeth Cohen, JoAnn Intili, and Edward DeAvila, *Multicultural Improvement of Cognitive Abilities* (Stanford, CA: Stanford University, 1982).

68. Bárbara Merino, *Evaluation of the Bilingual Interdisciplinary Computer-Assisted Curriculum (BICOMP)* (West Sacramento, CA: Washington Unified School District, 1986); Consuelo Coughran, Julie Hoskins, and Bárbara Merino, *The Bilingual Interdisciplinary Computer-Assisted Curriculum (BICOMP): Levels Third through Fifth* (West Sacramento, CA: Washington Unified School District, 1986).

69. Robert Karplus, *Science Teaching and the Development of Reasoning* (Berkeley: University of California, Berkeley, 1977); Joseph Nussbaum and Shimshon Novic, "Alternative Frameworks, Conceptual Conflict and Accommodation: Toward a Principled Teaching Strategy," *Instructional Science* 11 (1982): 183-200.

70. Roland Tharp and Ronald Gallimore, *Rousing Minds to Life: Teaching, Learning, and Schooling in Social Contexts* (Cambridge: Cambridge University Press, 1988).

71. Stephen Krashen, *Second Language Acquisition and Second Language Learning* (New York: Pergamon Press, 1981).

72. Merrill Swain, "Communicative Competence: Some Roles for Comprehensible Input and Comprehensible Output in Its Development," in *Input in Second Language Acquisition,* edited by Susan Gass and Carolyn Madden (Rowley, MA: Newbury House, 1985), pp. 235-256.

73. Michael Long, "Input and Second Language Acquisition Theory," in *Input in Second Language Acquisition,* edited by Susan Gass and Carolyn Madden (Rowley, MA: Newbury House, 1985), pp. 377-393.

74. Ramírez and Merino, "Classroom Talk in English Immersion."

75. Marta Ann Gardner, "Student Teachers' Perspectives toward Teaching in Culturally and Linguistically Diverse Settings: Three Case Studies" (Master's Thesis, Division of Education, University of California, Davis, 1991), p. 34.

76. Ibid.

77. Henry Trueba and Carol Barnett-Mazrahi, *Bilingual Multicultural Education and the Professional* (Rowley, MA: Newbury House, 1979).

78. George Spindler, "Transcultural Sensitization," in *Education and Cultural Process: Toward an Anthropology of Education*, edited by George Spindler (New York: Holt, Rinehart and Winston, 1974), pp. 449-462; George Spindler and Louise Spindler, "Teaching and Learning How to Do Ethnography of Education," in *Interpretive Ethnography of Education: At Home and Abroad*, edited by George Spindler and Louise Spindler (London: Erlbaum, 1987), pp. 17-36.

79. José Macías, "The Hidden Curriculum of Papago Teachers: American Indian Strategies for Mitigating Cultural Discontinuity in Early Childhood Schooling," in *Interpretive Ethnography of Schooling*, edited by Spindler and Spindler, pp. 363-380.

80. Concha Delgado-Gaitán, "Traditions and Transitions in the Learning Process of Mexican Children," in *Interpretive Ethnography of Schooling*, edited by Spindler and Spindler, pp. 333-359.

81. Bárbara Merino, personal notes, March, 1990.

82. Gardner, "Student Teachers' Perspectives toward Teaching."

83. Bárbara Merino, Douglas Minnis, and Rosalinda Quintanar, "Models for Training Student Teachers in Multicultural Education" (Paper presented at the Commission for Preparing Teachers for Cultural Diversity, Davis, California, 1989).

84. Pamela Tiedt and Iris Tiedt, *Multicultural Teaching: A Handbook of Activities, Information, and Resources* (Boston: Allyn and Bacon, 1986).

85. James Spradley, *The Ethnographic Interview* (New York: Holt, Rinehart and Winston, 1979).

86. Shirley Brice Heath, *Ways with Words: Language, Life, and Work in Communities and Classrooms* (New York: Cambridge University Press, 1983).

87. Spindler and Spindler, "Teaching and Learning How to Do Ethnography of Education."

88. Ellen Clark and Robert Milk, "Training Bilingual Teachers: A Look at the Title VII Graduates in the Field," *NABE Journal* 8 (1983): 1-41.

89. Ortiz, "The Use of Videotaping and Microteaching"; Gardner, "Student Teachers' Perspectives toward Teaching."

90. Judith Warren Little, "District Policy Choices and Teachers' Professional Development Opportunities," *Educational Evaluation and Policy Analysis* 11 (1989): 165-179.

91. Bruce Joyce and Beverly Showers, "Teacher Training Research: Working Hypotheses for Program Design and Directions for Further Study" (Paper presented at the Annual Meeting of the American Educational Research Association, Los Angeles, 1981).

92. Beverly Showers, Bruce Joyce, and Barbara Bennett, "Synthesis of Research on Staff Development: A Framework for Future Study and a State of the Art Analysis," *Educational Leadership* 69 (1987): 77-87.

93. Robert Politzer, Arnulfo Ramírez, and Carmen Hernández, *Training in English as a Second Language Methodology and Student Language Learning in Bilingual Elementary Schools* (Stanford, CA: Center for Educational Research, Stanford University, 1979).

CHAPTER VIII

A Look at Language as a Resource:
Lessons from La Clase Mágica

OLGA A. VÁSQUEZ

Over the past twenty-five years social scientists and educators have amassed vast amounts of knowledge about educating children who come from varying cultural and linguistic backgrounds, but this knowledge has remained distant from the classroom. In California, for example, the influence of research is evident at the public policy level.[1] However, theoretical and practical knowledge of sound, culturally relevant pedagogy has not been fully integrated at the instructional level. English continues to dominate every type of program offering in bilingual education, regardless of the students' linguistic needs.[2] At best, aspects of minority culture and language are randomly supplemented throughout all levels of schooling rather than forming the philosophical base of curriculum and instructional practices. Reyes's "one size fits all" description of teachers' approach to literacy instruction also adequately applies to education in general throughout the United States.[3] Regrettably, the common practice is to adapt the child to the pedagogy rather than to make the necessary adjustments to meet the cultural and linguistic, and, therefore, the cognitive needs of learners.

The shaping of children to fit one cultural mold has tremendous implications for minority children who will be the work force of the year 2000.[4] As it stands, the schooling profile of linguistic minority children—particularly Latino students—displays disproportionately high rates of dropping out, low academic achievement, and high enrollment in low academic tracks.[5] Given the demographic changes in the schoolroom and the disadvantages of a poorly educated work force, this country's future economic and social viability rests on its ability to provide optimal learning conditions for all children.

Olga Vásquez is an Assistant Professor in the Department of Communication at the University of California, San Diego, where she is also affiliated with the Laboratory of Comparative Human Cognition.

An important component for the success of this endeavor is the notion of language as a resource in the learning environment, which is the focus of this chapter. Understanding the way language plays out in learning activities and in the dynamics of an instructional interaction is key to making pedagogy relevant to the needs of diverse learners. In the next section, I sketch briefly the sociocultural perspective that helps us to understand that language is not merely a string of words independent of its sociolinguistic context. Rather, language is intimately tied to individuals' everyday situations, cultural values, and social relations. Next, I describe *La Clase Mágica* (The Magical Class), a bilingual/bicultural educational innovation that seeks to optimize the learning potential of Spanish-speaking children by restructuring activities to include knowledge and skills they bring from the various learning domains in which they participate. Finally, I discuss the insights on language and learning we have gained from providing children with free access to their own background experiences.

Language Acquisition from a Sociocultural Perspective

The sociocultural perspective views language acquisition as a complex process of learning to use language within the context of cultural and social meanings. The language that surrounds and involves children plays a critical role in their development; it is the means through which they are socialized and enculturated as well as a source they draw upon to fine tune their language skills. Language provides both the medium for communication and the context for cultural expression. Barring individual differences and learning disabilities, children develop a language system that reflects their own particular socializing experiences. In the course of meaningful interactions with those around them, children not only acquire the grammar, vocabulary, and sociolinguistic rules of a given language but they also learn their families' beliefs and values and the ways of the home culture. Through long exposure to social interaction with their caretakers, which is at the heart of language development, children also learn the basic requisites for membership in their community. Kennedy wrote:

Cracking the linguistic code of his community is thus no mere optional activity for the child. He is forced by circumstances to attempt to make sense out of the linguistic and social environment he is exposed to. Failure to do so would mean failure to join the community he finds himself in.[6]

The language that children use and the purposes for which they use it reflect their cultural background and by extension their access to particular socializing experiences. Individuals from different social and cultural backgrounds interpret and use language according to the norms of their particular group. What may be appropriate use of language in one culture may not be in another. For example, on a recent trip to Spain I inadvertently asked the hotel clerk to examine me physically when I used the Chicano version, "Me quiero registrar" to mean "I would like to check in." With a smirk on his face, the clerk promptly informed me that there was no such usage in Castellano (Castilian Spanish) and that I should have said, "Me quiero inscribir." The social situation that was created in this brief interaction communicated much about one man's perception of social inequalities. We don't know how much my physical appearance, my Chicano cadence, and my gender influenced his judgment of me, but it was clear that his command of standard Spanish positioned him at a higher status—enough to compel him to correct my usage. This is not an uncommon occurrence for Chicanos whose Spanish reflects a heavy influence of English vocabulary and grammar, much to the dismay of those who promote standard Spanish.

A number of factors that vary across cultures have been identified as sources of different uses of language. Studies such as those by Ochs, by Shieffelin and Ochs, and by Heath indicate that culturally specific views on child raising and language learning influence the ways parents and other adults interact verbally with children.[7] Middle-class Anglo parents, for example, who believe that language learning is facilitated by adapting the situation to their child, tend to assist their children's language endeavors by engaging them in conversations and by accommodating their own talk in a variety of ways. They talk about topics in ways that they feel take into account the child's abilities and interests. They often use a more simplified, repetitive, and affect-laden register known as baby-talk or motherese. They elicit clarifications and elaborations, expand and extend children's utterances, and regularly engage children in predictable conversation routines. Heath offers an example of how adults in an Anglo community seize upon a child's utterance to expand and interpret the child's speech:

Sally, banging on the backdoor, screamed "Go kool," and Aunt Sue responded "No, Sally, you can't go to *school* yet, Lisa will be back, come on, help mamma put the pans away." Aunt Sue assumed Sally both wanted to *go to school* and was commenting on the fact that Lisa had just *gone to school.*[8]

These patterns of verbal behavior have not been observed in some non-Western and working-class communities where parents believe that children learn best by adapting to their surroundings. Heath, Ochs, and Schieffelin have claimed that adults in these societies do not view young children as suitable or competent conversation partners. Instead, adults expect children to seek out their own opportunities to learn language by listening to and observing others. Models may be provided or cues used to help direct a child's attention. But attempts to support and enhance children's verbal contributions within the context of a conversation are not part of these groups' socializing experiences involving language. According to Heath, in the Afro-American community of Trackton it is the children who repeat after the adults, using the ends of adult utterances as practice.[9] In the midst of "their noisy multichanneled communicative environments" children are expected to be aware of what is happening around them and are not tutored or tested on discrete elements in their surroundings. Children are expected to become information knowers rather than information givers.

For language minority children who must learn English as a second language for schooling and for integration into the larger community, socialization in the use of language is influenced by their multicultural existence. The lines between language and cultures drawn by scholars cited above are not as clear-cut among Mexicano/ Latinos. In these homes, knowledge and skills of several languages and cultures often converge in family conversations as members attempt to negotiate their everyday life.[10] Some ways of using language (for example, story-telling, folklore, and oratory) are reminiscent of those brought from the old country.[11] Others, such as children acting as cultural and language brokers for members of their family's social network, emerge from life experiences in a multicultural world. For example, in the role of interpreter, children learn to make important decisions about the meanings of specialized vocabulary and to use language as a tool for advocacy. At other times, uses of language are reminiscent of ways language is used in Anglo middle-class homes. Pease-Alvarez, for example, found that the questioning strategies of adults in a Mexican immigrant community supported their children's contributions in conversations by prompting them to elaborate and clarify their oral expressions.[12]

The language milieu of these minority children is in sharp contrast to the range of experiences and world views offered in the classroom. The teachers across the United States are largely white, middle-class, monolingual, and English-speaking. They are faced with a growing diversity of class, language, and culture among their students for which they are not prepared. An evaluation of programs for speakers of other languages in California, for example, found a severe shortage of teachers trained for educating language minority students.[13] And if the low academic scores of language minority students and their loss of primary language are any indication, we can assume that what Kennedy admonished some twenty years ago might still be the case today: classroom processes and procedures "might actually interfere with the learner's capacity for language acquisition"[14] and, I may add, cognitive development. Frequently, outdated and erroneous assumptions about learning and teaching guide the instructional strategies and approaches teachers use in their classrooms. Moll notes that much "instruction for working-class students, be it in bilingual or monolingual classrooms, can be characterized as rote, drill and practice, and intellectually limited, with an emphasis on low-level literacy and computational skills."[15] Even when such potentially effective innovations as whole language, literature-based instruction, and writing processes are introduced in the classroom they often do not reflect the needs of diverse learners.[16] Instead, they are accepted uncritically and without appropriate modifications in a blind and lock-step approach that offsets any possible benefits.

Conceptions of language proficiency have had a major influence on ways educators have approached the schooling of minority students.[17] Fluency in a language other than English has historically been viewed as a problem rather than a resource in the classroom.[18] Instead of capitalizing on the language strengths of the children, educators have followed a policy of rapid transition into English in order to resolve the language "problem." As Cummins and Swain point out, the argument has been that if bilingual children are deficient in academic skills in English then they must need more exposure to English.[19] Learning the English language, rather than cognitive development and content matter, has become the primary object of instruction. What the students know before entering school is thus discarded. As a result, minority children have been misplaced in low academic tracks, inaccurately assessed, forced to lose their primary language, and disempowered in the school and broader community.[20]

Research has shown that focusing on surface-level features of language interferes with making meaning and with the development of a positive rapport among teachers and students. As Moll and Díaz have shown, children can achieve greater comprehension when the focus of instruction is on making meaning rather than on the correctness of the utterances.[21] But, how do we make the interaction, rather than how it is said, the focus of our concern? What kinds of educational activities can we as researchers create that will help minority children achieve their learning potential? How can we make language and culture a resource in the learning setting? And, what can we learn in an alternative after-school setting that will help teachers in their own classrooms? In the following section, I discuss how these questions shaped and continue to guide the research efforts of *La Clase Mágica* (The Magical Class), an after-school educational activity designed to provide bilingual children with a variety of literacy activities in both Spanish and English. I begin by briefly describing the historical and theoretical underpinnings that support the goals and objectives of this bilingually and biculturally adapted educational activity. Then I discuss the adaptation process that was undertaken to provide access to the children's own cultural and linguistic resources.

La Clase Mágica: *A New Form of Educational Activity*

Situated in a small Mexicano community established as a work camp at the turn of the century, *La Clase Mágica* is a computer-based literacy activity that brings together university and community resources to provide additional educational services to local children of elementary school age. It is a bilingual/bicultural manifestation of the "Fifth Dimension," the core activity of a six-team research consortium organized by the Laboratory of Comparative Human Cognition (LCHC) at the University of California at San Diego (UCSD). The Fifth Dimension brings together a research collaborative composed of various institutions of learning, six research sites spread across the country, and three target populations. Collaboration among the six teams is sustained primarily through electronic mail and telecommunication conferences.

The research collaborative is formally known as the Distributed Literacy Consortium and affectionately called the "Mellon Patch" by its participants as a reference to the funding agency (the Andrew Mellon Foundation). The goal of the research is to develop across-the-board, high-level literacy skills in a highly pluralistic, multicultural society in ways that induce and sustain intellectual excellence while at the same time supporting the diversity of America's people. The six teams are organized in partnerships that focus on three target populations. The partnership that serves two largely Anglo communities is headed by Michael Cole at the University of California at San Diego and by Pat Worden and Miriam Schustack at the California State University at San Marcos. The partnership that focuses on two Afro-American populations is directed by Gillian McNamee at the Erikson Institute in Chicago and by Catherine King at the University of New Orleans. The focus of this chapter is on one of the two Mexicano/Latino sites (called *La Clase Mágica*) that form the bilingual partnership. In collaboration with Margaret Gallego at the Julián Samora Research Institute at Michigan State University in East Lansing, *La Clase Mágica*, described later in this chapter, draws together two teams that focus on two distinct Mexicano/Latino populations at opposite sides of the country. Olga Vásquez heads *La Clase Mágica* efforts on the west coast.

Conceptually, the Fifth Dimension is a make-believe world loosely based on the game of "Dungeons and Dragons" in which children negotiate their way through a task-laden labyrinth in self-propelled and voluntary activity. The Fifth Dimension is represented by a maze-like structure composed of twenty rooms, each containing two computer games. Some of these are arcade-like games, but the majority use commercially available educational software. Heuristically, the Fifth Dimension is a "virtual culture of collaborative learning,"[22] designed to allow researchers to create and study new forms of educational activity in an after-school setting. Its stated goal is to provide local children with a wide variety of literacy-mediated activities supported by computer and telecommunication technology.

Theoretically, the motivational features of play, fantasy, and peer interaction are used to promote "collaborative learning, within which the children themselves are motivated to progress step-by-step through the maze." The object is for the children to become intrinsically and "actively involved in their own development rather than to simply receive information from other people."[23] Adults (in this case researchers, institutional representatives, and undergraduates taking classes taught by LCHC collaborators at the university) "guide and facilitate the children's development"rather than prescribe an appropriate course and content.[24] The undergraduates are encouraged to assume the role of an older sibling and to engage in the tasks themselves rather than providing quick answers for the children. Ideally, they collaborate with children in finding solutions to problems posed by the various tasks. The activities promote the children's growth within what Vygotsky called their zones of proximal development, that is, the difference between the learner's actual level of unassisted performance and the potential level of performance with assistance by a more experienced individual.[25] This approach makes cognitive and social development the by-products of meaningful interaction rather than its goals. Writing activities also help both children and adults reflect on their own learning. The children write about their progress through the maze in letters to the "Wizard," the Fifth Dimension's genial patron, and to other children in other locales. The adults write field notes and discuss their observations with each other.

The Wizard is a crucial motivating factor in the notion of a collaborative culture created by the activities in the system. It provides a playful way to maintain discipline in the Fifth Dimension so that the children and adults can interact on an equal level. It also provides a critical role in the literacy development of the children. Every activity in the Fifth Dimension promotes communication with the Wizard so that children can share life experiences, seek answers to their queries about progression through the Fifth Dimension, and unsuspectingly develop their literacy and language skills. At each site a computer designated as the Wizard's computer is equipped with a modem for children to communicate electronically with the Wizard who answers through a computer at the university. Children communicate on the average of once a week with the Wizard via short letters or an electronic live-chat. The latter is a direct conversation with the Wizard by telecommunication.

To maintain the mysterious allure, the identity of the Wizard is one of the best kept secrets in the system. In fact, no one really knows who the Wizard is. We do know, however, that some undergraduates assist the Wizard in answering the letters and occasionally take the Wizard's place in doing the live-chats on the university computers. We call this assignment "wizarding."

The overlapping contexts of the individual games and the collaborative culture of the Fifth Dimension provide the structure and authority for the children. The rules of behavior and direction of the children's activities are part of a dynamic process that is negotiated with a playful and benevolent—if forgetful—Wizard. The Wizard is an electronic entity to whom the children must report their progress and the one they ask for assistance with problems posed by the technology or the games. Placing the only authority in the system outside the local site serves to reduce the power relations between the adults and the children. This complex role structure makes it possible for the children, who often have greater experience with the conventions of the Fifth Dimension and knowledge of the games than the adults, to assume the role of expert periodically. Ideally, it equalizes role relationships, allowing adults and children to collaborate as partners in solving game-related problems.[26]

The Bilingual/Bicultural Adaptation of a Learning Environment

In 1989, La Clase Mágica grew out of a commitment among LCHC collaborators to serve linguistic minority children living less than a mile, yet worlds apart, from an already established Fifth Dimension site. It began to take shape in front of an altar of a small Catholic mission serving a Mexican-origin community that extends into the surrounding areas of an upper-middle-class town in southern California.[27] As the program grew, it moved from inside the church to the kitchen where the equipment was set up and broken down for every site visit. Its present and most permanent location is a large portable trailer in the back of the mission grounds, along a wall of a Headstart classroom. For most of this time, ten to fifteen children from two of the surrounding elementary schools have attended La Clase Mágica, which is open three times a week for a period of an hour and half after school. On the average, children attend twice a week and typically stay with the program for the entire year. Some children have been in the program since its inception.

From its beginning, the team of two site coordinators (women from the community), myself, and a small cadre of UCSD undergraduate students taking my classes at the university made the Mexicano/Latino community the focus of the transformation of the Fifth Dimension into La Clase Mágica. Over the course of eight academic quarters and with the collaboration of a research team directed by Margaret Gallego at Michigan State University, La Clase Mágica deliberately evolved to reflect both Anglo and Mexicano/Latino culture. Although it retained the conceptual and theoretical principles of the Fifth Dimension, language and culture became its key features. Inspired by on-going deliberations across and within research groups, Spanish language and Mexican cultural knowledge were slowly integrated into written materials. When available, computer software in Spanish was also purchased.

In redesigning the Fifth Dimension, the primary aim was to make the system and its activities contextually relevant to the children's lives. It is important to emphasize, however, that we made the changes in a larger environment of restricted resources, a situation that mirrors most classrooms in the United States. Original tasks were constructed in English to serve an Anglo middle-class population, omitting references to the life experiences of minority children. Only three of the original computer games were in Spanish. The undergraduates, as well, reflected the racial and linguistic composition of the nation's teachers. Relatively few spoke Spanish and fewer still were of Mexican origin. The Mexican-origin children, on the other hand, came from various linguistic, regional, and generational backgrounds. Some came from families who had lived in the area for generations, and others came from families who had recently migrated to the United States, making the adaptation a greater challenge.

Transforming the Fifth Dimension was not a simple act of translation from English to Spanish but a fundamental change in the approach to the organization of the pedagogical activity. Although informed throughout by traditional Mexican cultural knowledge, the Fifth Dimension's evolution into *La Clase Mágica* was not based solely on the children's home culture. Rather it tapped the multiple knowledge sources available in the children's everyday life. Whenever possible, content knowledge and skills from such learning domains as the family, church, sports, and dance groups were written into the tasks accompanying the games.[28] The goal was to build upon the background knowledge of the children at the same time that a new set of experiences and a second language were introduced. The meanings and experiences cued by references to traditional Mexican folk tales, family histories, and notable figures in Mexican history gave children a starting point for writing electronic messages and using the vocabulary of modern technology. In this way, children could draw on their personal experiences to write to *La Clase Mágica's* Wizard and have a basis to interact with the adults around them.

These changes did not occur overnight, nor were they considered permanent adaptations. They came about through a series of deliberations in research meetings, in-class discussions, and teleconference discussions among the students and researchers at opposite sides of the country. We learned that these on-going deliberations are an essential part of the adaptation process. Rather than searching for a product that could be generalized to other locales, we chose instead to focus on the dynamic process of continual adaptation. We sought explanations for linguistic trends noted among the children and raised concerns about adequate evaluation of the effects of our efforts. Slowly, through the collaborative efforts of the participants, *La Clase Mágica* gained its culturally relevant character.

New names for the rooms, the Fifth Dimension, and even the Wizard, for example, were selected over simple translations. The two site coordinators lobbied for the name, *La Clase Mágica*; they thought that the concept of the Fifth Dimension might elude the children. After much discussion over the Wizard's new name, it was decided to construct a new word in Spanish. The consensus was reached that *El Maga* would serve the dual purpose of disclaiming gender specificity to the only authority figure in the system (since it combines the Spanish masculine and feminine cases in a single term) and provides for the flexible use of any one of four options: *El Mago, La Maga, La Mago,* or *El Maga.*[29]

Our goal was to create an environment that would reflect the children's multicultural experiences, including aspects of transculturation (i.e., the exchange and appropriation of cultural artifacts among adjacent cultures such as those of Mexico and the United States[30]). Transculturation is a significant knowledge source in the life of Mexican-origin individuals and is best exemplified in *La Clase Mágica* by the names for two of the rooms in the maze. Each is named after a character from children's television programs popular on both sides of the border: Kermit, the famous frog character in "Sesame Street," and Chapulín Colorado (Red Grasshopper), the equally well-known child character in "El Chavo del Ocho." Familiar names and situations were strategically used to help children make cognitive connections between the task and their own background experiences. It was hoped that this strategy would provide a stepping stone for the comprehension of the tasks.[31] At minimum, it was hoped that these "flags" would hook children into a conversation with the adults around their significance and thus provide the meaningful interactions found to be so crucial to language acquisition. One such conversation around the room named "Malinche" was initiated by *El Maga*, who asked the child who this historical figure was. Not knowing the response, the child was asked to find out. Through her queries of several adults she learned about a notable figure in Mexican history and her counterpart (roughly speaking) in American history, Benedict Arnold.

Task cards or guide sheets that accompany each of the games were a major focus of our adaptation efforts. Each card was adapted to combine some background knowledge of the children with the setting of the game. The task card of "Botanical Gardens," a commercially available computer game, is an example of the type of alterations that we made. The game asks children to experimentally manipulate soil, water, sun, and air on the screen in order to determine the optimum conditions for growing a plant to a specified height of 100cm. In the adapted task card, the game entitled *El Jardín de Abuelita* (Grandmother's Garden), the children are asked to think of themselves as *abuelita's* helpers, learning her garden secrets for manipulating the elements. This is a likely real life situation for the cross-generational exchange of the kind of information that Moll and his collaborators call a community's "fund of knowledge."[32] The adapted card gives the children the opportunity to apply knowledge and skills they may have already acquired from their own *abuelitas.* The card asks them to grow plants for culinary, medicinal, or environmental purposes. Again, these are real social and familial goals common in these children's homes and community. In reporting to *El Maga* their success or failure in achieving their desired goals, the children are able to draw knowledge from their own personal experiences as well as from knowledge they gain as they play the game.

As the project grew to include two sites in different parts of the country, the two teams of site coordinators, students, and researchers continually looked for alternative ways of connecting the children's existing knowledge base and language to new knowledge and new linguistic skills. As Krashen and Biber point out, "background knowledge helps make input comprehensible" and "language acquisition results from comprehensible input."[33] Our concern, then, was not solely the acquisition of English. We were also seeking to draw connections between the children's multiple skills and knowledge of the primary language and the many other uses of language and literacy newly available to them and represented at *La Clase Mágica*. In the next section, I share some insights concerning our attempts to make the children's linguistic and cultural background a resource for learning.

DISCURSIVE SPACES IN A BILINGUAL SETTING: DOMINANCE OF ENGLISH

In the initial stages of *La Clase Mágica* we made an error of judgment common to many bilingual classrooms. Although we promoted *La Clase Mágica* as a bilingual/bicultural setting, English and mainstream knowledge were featured prominently. Almost from the beginning of their participation in *La Clase Mágica*, the undergraduates noted the children's tendency to choose English. In the fourth quarter of operation, well into the adaptation process, a dramatic shift to the use of English by the children puzzled the students and me. Although the shift to English was not unwelcome, it raised questions about the project's support for dual-language acquisition. Why, we wondered, do children, including recent arrivals whose fluency is minimal, seem to choose freely to speak English in a bilingual/bicultural setting? Why do balanced bilingual children refuse to use Spanish with bilingual adults? Why did we occasionally hear the children admonishing one another to "Speak English!" Did certain structural features favor one language over the other? A close examination of the discursive spaces—portions of conversations when two or more individuals are engaged in face-to-face interaction—provided some key insights into why, at least in the initial stages of the project, children seemed to think that they should use English at *La Clase Mágica*.

INFLUENCES ON LANGUAGE CHOICE

English dominates most of the children's everyday experiences, and it is certainly the language of choice at school. Although participation in *La Clase Mágica* is voluntary, some aspects of the tasks are unavoidably formal and school-like. These elements were not lost on the children who, for the first several quarters of the project, addressed all of the adults as "Teacher." In the later quarters, when *La Clase Mágica* had finally been assigned a permanent home in the Headstart classroom, the environment became, if anything, more school-like. Thus, it was not surprising that the children identified *La Clase Mágica* as a type of school, which in turn prompted them to favor English. Another plausible explanation for the children's shift to English is the low status accorded to Spanish in the schools and the community at large.[34] Children learn quickly that their use of that "funny" language earns them ridicule rather than prestige.

A careful and critical analysis of our own initial efforts, however, showed that the most definite and formidable obstacle to the children's free use of Spanish lay in the structural relations among the participants. Midway into our adaptation process, the use of English was still being favored in almost all situations. When a bilingual adult engaged a child in Spanish, the interaction was likely to shift to English if they turned their attention to the computer (much of the software was in English), written materials (task cards and accompanying activity sheets were in English), or to other undergraduates. Even *El Maga* had not sustained extended fluent conversations in Spanish with the children. On those occasions when Spanish was used, it tended to be employed in short discursive spaces. For example, since the students "wizarding" for *El Maga* had only limited Spanish fluency, replies to the electronic entries that the site coordinators had insisted on writing in Spanish for the children became stilted and produced tensions in which the message lost the character of dialogue. What had been intended as a live exchange (live-chat) between the children and *El Maga* via telecommunications resembled instead a series of alternating monologues.

We also began to realize how the children's choice of language was dictated by factors outside their control but well within ours. For example, among the adults ideological tensions arose over which language the children should use. When the site coordinators—bilinguals dominant in Spanish—helped the children write letters to *El Maga*, they insisted on Spanish in order to understand and therefore write the letters. Thus, unintentionally, but nevertheless quite decisively, the children's free choice of language was subverted, as can be seen in the example below. After one of the initial letter-writing sessions, one of the site coordinators made this entry in her fieldnotes:

. . . cuando los niños empezaron a decir lo que querían que yo le dijiera al mago la niña era la que le decía al oido lo que dijera y empezó a decirlo en inglés, pero le dije que tenía que irme diciendo en español porque yo no sabía escribir inglés.

(. . . when the children started to tell me what they wanted me to say to the wizard, the little girl was the one to whisper in her brother's ear, and he began in English, but I told him that he had to tell me in Spanish. I could not write in English.)

The message to the children from the coordinator was clear. She was not going to make an effort to write the letter in a language she did not know and that she did not want the children to practice so freely. In another note, this same coordinator decried the loss of Spanish by children whose parents did not insist that they speak to them in their native language. She was voicing concerns similar to those of parents from many other ethno-linguistic minorities who fear that communication between them and their children will be impaired if the native language is lost.[35]

In their interactions with the undergraduates, on the other hand, the children were clearly forced to use English. This was a practical necessity because the majority of the undergraduates were not bilingual.[36] But as the following comment, voiced in many class discussions, indicates, at least some of the undergraduates may also have had underlying ideological reasons for urging the children to speak English: "I think that we should do everything we can to teach the children English so they can compete in the outside world. We should take advantage of the time we have with them" (stated by a student in class). As assistants to *El Maga*, the students saw themselves as tutors. Although they were encouraged to participate as "older siblings," in their minds the implicit association to authority that the title of "assistant" engendered overshadowed their assigned role. However, a more subtle, underlying ideological tension tempered their assumptions about the children's use of English. Many undergraduates assumed that English was learned only through formal instruction rather than through meaningful and comprehensible interactions around real-life situations. Many noted the use of English all around them, but they had difficulty accepting that the problems posed by the games were the object of their interactions. They could not see that making the problems comprehensible by using a language that the children could understand would actually facilitate the problem solving and the learning of English.[37] Instead, they thought that the children should be exposed to more English and cited the children's language "problem" as an explanation for their inability to progress through the games or the maze itself. Others noted "language interference" in the children's attempts to pronounce words on the screens. As much as I insisted that "the key was their meaningful interactions with the children" and that "the direct teaching of literacy skills and English was not the purpose of their site visits," their approach to the children was redirected by their own experiences in education. They had little experience with minority children or their communities. Ethnic communities, even those in their own cities, were places the students entered only to visit the restaurants.[38] In school they had been separated from children who could not speak English or came from working-class backgrounds. Even their Spanish foreign language classes consisted of privileged, mostly college-bound, Anglo, middle-class students.

It was obvious that directing the undergraduate students in class to focus on helping the children move through the games and ultimately through the maze was not enough to discourage them from falling back on ideas and instructional strategies they themselves had learned in school. Their pedagogical perspective was driven by their own experiences of direct instruction (for example, on letter-sound correspondence, vocabulary words, and syllabication) instead of relying on the assistance of the bilingual children at *La Clase Mágica* as valuable resources. Many more changes were needed to create an optimal learning environment for the children and the undergraduates.

The first major change was to reinforce Spanish whenever resources were available. Bilingual undergraduates were asked to use Spanish exclusively at site, unless the children themselves pursued the interaction in English. Bilingual or monolingual Spanish language games were added to many of the rooms in the maze.[39] Two rooms were designated to specifically encourage language activities found in the homes and community. The story room, *Historiateca*, for example, was designed to encourage children to create stories in either language, bring some from home, or read others collected by the staff. The game room, *Actividades Tradicionales*, encouraged children to share with other participants games and diversions such as *lotería* (a bingo-type board game) and *víboras y escaleras* (snakes and ladders) that were practiced in their homes. Students with the greatest command of Spanish were asked to do the "wizarding" for *El Maga*.[40] As these revisions became part of the daily routine of the project, the children's choice of language gradually shifted from the sole use of English to the use of English for specific purposes. And, ultimately, as I illustrate below, they used either language by choice as a result of further changes.

THE USE OF LANGUAGE FOR SPECIFIC PURPOSES

The most notable change that appeared after these adaptations were instituted was the decrease in the children's heavy reliance on English. We began noticing the use of both languages within specific contexts. Their shift to English for speaking with the undergraduates around problem-solving activities was reported in the undergraduate students' field notes in the seventh quarter of the project. As the following excerpts from these unedited field notes indicate, the children were by this time making conscious decisions about which language to use with whom and in which domain. Although during this academic quarter, half of the undergraduates spoke some level of Spanish, the children continued to use English with them. At the same time, however, we began to witness more freedom in the children's choice of Spanish when they were collaborating among themselves to solve game-related problems. By creating equal access to either language and cultural affiliation, we were providing opportunities for children to exercise a choice. Cummins would call this "student empowerment."[41]

Sara, possibly feeling excluded from our game, continued to interject while Nidia was playing. She spoke in Spanish to Nidia when Mary (undergraduate student) was not directly helping her to solve the problem, or when she was just talking about the game, but when Mary became involved in the problem-solving, she used English and pointed to the items on the screen.

José, who I have not seen at *La Clase* until this time, was yelling at one of the kids in Spanish—a long tirade which culminated in him calling the other boy a "maricon." José had been unaware of my proximity and when he looked up right after he called the name, he saw me standing right next to him. He said "Just kidding" and ran off. This is a very interesting language switch for a few reasons. First, it seems that English was chosen to address authority. The argument might be made that he switched to English because I am an English speaker. I look "white," and I had never met José before. This does not hold up very well, however, because implicit in his face-saving remark is the fact that I must have understood his tirade, which was in Spanish. If I did not understand the tirade, then there would have been no need for him to make the statement in English when he saw me.

Undeniably, these children, with their varying degrees of fluency in Spanish and English, were making decisions about which language to use based on their previous experiences; presumably their experiences in school were the most influential. What was most striking about their choice of language was that it was not based solely on the availability of proper linguistic resources but instead reflected subjective perceptions of such factors as their interpretation of their physical surroundings and their understanding of the roles and status of the adults present. Perhaps most important, they seemed to base their language choice on the specific purpose for which the language was to be used. For example, the children made a distinction between play activities and learning activities. When they played together outside (a half-hour of organized activities before sessions of *La Clase Mágica* began) or when they talked casually with members of their social group, they used Spanish. And, when they were engaged in activities that resemble the activities of their homes and community—playing tag or *lotería*—they used Spanish. When they interacted with the undergraduates to solve computer game problems, the children perceived themselves as learners. They shifted into a "school mode" and therefore used English. This code-switching tendency to use the home language in socio-emotive contexts and the second language in academic contexts has been recorded among other ethnolinguistic groups.[42]

The realization that the children, and the undergraduates as well, were juxtaposing learning with problem solving in the games, and the role of *El Maga's* assistants with teachers, spurred us to make yet more revisions. To dispel any residual hierarchy in the notion of Wizard Assistant, the role was redefined and renamed: Assistants became simply *Amigos* or *Amigas*. Improvements were made with *El Maga* as well, so that when we began the eighth quarter, adults were defined as friends and *El Maga* was a masterful, bilingual Wizard, whose manipulation of regional varieties of Spanish instantly touched a responsive chord in at least one child who exclaimed, "Ah, ahora tenemos una Chola para maga." ("Oh! Now we have a Chola [female member of a Chicano youth culture] for Wizard!")

These changes made further difference in the use of Spanish and English at *La Clase Mágica*. We began noting that the children's use of Spanish was in transition from the social sphere into the literacy activities. Their previous reluctance to use Spanish had prevented us from observing their literacy skills in the first language, an event that was possible when they began writing to *El Maga* unassisted in Spanish. We also began noting that children were relying more on the written language on the computer monitor and on the task cards. Children were taking more time to read the directions on the monitor instead of incessantly pressing on the keys to move forward. On one occasion, we observed a nine-year-old boy spend three site visits on the incomprehensible game manual trying to figure out how to play the game. The adult English speakers were of no help in deciphering the technical language of the text.

While we have a long way to go before our project structurally supports the use of either language in advanced critical thinking skills, the children's responses at *La Clase Mágica* indicate that they perceive themselves as having a choice concerning which language to use. For example, in an impromptu question-answer period at the drawing table, several children indicated by their responses that they not only spoke both languages but that they had a fair assessment of the adult's language competencies. The example below illustrates eight-year-old Rina's conception of the language competency of the *Amigos* with whom she uses English to make life easier for them:

> OV: ¿Que idioma se habla aquí? (Which language is spoken here?)
>
> Rina: A veces inglés, a veces español. (Sometimes English, sometimes Spanish.)
>
> OV: ¿Por qué? (Why?)

Rina: Los estudiantes vienen y hablan inglés y nosotros hablamos inglés con ellos. (The students come and speak English and we speak with them in English.)

OV: ¿Por qué usas inglés, si unos estudiantes hablan español? (Why do you speak English with them when some of them speak Spanish?)

Rina: Para que entiendan. (So they understand.)

Rina's responses indicate that she knows that both languages are valued at *La Clase Mágica* and that her choice of English with the undergraduates is to facilitate their efforts to communicate with her. In another conversation with two five-year-olds, Jesús and Elías, I found the children's playfulness in responding to my queries an expression of the comfort they felt at *La Clase Mágica* and with me, as well as with choosing which language to use. It is clear that Elías finds their experience at *La Clase Mágica* qualitatively different from their experience at school:

OV: ¿Que idioma usas aquí? (Which language do you speak here?)

Elías: Español. (Spanish.)

OV: ¿Por qué? (Why?)

Elías: Yo no se. (I don't know.)

OV: ¿Y tú Jesús? (And you, Jesús?)

Jesús: Inglés. (English.)

Elías: No es cierto, no. ¡Estas hechando mentiras! [a Jesús] (It's not true! You're lying! [to Jesus]).

Jesús: Tu eres el que hechas mentiras. (You are the one who's lying.)

OV: ¿Cuándo usas inglés? [a Jesús] (When do you use English? [to Jesus]).

Elías: ¡En la escuela! [yells] (In school!)

Jesús: ¡En la escuela! [yells back] (In school!)

OV: ¿Por qué hablas inglés en la escuela? (Why do you speak English in school?)

Elías: Porque hablan puro inglés, no hablan chino. (Because they speak only English and not Chinese.)

OV: ¿Y aquí? (And, here?)

Elías: Hablamos en el español, ¿verdad? [to Jesús] (We speak
      Spanish. Isn't it true?)

Here Elías communicates that he is not sure why Spanish is spoken at
La Clase Mágica, but he does know that English is the language of the
school. After all, he says, "They only speak English and not
Chinese."

While children at *La Clase Mágica* continue to use English with
Amigos and *Amigas*, it is clear that Spanish is increasingly the language
of choice in their interactions. Children are no longer refusing to speak
Spanish with bilingual adults nor do they tell each other to "Speak
English!" In fact, a look back at the initial concerns of an *Amiga*, as
cited in her field notes, demonstrates the changes in the attitudes of the
children toward using Spanish at *La Clase Mágica*:

> . . .I explained (to Andres and Nellie) that I only spoke English. He was
> very proud in telling me that he spoke both Spanish and English. He
> explained that he went to all English-speaking classes, but spoke mostly
> Spanish when he was away from school.

As the above discussion points out, children learned that either
language was valued at *La Clase Mágica* and used them both
accordingly. They used English to facilitate communication with the
undergraduates and Spanish to establish camaraderie with their peers.
In numerous instances they also used Spanish to gain an upper hand
over the adults. Their linguistic competence was clearly demonstrated
in a field note reporting how a child used Spanish to subvert the
adult's mastery of English spelling and vocabulary:

> This example occurred during a game of hangman in which nine-year-old
> Ana was playing with Nina, an Amiga. When it was her turn to make the
> puzzle, Ana chose to use Spanish so that the puzzle would be difficult for the
> monolingual English-speaking Amiga and give Nina a better chance of
> winning.

They had acquired confidence in the communicative value of speaking
two languages. For example, when asked why she wanted to speak
both languages, seven-year-old Rina responded:

> . . . y a mi me gusta hablar inglés. Yo debo hablar inglés por que a veces no
> me acuerdo de un bombero como decirlo en español.

> (. . . I like to speak English. I should speak English because sometimes I can't
> remember how to say [the word for] fireman in Spanish.)

Rina understood that by speaking two languages, she had a broader system from which to make meaning. If she did not know the word in one language, she could rely on her other language to help make herself understood.

While we are currently in the preliminary stages of the analysis, the adults' field notes and the informal interviews of the children have already given us valuable insights into what influences language choice and the ways in which language is a resource in the learning setting. At the present time, evaluation measures indicate that our efforts are creating some impact at various levels of the system. For example, analyses of data sets on attendance, institutional support, and parent involvement provide strong evidence that our program is highly valued in the community. Analyses of field-developed "skills assessments" (pre and post quizzes on several cognitive skills promoted by the games) and record sheets of children's activities also indicate their progress in some domains. The latter indicate that children are progressing successfully through the maze. The undergraduate students' field notes clearly demonstate their own development of observation and writing skills as well as an increasing understanding of theory and, in some cases, their own identity.

While we find that we have many ways in which to prove that children are acquiring literacy and language skills, we also must contend with demonstrating the validity of the program's effects to outside institutions. This is not an easy task for a voluntary after-school program. In fact, we have had to develop methodological extensions to standard evaluation measures in order to make comparisons with a control group possible. We have gone outside the system to the schools to obtain scores on standardized achievement tests on the children, each of whom is matched with an equal-achieving "blind control" child from the school records. Our rationale was to provide a "far transfer" measure of the system's impact through differential change in achievement at the end of the school year (if, of course, there were any change).[43] These strategies will allow us to make judgments about the suitability of school-administered tests and possibly corroborate our findings if there is any positive differential in the results of the participants in *La Clase Mágica*.[44]

In Summary

As an after-school activity, *La Clase Mágica* is not under the institutional constraints that are placed on schools to demonstrate growth in subject-area content and mastery of grade-level skills, nor does it have to comply with hierarchical relationships imposed by the school structure. Children are not subject to an adult authority who has all the answers. In fact, on many occasions, it is the children who are the experts. However, in many ways, the conditions at *La Clase Mágica* resemble the reality of this country's schools. *La Clase Mágica* is an example of an educational effort that attempts to implement a culturally relevant curriculum and provide a learning environment within the context of limited resources. We continue to experience a shortage of qualified bilingual personnel and adequate bilingual instructional materials. Granted we have the flexibility to make sweeping changes to accomplish our goals (which most teachers do not have); still we believe we have some insights concerning the use of language and culture as a resource in the learning setting from which other teachers could benefit.

Our experience has taught us that the child's language must be perceived as one of the most important components of the instructional setting. As the voices of the children from *La Clase Mágica* testify, these children do not come from impoverished "language environments." They come with language experiences that draw on a variety of contexts and knowledge sources. Their linguistic repertoires and cultural affiliations draw on their experiences in home, school, and community. And, in contrast to previous conventional wisdom, children in a bilingual/bicultural environment are able to learn and flourish using two languages. In fact, when children at *La Clase Mágica* indicated that they could speak only English, their facility in communicating with those around them and their access to important information and skills were visibly restricted. Our experience clearly supports what Pease-Alvarez and Hakuta propose for teaching bilingual children:

Don't worry about English; they are all learning it; instead, worry about the instructional content; if you are going to worry about language, worry about the lost potential in the attrition of the native language, for all of the languages of the world are represented in this country.[45]

If measures are not instituted to prevent it, as the initial stages of the adaptation showed us, the likelihood of losing the first language is very high.[46] In this age of the global village, the children's primary language is a national resource which must be given status and recognition as a viable tool in the learning process.

When children experience complete freedom of language choice, an optimal learning condition is created that directly influences their ability to perform in a wider zone of proximal development. Given the opportunity to freely tap their cultural and linguistic resources, children will, as little Rina demonstrated, choose communicative value over form. They can push the limits of their ability to express themselves rather than staying bound to an incomplete message shaped by the lack of fluency in a language. Their critical thinking skills are enhanced not by speaking a variety of languages but by the ability to use resources at their disposal to negotiate meanings in problem-solving activities.[47] Our work has shown that capitalizing on the cultural and linguistic background resources that children bring to the learning environment makes more sense than beginning with a clean slate. Using the multiple skills and knowledge of the primary language in the learning setting not only facilitates the acquisition of the second language but also sets the stage for the empowerment of minority children.[48]

Finally, another important lesson we have learned from our efforts is that serving the needs of a diverse student population is a complex, deliberate, and dynamic process. It is not a packaged approach that can be applied intact to every situation and regional location. It requires cross-level effort involving relevant local institutions such as the home, the school, and the university, and all adaptations must be grounded on the linguistic and cultural resources available in the local community. Importantly, it must be a project in which all participants—parents, paraprofessionals, children, amigos, and researchers—help to shape its goals and objectives and therefore the process of change. Teachers cannot do it alone. They must form partnerships with representatives from local institutions for social and economic support.

I wish to acknowledge the contributions of students in my courses ("Literacy Issues in a Minority Setting" and "Communication in the Community") offered through the Department of Communication at the University of California at San Diego. Their class discussions and course papers gave birth to many of the ideas developed in this chapter. In particular, I wish to acknowledge Maria Lourdes Durán and María Nieves, two community representatives, who have played a critical role in the adaptation process and the overall success of La Clase Mágica. Finally, I thank Arturo Vásquez, bilingual consultant for the California Department of Education, for his insightful comments.

NOTES

1. California State Department of Education, Schooling and Language Minority Students: A Theoretical Framework (Los Angeles: Evaluation, Dissemination, and Assessment Center, California State University, 1981); idem, Beyond Language: Social and Cultural Factors in Schooling Language Minority Students (Los Angeles: Evaluation, Dissemination, and Assessment Center, California State University, 1986).

2. Dorothy Legarreta-Marcaída, "Effective Use of the Primary Language in the Classroom," in California State Department of Education, *Schooling and Language Minority Students: A Theoretical Framework* (Los Angeles: Evaluation, Dissemination, and Assessment Center, California State University, 1986); James Crawford, *Bilingual Education: History, Politics, Theory, and Practice* (Los Angeles: Bilingual Educational Services, 1991); J. David Ramírez, Sandra D. Yuen, Dena R. Ramey, and David J. Pasta, *Longitudinal Study of Structured English Immersion Strategy, Early-exit, and Late-exit Transitional Bilingual Education Programs for Language Minority Children*, Final Report (San Mateo, CA: Aguirre International, 1991).

3. María de la Luz Reyes, "The 'One Size Fits All' Approach to Literacy" (Paper presented at the Annual Meeting of the American Educational Research Association, Chicago, 1991).

4. David E. Hayes-Bautista, Werner O. Schink, and Jorge Chapa, *The Burden of Support: Young Latinos in an Aging Society* (Stanford, CA: Stanford University Press, 1988).

5. Thomas P. Carter and Robert D. Segura, *Mexican Americans in School: A Decade of Change* (New York: College Entrance Examination Board, 1979); Richard Valencia, *Chicano School Failure and Success: Research and Policy Agendas for the 1990s* (New York: Falmer Press, 1991).

6. Graeme Kennedy, "Conditions for Language Learning," in *Focus on the Learner: Pragmatic Perspectives for the Language Teacher*, edited by John W. Oller, Jr. and Jack C. Richards (Rowley, MA: Newbury House, 1973), p. 70.

7. Elenore Ochs, *Culture and Language Development* (Cambridge: Cambridge University Press, 1988); Bambi B. Schieffelin and Elenore Ochs, "Language Socialization," *Annual Review of Anthropology* 15 (1986): 163-191; Shirley B. Heath, *Ways with Words: Language, Life, and Work in Communities and Classrooms* (Cambridge: Cambridge University Press, 1983).

8. Heath, *Ways with Words*, p. 125. Emphasis in original.

9. Heath, *Ways with Words*.

10. Olga A. Vásquez, Lucinda Pease-Alvarez, and Sheila M. Shannon, *Pushing Boundaries: Language in a Mexicano Community*, in preparation.

11. Olga A. Vásquez, "Connecting Oral Language Strategies to Literacy: An Ethnographic Study among Four Mexican Immigrant Families" (Doctoral dissertation, Stanford University, 1989); Juan Guerra, "The Acquisition and Use of Literacy Skills and Literate Behaviors in Families of Mexican Origin" (Doctoral dissertation, University of Illinois at Chicago, 1991).

12. Lucinda Pease-Alvarez, "Home and School Contexts for Language Learning: A Case Study of Two Mexican-American Bilingual Preschoolers" (Doctoral dissertation, Stanford University, 1986).

13. Paul Berman, Jay Chambers, Patricia Gándara, Barry McLaughlin, Catherine Minicucci, Beryl Nelson, Laurie Olsen, and Tom Parrish, *Meeting the Challenge of Language Diversity: An Evaluation of Programs for Pupils with Limited Proficiency in English*, vol. 1, Executive Summary (Berkeley, CA: BW Associates, 1992).

14. Kennedy, "Conditions for Language Learning," p. 68.

15. Luis C. Moll, "Bilingual Classroom Studies and Community Analysis: Some Recent Trends," *Educational Researcher* 21, no. 2 (March, 1992): 20.

16. Reyes, "The 'One Size Fits All' Approach to Literacy."

17. Birget Harley, James Cummins, Merril Swain, and Patrick Allen, "The Nature of Language Proficiency," in *The Development of Second Language Proficiency*, edited by Birget Harley, Patrick Allen, James Cummins, and Merril Swain (Cambridge: Cambridge University Press, 1990).

18. For a review, see Bárbara M. Flores, "Language Interference or Influence: Toward a Theory for Hispanic Bilingualism" (Doctoral disseration, University of Arizona, Tucson, 1982).

19. James Cummins and Merril Swain, *Bilingualism in Education* (New York: Longman, 1986).

20. James Cummins, *Empowering Minority Students* (Sacramento, CA: California Association for Bilingual Education, 1989).

21. Luis C. Moll and Estephen Díaz, "Change as the Goal for Educational Research," *Anthropology and Education Quarterly* 18, no. 4 (1987): 300-311.

22. Mike Cole and Agiliki Nicoloupoulo, *Creating Sustainable New Forms of Educational Activity in After-school Settings*, Final Report to the Spencer Foundation (La Jolla, CA: Laboratory of Comparative Human Cognition, University of California, San Diego, 1991).

23. Ibid., p. 41.

24. The undergraduates are drawn from students taking courses on child development and literacy offered through the Department of Communication at the University of California, San Diego. Participating in the Fifth Dimension allows the students to put into practice theories about learning, language, and literacy that they are learning in their courses. After each site visit, they use electronic mail to submit their observations (as field notes) to the professor.

25. Lev S. Vygotsky, *Thought and Language* (Cambridge, MA: MIT Press, 1978).

26. Every quarter (that is, every ten weeks) a new group of undergraduate students comes to *La Clase Mágica* unfamiliar with the culture of the Fifth Dimension and the games. Thus, the children are in a much better position to be the "experts" in the learning situation.

27. The designation "Mexican-origin" includes immigrants and subsequent generations of individuals who trace their ancestry to Mexico. Chicano/a is a self-designation used by Mexican Americans who identify with the historical and political struggles of Mexican-origin individuals in the United States.

28. Luis C. Moll, Cathy Amanti, Deborah Neff, and Norma González, "Funds of Knowledge for Teaching: Using a Qualitative Approach to Connect Homes and Classrooms," *Theory Into Practice* 31, no. 2 (Spring, 1992): 132-141.

29. In a literal translation of *wizard*, "el" (the article specifying masculine gender) is needed. Thus, *wizard* would translate literally as "the male wizard" in Spanish, an option we wanted to avoid.

30. José Cuellar, personal communication, 1987; Renato Rosaldo, *Culture and Truth: The Remaking of Social Analysis* (Boston: Beacon Press, 1989).

31. John Bransford, *Human Cognition: Learning, Understanding, and Remembering* (Belmont, CA: Wadsworth, 1979).

32. Luis C. Moll, Carlos G. Vélez-Ibáñez, James Greenberg, K. Whitmore, E. Saavedra, J. Dworin, and R. Andrade, *Community Knowledge and Classroom Practice: Combining Resources for Literacy Instruction* (Tucson, AZ: College of Education and Bureau of Applied Research in Anthropology, University of Arizona, 1990).

33. Stephen Krashen and Douglas Biber, *On Course: Bilingual Education's Success in California* (Sacramento, CA: California Association for Bilingual Education, 1989), p. 210.

34. Nancy L. Commins, "Dilemmas of Bilingual Teachers: Planning for Instruction in Two Languages" (Paper presented at the Annual Meeting of the American Anthropological Association, Chicago, 1991).

35. Lily Wong Fillmore, "When Learning a Second Language Means Losing the First," *Early Childhood Research Quarterly* 6, no. 3 (1991): 323-346.

36. Few of the students enrolled in the University classes speak Spanish; even fewer are Mexicano/Latino. For the most part, the Mexicano/Latino students do not speak Spanish as their first language.

37. Cummins and Swain, *Bilingualism in Education*.

38. David Franke and Kristen Janikas, "Ollie-popping over the Walls of Eden Gardens," in *And the Walls Came Tumbling Down: New Perspectives on Learning*, a compilation of students' papers for the course on "Communication in the Community," edited by Olga A. Vásquez (La Jolla: University of California, San Diego, 1992).

39. Several of the bilingual/monolingual programs were created by Bilingual Instructional Technology (BIT), a federally funded Title VII project at San Diego State University, in courses taught by Bernie Dodge, Associate Professor of Educational Technology. The abject lack of educational software in Spanish is a serious constraint in providing equal access to both languages.

40. Acting as assistants to *El Maga*, designated bilingual students answered her mail and chatted with the children in her behalf. They also were asked to submit debriefings in writing about their thoughts on the way they responded to the children in terms of language choice and use of content knowledge.

41. Cummins, *Empowering Minority Students*.

42. Crystal Shannon-Morla, "Effect of Emotion on African-American Black English and Standard English Code-shifting Bilinguals" (Doctoral dissertation, California School of Professional Psychology, San Diego, CA, 1992).

43. "Far transfer" here refers to the ability to apply skills and knowledge learned in one activity to a different activity. At *La Clase Mágica* we want to know if participation in our program affects children's performance in school-type activities, such as taking standardized tests. "Near transfer" is the application of skills learned in one activity in another similar activity. For example, near transfer occurs when skills learned in a mathematics class can be applied in a standardized test on mathematics.

44. The research team assisted the director of special programs at the local school in administering the Language Assessment Scale to almost a hundred students. A rank-order comparison between *La Clase Mágica's* participants and their school peers with similar backgrounds will be made to assess the effects of *La Clase Mágica* on the participants' fluency in both oral and written English and Spanish.

45. Lucinda Pease-Alvarez and Kenji Hakuta, "Enriching Our Views of Bilingualism and Bilingual Education," *Educational Researcher* 21, no. 2 (March, 1992): 6.

46. Fillmore, "When Learning a Second Language Means Losing the First"; Judith Lessow-Hurley, *The Foundations of Dual Language Instruction* (New York: Longman, 1990).

47. Dell Hymes, "Introduction," in *Functions of Language in the Classroom*, edited by Courtney B. Cazden, Vera P. John, and Dell Hymes (New York: Teachers College Press, 1972).

48. Cummins, *Empowering Minority Students*.

CHAPTER IX

The Home-School Connection in Bilingual Education

CLAUDE GOLDENBERG

Over the last thirty years, a vast literature has emerged documenting the relationship between children's homes and their school achievement. Researchers have investigated perhaps hundreds of links between home and school, and a clear consensus has appeared: children's experiences at home profoundly influence their chances for success at school. Whether overtly acknowledged or not, homes and schools are inextricably linked.[1]

Some home-school links are based upon factors that cannot be readily influenced by educational policy and practice. Parents' economic or educational status, for example, are strongly related to children's school outcomes. But these are extremely difficult to change, at least in the short term. The connections between family social status and school achievement, as powerful as they might be, offer educators very little they can use to help students succeed in school.

In contrast, a wide range of factors that educators and families *can* influence—Bloom has called them "alterable variables"[2]—can promote productive home-school links, which in turn can help produce higher levels of academic achievement or other desirable outcomes. Accordingly, researchers, policymakers, and educators themselves have increasingly been calling for practices and policies to encourage such home-school connections.

Home-school links are no less important for Spanish-speaking children in U.S. schools. Indeed, forging such links is perhaps especially important for these children, since most of their parents were born and educated outside the United States and are therefore unlikely to be familiar with the U.S. educational system and unable to make such links on their own. Ramírez and associates found that only 19 percent of the parents of Spanish-speaking school children were born in the United States. For the other 81 percent, whatever formal

---

Claude Goldenberg is Associate Research Psychologist, Department of Psychiatry and Biobehavioral Sciences, University of California, Los Angeles.

schooling they received (average for all parents was seven years) appears for the most part to have taken place in Latin America.[3]

Even if not born outside the United States, disproportionate numbers of Latino students come from families of low socioeconomic status.[4] For various reasons, these families have traditionally had little contact with schools.[5] Meaningful and productive home-school connections among this population are therefore especially likely to benefit children, families, and the schools they attend.

This chapter will focus on what educators of Spanish-speaking language-minority children have been doing to promote productive links between the home and the school. I will first provide an overview of research and practice in the area of home and school connections more generally, not just among language-minority children and families. This area has become extraordinarily productive over the past decade, and it is useful to consider the larger context before turning more specifically to home-school connections for Latino populations.

Home and School: Making the Connection

The importance of home-school collaboration has not always had the widespread recognition it now enjoys. Consider what the 1929 yearbook of the National Society for the Study of Education said:

> The importance of the family *as a social influence* is generally conceded. In spite of this we find scant attention given to the study of the family *as an educational institution.* As a result, our knowledge, compared with what might be expected, is hazy and inadequate. . . . In practice, in spite of eloquent eulogies of the home, *the family is little recognized as a chief educational agency.*[6]

The neglect of the family as an educational institution in the early part of the century was probably not merely an oversight. Epstein points out that early and highly influential sociological theories, such as those of Weber, Waller, and Parsons, emphasized the importance of keeping the authority and influence of the home and the school distinct and separate from one another.[7] It was assumed that because the two institutions differed in goals, outlook, and functioning, families and schools would both be better served if each institution operated more or less independently.

What a difference sixty years make. Today, the observations in the NSSE 1929 yearbook could hardly be more dated. Although there were signs of a shift in thinking even then—which was, however, largely centered on parent involvement in the preschool years[8]—our regnant theories have changed, as have our practices and attitudes toward the home as an educational institution. As a result of research, innovative practice, and general shifts in public attitudes, particularly over the last decade, the importance of home-school collaboration is now widely acknowledged. Moreover, educators have at their disposal a wide range of strategies and approaches they can use to promote home-school connections, as well as an unprecedented number of sources for ideas and suggestions.

An astonishing number of publications have appeared over the past decade providing educators and parents with hundreds of possible ways to promote children's school success through home-school collaborations. The September, 1991, issue of *The ERIC Review*, a publication of the U.S. Department of Education, contained titles, summaries, and information on how to obtain about three dozen different books and pamphlets, some in Spanish, dealing with parent involvement in children's education. Examples of other publications from diverse sources are:

• Arizona Department of Education (1986), *Parent Participation for Effective Schools* (three handbooks for parents, teachers, and administrators);

• U.S. Department of Education (n.d.), *Help Your Child do Better in School*;

• California State Board of Education (1989), *Parents and Schools Make a Difference!* (also available in Spanish);

• The Center for the Study of Reading, University of Illinois at Urbana-Champaign (n.d.), *10 Ways to Help Your Children Become Better Readers* (also available in Spanish);

• American Association of School Administrators (1982), *Parents . . . Partners in Education* (also available in Spanish).

Amidst this avalanche of suggested and promising activities, Epstein[9] has provided a useful conceptual scheme for organizing the many approaches to home-school connections or, as she terms them, types of "school and family partnerships":

Type 1. <u>Fulfilling the basic obligations of families (*parenting*)</u>. Families have basic responsibility for assuring the physical and emotional well-being of children. By providing for proper nutrition, health care, and socioemotional development, families also make positive contributions to children's school success. If families cannot or do not fulfill these obligations, schools can help by providing information or resources.

Type 2. Fulfilling the basic obligations of schools (*communicating*). Schools have an obligation to inform parents about school programs and children's progress. Even early theorists who took a dim view of overlapping responsibilities between schools and homes acknowledged the need for schools to communicate basic information to parents through, for example, notices or report cards.

Type 3. Encouraging involvement at school (*volunteering*). Parents' involvement at the school site includes a wide range of possible activities, from attending school functions and events to helping teachers with clerical or instructional duties. Schools can promote these home-school connections by providing information, accommodating to parents' schedules, and offering training when needed.

Type 4. Promoting learning activities at home (*home learning*). Extending children's learning opportunities beyond the regular school day is a fourth way to forge productive home-school connections. Examples include assigning homework, providing parents with guidance or training for helping their children, and suggesting appropriate home learning activities. By definition and design, promoting home learning is likely to have the most direct effects on achievement.

Type 5. Involving parents and the community in decision-making and advocacy (*governing*). Parents serve on local school boards, advisory councils, school site councils, and other bodies that either formulate policy or contribute to it. Schools can help provide parents with the knowledge and skills that will contribute to their success in these roles. To the extent they do, schools can find effective partners for their improvement efforts.

Type 6. Collaboration and exchange with community organizations. Schools can help coordinate services or programs provided by other community groups or agencies, for example, after-school care, health services, public libraries, and cultural or other groups. Although this type of home-school collaboration has not been actively investigated, it is possible that it too can contribute to children's learning, school success, and general development.

In addition to Epstein's six, there is a seventh possible way to promote productive home-school connections, this one suggested by educational anthropologists and other social scientists long concerned with the underachievement of some cultural minorities in the United States:[10]

Type 7. <u>Accommodation of the school program to children's home cultures</u>. As with the other types of home-school connections, this represents a heterogeneous category covering a wide spectrum of possible actions by the school. Some possible accommodations are fairly straightforward, even if they remain controversial—for example, the use of the home language for instruction (as in bilingual education programs) and recognition of the holidays, history, and traditions of minority children's culture.[11] Other accommodations are more subtle and complex, such as the use in school of the home culture's social/interactional patterns,[12] use of linguistic forms and functions from children's homes,[13] and use of family and community knowledge and resources.[14]

The Home-School Connection for Spanish-speaking Children

A relatively small but significant portion of the research investigating home-school connections has included language-minority children. This research strongly supports the underlying thesis of this chapter: by encouraging and promoting productive home-school links of the various types outlined above, educators can help all children—including students from Spanish-speaking homes—be more successful at school. Four studies of effective school programs—one in preschool, one in the early elementary grades, one in the later elementary grades, and one in high school—provide cases in point:

• Campos and Keatinge report on a Title VII preschool program for low-income, Spanish-dominant students.[15] A strong parent involvement component was a major feature of the program. Parents were encouraged to participate as volunteers and to visit the classroom whenever they wished. In addition, the preschool teacher held monthly workshops to provide information and suggestions for the parents on a variety of topics (chosen by parents themselves) and to show them how they could increase children's learning opportunities at home.[16]

Campos and Keatinge report that children who attended the experimental preschool—which emphasized linguistic and conceptual development *in Spanish*—were more advanced than comparison children on measures of school readiness, early academic achievement, and *English* oral language.

● Goldenberg and Gallimore report on a predominantly Hispanic elementary school where first- and second-grade children's reading achievement (in Spanish) improved substantially over a two to three year period as a result of several changes in the school's early literacy program.[17] One of the changes involved increased parent and home involvement in children's beginning literacy development. Whereas in previous years there had been no systematic attempts to involve parents in helping their children learn to read, teachers began sending home books and other reading materials, including homework and other assignments designed to promote literacy.

As a result of these and other changes, early reading achievement at the school improved markedly. Whereas prior to 1986, second and third graders at the school were at about the 30th percentile in their reading achievement, by 1986 they were at about the 60th percentile.

● Carter and Chatfield describe another effective elementary bilingual education program.[18] Sixth graders at the school achieved at higher levels in reading and mathematics than students at comparable schools in the state for most years from 1980 to 1985. Other test results also suggest that the students are achieving well.

The study identified a number of features of the school's program that help explain the relatively high levels of student achievement, for example, a positive climate for learning, a staff that is focused on outcomes, and high expectations for student achievement. The researchers also found that an "ongoing community/school process" was an important part of the school's success equation. Overwhelming majorities of both parents and teachers felt there were good home/school relations. Volunteers from the community worked in the school, both directly with children and in helping teachers make classroom materials. Carter and Chatfield report that the school's staff was trying to enhance the already strong home-school connections by improving the quality of homework teachers assigned.

● Finally, Lucas, Henze, and Donato report case studies of six effective high schools (using various criteria for "success"—attendance rates, dropout rates, postsecondary attendance, standardized test scores) with large Latino populations.[19] These authors identified eight factors that helped explain these schools' apparent success with language-minority students. One of the factors had to do with encouraging parents to become involved in their children's education. This was accomplished in different ways at the different schools, for example, parent advisory committees, newsletters, monthly parent nights, evening student performances, teacher-parent meetings, student-of-the-month breakfasts, honors assemblies, and community liaisons.

In addition, Lucas et al. report that the successful high schools placed a great deal of value on students' home languages and cultures. While recognizing, celebrating, and building upon cultural knowledge and experiences students brought from home, the school staffs also worked to break down stereotypes about Latino students. Students were treated as individuals, not as members of an undifferentiated cultural or ethnic group. One assistant principal offered this observation: "Basically, Hispanic kids are no different from other kids; they want to learn. Those who fall by the wayside arc those whose needs aren't being met. Who wants to fail everyday?"[20]

We should keep in mind that strong home-school links in these successful programs were not the only factors at work. Various other features also played important roles. For example, the schools had strong substantive learning programs that provided appropriate opportunities for academic and cognitive growth. They also promoted use of students' primary language and skill development in the primary language. Productive home-school links were part of a larger constellation of factors that made the programs successful. The point might be obvious, but it bears highlighting: effective schools do a number of things, not just one, that help promote language-minority students' success.

Nonetheless, home-school connections played important roles. They were important even in high school, although Lucas et al. report that parent participation was the "least developed component" in the high schools they visited.[21] Perhaps this reflects the fact that parents' direct involvement in children's schooling declines as children get older,[22] and therefore parents are less likely to have a strong impact on school performance when children reach high school. Different types of home-school connections might thus be relevant at different levels of schooling. In any case, across the four studies, we see a wide variety of types of home-school connections, such as helping parents fulfill basic obligations of parenting (type 1); schools communicating with parents (type 2); community volunteers in school (type 3); promoting home learning (type 4); and placing a high value on children's home cultures and experiences (type 7).

Home-School Connections: Opportunities to Promote Success

Clearly, home-school connections offer educators an important set of opportunities and strategies for promoting success among language-minority students.

Why is this? One reason is straightforward: home-school connections have generally been shown to influence children's academic achievement across a wide range of cultural, ethnic, and social class groups, as well as the achievement of high-, middle-, and low-achieving students, and of students in countries other than the United States.[23] What works in general is likely to work for the specific groups that concern us here—language minority students from Spanish-speaking homes.[24]

But at least two other factors appear to make productive home-school connections particularly important in the case of language-minority populations. First, despite clear interest in their children's education and their desire to help children succeed in school, many parents either feel limited in their ability to help or do not know that their children would benefit from such assistance.[25] Foreign-born parents especially are likely to be unfamiliar with school programs in this country and to be somewhat wary about intruding on a process they feel they do not understand. In many cases, however, they are fully capable of helping their children, either academically or behaviorally, and many potentially productive opportunities are probably missed.

A clear instance comes from a study, in which a mother from Mexico told me she had stopped teaching her first-grade daughter the letters of the alphabet because the teacher told her this was not the way they taught reading at the school. Since the teacher did not provide the mother with alternative suggestions or guidelines for helping her child, the mother stopped altogether: "*No es igual aquí como en el país de uno*" ("It's not the same here, as it is in one's own country"). In the case of another child, the father (Puerto Rican) told the mother (Salvadoran) to stop trying to teach their son to read and to let the teacher do her job. "*Los métodos de la maestra son distintos*" ("The teacher's methods are different [from what we know]"), the father said.[26]

In both cases, the children ended first grade far below level in their reading achievement. The irony was that the parents were fully literate and capable of helping their children succeed. They most likely would have, had they been informed by teachers how to do so. The problem becomes compounded as children advance in school, and their schoolwork becomes more difficult and is in English. Parents feel increasingly incapable of helping.[27] It becomes even more critical for schools and teachers to help parents understand the other ways they can support children's continued learning, such as reading with them in the home language, making sure homework and other assignments are done, setting regular study times, limiting television viewing, and generally taking an active interest in children's school performance.

Second, Latino parents might be especially motivated to help their children do well in school because of the role they accord formal schooling in helping their children achieve social and economic mobility.[28] Parents universally have as one of their goals for children the acquisition of "economic capabilities."[29] Because many Latino parents blame their own socioeconomic status on their lack of formal schooling or their inability to speak English, or both, they want their children to go much further in their education than they did.[30]

Consider what this Mexican mother with a third-grade education answered when I asked how she felt about her own level of formal schooling:

Yo siento que no fue suficiente. Yo habría (sic) *querido estudiar mas, ser alguien en la vida. Con este poquito que estudié, no es suficiente. (I: ¿Y porqué cree que no fue suficiente?) . . . Batalla uno mucho por lo que no sabe uno de que no estudió. Batalla uno mucho para buscar trabajo.* ("I feel it was not sufficient. I would have liked to study more, to be somebody. With the little I studied, it's not enough. [I: And why do you think that it was not enough?] . . . You really struggle because of what you do not know from not having studied. You must really struggle to find a job.").[31]

Parents want their children to have good jobs and be economically secure, and they see schooling as an important (although not exclusive) means of accomplishing this. A Mexican mother with a sixth-grade education put it this way:

Yo trato de inculcarles [a los niños] que ellos deben estudiar, porque ya todo lo que sirve más bien es la preparación. Porque cada día están pidiendo más cosas en los trabajos. Depende de lo que dice uno—hasta que fue a la escuela—así le dan a uno la oportunidad de trabajo. Es lo que siempre le digo a mi hijo. ("I try to inculcate in them [her children] that they should study, because what is most valuable is your preparation [that is, academic preparation] . . . every day they require more and more at [different] jobs. It depends on what you tell them—how far you went in school—as to whether they'll give you the chance of a job. This is what I always tell my son.").[32]

We would expect that if Hispanic parents were regularly informed about how they can help their children succeed in school, many would take positive steps toward doing so, particularly when children are young and parents feel they can have a direct hand in assisting children's learning. Indeed, this is what I found earlier: when parents found out how they could help their first-grade children learn to read, the result was improvement in children's reading achievement.[33]

Other Efforts to Promote Home-School Connections with Latino Families

The four studies of successful programs for Hispanic students cited earlier suggest that home-school connections and parent involvement can have substantial effects on student success program-wide. Other projects around the country, using many types of home-school connections, suggest other promising approaches.

Moll and Greenberg[34] and Moll, Amanti, Neff, and González[35] describe a project in Tucson, Arizona, with elementary-age Mexican and Mexican-American students. The purpose of this work is to discover the "funds of knowledge" in children's homes and

to develop innovations in teaching that draw upon the knowledge and skills found in local households. Our claim is that by capitalizing on household and other community resources, we can organize classroom instruction that far exceeds in quality the rote-like instruction that these children commonly encounter in school.[36]

The investigators use an innovative design in which teachers develop study themes and classroom practices based upon what they learn from ethnographic studies of students' homes (conducted by teams of teachers and researchers). This is a very clear example of the seventh type of home-school connection described previously, accommodating classroom practices to reflect children's home cultures and experiences. Parents also come to classrooms to share their relevant expertise about topics the class might be studying, an example of home-school connection type 3 (parents' volunteering at school). But as Moll et al. point out, this is not a typical parent visit to correct or sort papers; the purpose of the parent's visit was to contribute intellectually to the students' academic activity.[37] Moll et al. are currently developing procedures to determine whether their project produces academic benefits for children in participating classrooms.

Taking a different tack, Ada (working in Northern California) and Delgado-Gaitán (working in Southern California) describe similar projects where parents participated in monthly meetings to discuss children's literature and to learn how to read with their elementary-age children.[38] These projects represent various types of home-school connections. The parent meetings and training sessions probably helped promote home learning activities (type 4, home learning); parents seemed to have become actively involved in community groups and parent networks affecting school policies and functioning (type 5, governing); and the home language was used for readings and discussions (type 7, accommodations to home cultures).

Ada reports that her monthly meetings drew sixty to a hundred parents (from a total student population in the district of 14,500). In Delgado-Gaitán's project, teachers nominated middle-elementary students whom they felt could benefit from added support in reading. Eleven families participated and were paid a nominal sum.

The respective reports suggest that participating parents and children found the experience extremely beneficial, although neither study reports data indicating effects on children's reading achievement. There seemed to be an increased appreciation among the parents for the importance of reading with children, and the amount of reading in the home, particularly for the children, probably increased accordingly. Ada and Delgado-Gaitán both report that parents came to feel increasingly empowered to take an active role in community and educational matters affecting them and their children.

In Delgado-Gaitán's project, parents who were trained in how to read with their children began asking children more questions during the reading sessions. In contrast to the baseline session, where parents interacted minimally with children, subsequent readings involved more frequent questioning by the parent. In a sense, this study confirms earlier studies, such as one by Henderson and García where Latino parents were trained to change aspects of their interactional patterns with children.[39] More generally, these studies confirm many other findings that parents can be trained to read and interact with their children in specified ways.[40] How well these changes are sustained after the intervention has ended is not known.

Several preschool programs have also explored various home-school connections to support children's development. In 1985, Dade County (Florida) instituted the Home Instruction Program for Preschool Youngsters (HIPPY) to serve Latino as well as black and Haitian children in low-income areas in Miami.[41] Paraprofessionals visit children's homes every other week and model activities that parents and children will work on for fifteen minutes daily. Evaluations of the original program model (developed in Israel) have been extremely favorable, and evaluations in the United States are currently underway. Another preschool program, this one for black and Puerto Rican preschoolers in Philadelphia, is based in a neighborhood Head Start center. The Parent-Child Learning Project (PCLP) will assist parents and children to develop literacy skills and help parents support their children's learning when they enter school.[42] No evaluation data are yet available.

Finally, the McAllen (Texas) school district has instituted a comprehensive parent involvement program districtwide.[43] The pre-K to 12 heavily Hispanic (88 percent) district uses a very wide range of parent involvement strategies at all levels, using the framework of activity types described earlier in this chapter. All parents sign contracts saying they will make certain that children do homework, that they will discuss with children what they learned at school each day, remind them of the need for discipline, and provide a minimum of three hours per week (without TV) of uninterrupted time devoted to a learning activity. The district offers classes for effective parenting, parent/student community evening study centers, and a wide range of special programs and activities too numerous to list. While each campus and the district office keep logs of all activities and survey data are analyzed to look for areas needing improvement, no evaluation data have yet been reported. Nonetheless, the district's clear commitment to productive and multidimensional home-school links is very impressive.

Gauging and Comparing the Effects of Home-School Connections

We have seen that home-school connections played a role in the successful school programs described earlier. Further, educators around the country are exploring various ways to bring schools and families into productive partnerships to help educate children from Spanish-speaking backgrounds. What are the relative effects of the various types of home-school connections? Which are the most "potent" or "effective"? These are important questions, particularly for educators wanting to find practices with the highest probability of helping students succeed.

Unfortunately, there is no simple answer. Hess and Holloway confronted the same problem when they posed a related question: Which family variables are the most important for affecting student achievement?

It is not possible to answer this question with results available at the present time. Not only is family research faced with problems of measurement error, experimenter effects, and generalizability, but variables with similar labels are defined in quite different ways, intensive studies use populations that differ from one another in socioeconomic and cultural properties, and statistical procedures of different studies often are not comparable.[44]

The situation is even more complex for the educator who wants to know which type of home-school connection is most likely to have the greatest positive effect on schools and students.

One reason is that different types of activities to promote home-school connections are likely to yield different types of results, which will defy direct comparisons.[45] Davis, a principal at a multicultural school, describes how he and his staff use various forms of written communication in four languages to keep parents informed and to solicit their ideas and suggestions.[46] But the effects of newsletters and notes home (type 2, communicating) cannot be compared to the effects of homework or other attempts to promote home learning (type 4). The latter are much more likely to help improve student achievement directly.[47]

The same can be said for the other types of strategies.[48] Their effects are likely to be fairly specific to the activities they promote. Information and training in child development and child discipline (type 1, parenting) are likely to affect parents' knowledge about and use of disciplining and child guidance techniques.[49] Promoting shared governance with parents (type 5, governance) can lead to parental empowerment, collaborative problem solving, and a more productive environment for school improvement.[50] Encouraging and training teachers to use interactional styles familiar to minority-group children (type 7, accommodation to home culture) can lead to increased participation of students in classroom lessons and activities.[51]

Each of these is a valid type of home-school connection, *but each is valid for different reasons*. The first question educators must ask themselves, therefore, is "What do we want to accomplish by promoting home-school connections?" They can then turn to deciding what type of home involvement, or home-school connection, is likely to accomplish their goals. Perhaps the most desirable, if ambitious, home-involvement program would involve a combination of types of home-school connections accomplishing a combination of goals. The McAllen, Texas, program appears to be an example of just such an ambitious effort.

Yet another problem in gauging the effects of different home-school connections is that while hundreds of practices exist, the effects of most have not been well evaluated, particularly with respect to their effects on student achievement.[52] Student achievement, of course, is what many educators consider the most important criterion for determining the effectiveness of any program or intervention. At the moment, it appears that promoting learning activities and opportunities to learn in the home (type 4, home learning)—in other words, influencing what is sometimes called the "curriculum of the home"— is likely to have the most direct effects on children's learning.[53] Other types of home-school connections probably accomplish other goals. Together, several types might have a multiplicative effect on important aspects of family and school functioning and on children's learning, growth, and development.

One clear message from the brief review of successful programs and promising practices is that more research and ongoing evaluations are needed to document the effects of various types of home-school connections on various outcomes. In particular, educators need to know which types have the strongest effects on student learning and school success in general. Further, since self-selection is often at work, particularly in projects that require large time commitments from parents, it would be important to determine the generalizability of some of the approaches discussed above. Parent training, for example, might get very strong effects, but if many parents are unwilling or unable to participate, its feasibility on a large scale becomes doubtful, and other approaches must be used to involve most, or ideally all, parents in one way or another.

For the moment, we can suggest three working hypotheses to guide educators and researchers, regardless of the student population.

(1) *The effects of various types of home-school connections are probably fairly specific; different types will yield different outcomes.* Newsletters

can make parents knowledgeable about what is happening at the school, but we should not expect them to improve student achievement unless they contain information that parents then actually use to influence, for example, TV viewing, time spent reading or doing homework, or trips to the library or museums. Similarly, parent participation in school governance is likely to help parents feel empowered, but we should not expect it to make parents more knowledgeable about disciplining or motivating children or helping them with homework, unless in the course of their governance activities parents are provided with pertinent information or training.

(2) Following from the first hypothesis, *cognitive or academic effects are most likely to be the result of home-school connections that specifically focus on cognitive or academic learning at home.* Although other types of home-school connections probably make a number of important contributions, student learning is most likely to be directly influenced by increasing and improving home learning opportunities through the use of homework or other organized activities designed to promote learning.

(3) As Epstein suggests, *schools with comprehensive home involvement programs encompassing various types of home-school connections probably help families and children in a large number of important ways.* If so, the more types of productive connections homes and schools can forge—in other words, the "thicker" and the more positive the network of relationships between homes and schools—the more positive and powerful the effects on children, families, and schools will be.

Issues in Forging Home-School Connections with Language-minority Families

Despite the promising approaches that have been described and the importance Hispanic parents attribute to their children's education, various studies and commentators suggest these parents are less involved in their children's schooling than are their middle-class Anglo-American counterparts.[54] Why this is so is unclear, but one set of reasons has already been suggested. Whether due to low educational levels or their unfamiliarity with U.S. schools, Hispanic parents tend to feel uncertain about helping their children in school. This suggests that providing them with useful and timely information about how they can support their children's learning is likely to increase their participation in children's education, thereby strengthening home-school links in ways that are likely to influence children's academic achievement.

CULTURAL OR SOCIOECONOMIC OBSTACLES

Another possible explanation for low levels of parent participation is that cultural or socioeconomic gaps separate families and schools, gaps that are inimical to productive home-school connections. Various commentators have suggested that culturally and economically marginalized groups feel unwelcome at the school and therefore make few efforts to establish contacts or respond to initiations from the school.[55] Because of the correlation between culture and educational or social status for some language minority populations, it is often difficult to distinguish which set of factors is responsible for observed behaviors. Moles, however, reports survey results that suggest the obstacles have more to do with limited education and low economic status, rather than with minority or ethnic group membership.[56] Parents with less than a high school education and very low incomes were two or three times as likely to have low levels of contact with the school; however, when these factors were controlled, there were no differences among whites, blacks, and Hispanics in their school-family contacts.[57]

LANGUAGE AND PARENT PARTICIPATION

Language is, of course, an extremely important issue when considering home-school connections with Latino families. Clearly, if parents do not understand newsletters or their children's homework, they will be unable to respond appropriately. Similarly, if parents cannot communicate with the school staff, other important avenues for productive home-school links will also be closed off.

Yet issues of language, culture, or social class can be dealt with, as the studies and projects cited previously strongly suggest. Parent participation will increase, for example, if language barriers come down. Ramírez, Yuen, and Ramey found that Latino parents of students in late-exit bilingual programs—where students' academic work was in their native language until late elementary school—were more likely to be aware that their children had homework and were more likely either to help with or monitor homework than parents of children in early-exit or immersion programs.[58] Ramírez et al. suggest this difference is due to the greater use of Spanish in late-exit programs, which permits greater parental involvement in home academic learning. (This interpretation must be accepted cautiously, however, since

Ramírez et al. also found that late-exit teachers assigned homework more frequently than teachers in the other types of programs.)

Many school districts are trying to accommodate to parents' language and schedules. For example, notices are sent home in both English and Spanish. Teachers might stay at school for extended hours during parent-teacher conference days. Under these circumstances, attendance at parent conferences or other school activities can be very high. A survey at one school in Southern California, in a very low-income area with a 90 percent Latino enrollment, revealed that 92 percent of parents attended the fall conference, and teachers made up an additional 5 percent subsequently; at another school in the same district, attendance was 88 percent, with 8 percent made up within a week.[59] Parent attendance at school functions such as open houses or evening student performances has traditionally been high in the district.[60] Some teachers hold meetings or workshops for parents, where they report that upwards of 50 percent of their students' parents attend.[61] One school also has a bilingual "homework liaison" that contacts parents when children are having difficulty turning in homework. Teachers report that this direct and immediate contact with parents, in a language they can understand, has helped improve the homework return rate.[62]

LANGUAGE USE IN THE HOME

There is, as well, another aspect to the language issue. In the past, educators often recommended to Spanish-speaking parents that they speak to their children in English to the extent possible. This, of course, was in an effort to help children acquire English quickly.[63] The most celebrated instance is found in Richard Rodríguez's moving but controversial memoir.[64] Rodríguez recounts how three nuns from the school he attended visited his parents one Saturday morning when he was in first grade and suggested to Mr. and Mrs. Rodríguez that they encourage their children to practice English at home. "In an instant," Rodríguez writes, his parents "agreed to give up the language (the sounds) that had revealed and accentuated our family's closeness. The moment after the visitors left, the change was observed. '*Ahora*, speak to us *en inglés*, my father and mother united to tell us" (p. 21). Whatever its other consequences, the switch was not without cost, however:

The special feeling of closeness at home was diminished. . . . We remained a loving family, but one greatly changed. No longer so close . . . [there] was a new quiet at home. The family's quiet was partly due to the fact, as we children learned more and more English, we shared fewer and fewer words with our parents. . . . [At dinner] my father at the other end of the table would chew and chew at his food, while he stared over the heads of his children (pp. 22-23).

Rodríguez became highly successful academically, and he is now a writer and commentator of some reputation. He certainly learned English very well. In his memoir, he attributes his success partly to his parents, who helped him become a "public" person, that is, someone who could participate fully in mainstream American society. Despite his initial anger and resentment over the abandonment of Spanish in his home, Rodríguez writes, the nuns and his parents did the right thing.

Although Rodríguez's memoir was highly publicized, it would be dangerous to generalize from this one case. First, it is impossible to establish that Rodríguez's success was related to his parents' decision to stop speaking Spanish with their children. Several studies challenge the notion that Spanish-speaking children do better in school if their parents speak to them in English.[65] Second, it is questionable how many parents would be as willing as the Rodríguezes were to abandon their native language when communicating with their children. Consider, for example, the findings of the National Commission on Secondary Schooling for Hispanics, which found that although "Hispanic parents are staunch supporters of solid English instruction" . . . they do object to instructional approaches "that deprive their children of Spanish, which often is the language of communication in their families. Parents fear that they will not be able to guide their youth and pass on their values."[66]

We do not, in fact, know what the effects would be if large numbers of parents and teachers did what Richard Rodríguez did— other than accelerating the loss of the native language in the United States[67] and probably interfering with important communicative and affective links between parents and children, as indeed happened in the Rodríguez family. In any event, this type of home-school connection is at best likely to be a two-edged sword, with the sharper edge likely to cut more deeply into important family, linguistic, and cultural ties.

RECENT EDUCATIONAL TRENDS AND HOME-SCHOOL CONNECTIONS

Many recent calls for educational reform are based upon the view that "learning is an active, constructive, and goal-oriented process"[68] rather than one in which individuals progressively acquire additional skills.[69] Despite these shifts in educational thinking, there is evidence that many working class families place a higher value on their children's acquisition of skills than on the construction of meaning. In the area of literacy acquisition, many minority parents and parents from a low socioeconomic level construe learning to read as a process of learning decoding and other skills, not as a process driven by children's interest in making meaning from text.[70]

When we consider home-school connections, we cannot ignore parents' own constructions about how children learn. I will illustrate with a recently completed intervention that yielded some unexpected results.[71]

For a study of home and school effects on early literacy development, we created a set of simple, photocopied story books in Spanish ("Libros") for teachers to read with children at school, then send home. Other than a brief video some of the parents saw, there was no real parent training involved. The teachers suggested to parents during the fall conference that they read the books with the children as they would any other children's book. Parents were told that repeated readings, accompanied by conversation focusing on the meaning of the texts would be especially helpful, and that if the children memorized the texts that would be fine. (Teachers made a point of saying this to parents since in a pilot study we found that parents expressed skepticism over the value of children simply memorizing texts.) The teachers also used the books in their classrooms, along with other materials developed to accompany them.

As expected, we found that children in kindergarten classrooms using the books were more advanced in their literacy development than children in classrooms using the district's basal program supplemented by phonics-oriented worksheets provided by our study.[72] We were surprised, however, by a second finding, this one coming from our direct observations over the school year in ten homes (five in each condition). Although children in the "story book" classrooms had higher levels of early reading development than children in the "readiness and phonics" classrooms overall, use of the story books at home was *unrelated* to individual children's literacy development. In contrast, use of the phonics worksheets was *strongly related* to individual children's literacy development.

We think the reason for these paradoxical findings has to do with parents' own understandings of how children learn to read. The Latino parents with whom we work equate learning to read with learning to decode and not with learning to construct meaning from written texts.[73] From the standpoint of learning to read, they attach less importance to children hearing books or having opportunities to "pretend-read" or talk about books, and more importance to children engaging in repetitive, drill-like activities—*"para que se les grabe"* ("so that they [letters or words] become 'recorded' [in children's minds]").[74] Consequently, whether they used the "Libros" or the worksheets, parents constructed literacy events heavy with repetition and largely devoid of attention to meaning. (This description of the parents' reading behavior with their children is consistent with the baseline readings in Delgado-Gaitán's study.[75] Before the training, there was minimal interaction between parent and child about the book being read.)

The booklets did not lend themselves to this sort of drill-like usage; consequently, their use at home was unrelated to kindergarten literacy attainment. In contrast, there was a congruence between the worksheets and parents' beliefs about learning to read; this congruence led, we believe, to their more effective use in the homes. The more children used the worksheets at home, the higher their literacy attainment (on a broad spectrum of measures) at the end of the school year.

These results do not suggest that teachers ought not send home books and other "real" reading materials. But they do underscore the importance of considering the family context that will receive materials from school or receive some other form of intervention. If parents do not construct the process of literacy (or numeracy) development in the same way that many educators and researchers are now constructing it, this should be taken into account as we seek to forge productive home-school links.

One possible resolution to the dilemma uncovered by our study is parent training. But although training parents how to read to their children can produce at least short-term changes, as we have already seen, we must be concerned about whether training programs will tend to exclude substantial numbers of parents who are unable or unwilling to participate. If home-school connections are to make a serious impact on the school success of large numbers of language-minority youngsters, rather than helping only a select few, schools need to reach all families. This is one reason why it is so important to be mindful of the various types of connections that can be forged, and within those types, of the wide range of possible activities that can be used to include as many families as possible. Moreover, it underscores why educators must have reliable information about the effects of various types of home-school connections so that they can use strategies that fit their particular situation and have a reasonable chance of producing desired effects.

For many educators, whether home-school connections affect student achievement is no longer an issue. Nor do many doubt they can help improve language-minority students' chances for school success by forging and nurturing productive home-school relations, particularly those that influence the "curriculum of the home." It is difficult to imagine, in fact, any serious attempt to improve language-minority children's school achievement that does not involve efforts to link the home and school productively.

Educators have available a wide range of possible ways to promote home-school connections for the purpose of helping to improve these students' chances of success in school. Different types of home-school connections probably lead to different types of effects; comprehensive programs to link home and school, utilizing a variety of types of connections, probably have the greatest possibility of producing comprehensive, meaningful, and substantive effects. The real question now is, How can educators mobilize the resources most homes possess—including the interest and ability of most parents—in order to help all language-minority children be as successful as possible at school? This is clearly the agenda for the 1990s.

This chapter was made possible by grants from the Spencer Foundation and the National Institute for Child Health and Human Development. My thanks to Joyce Epstein for her valuable assistance and to Ellen Dorfman Goldenberg, Ronald Gallimore, Leslie Reese, and Javier Tapia for their comments and suggestions. Thanks also to the many colleagues who shared their work with me.

Notes

1. Robert D. Hess and Susan H. Holloway, "Family and School as Educational Institutions," in *Review of Child Development Research, vol. 7: The Family*, edited by Ross D. Parke (Chicago: University of Chicago Press, 1984), pp. 179-222.

2. Benjamin Bloom, "The Effect of the Home Environment on Children's School Achievement," in Benjamin Bloom, *All Our Children Learning* (New York: McGraw-Hill, 1981).

3. J. David Ramírez, Sandra D. Yuen, Dena R. Ramey, and Bárbara J. Merino, *Longitudinal Study of Immersion Programs for Language Minority Children*, First Year Report (San Mateo, CA: Aguirre International, 1986). These authors report that foreign born parents of Spanish-speaking children have been in the United States an average of fifteen to sixteen years and that their average years of schooling is seven (pp. 196-197). This suggests that, in general, foreign born parents received their formal education in their native countries.

4. U.S. Bureau of the Census, *The Hispanic Population in the United States: March, 1991*, Current Population Reports, Series P-20, no. 455 (Washington, DC: U.S. Government Printing Office, October, 1991).

5. Oliver Moles, "Disadvantaged Parents' Participation in Their Children's Education" (Paper presented at the Annual Meeting of the American Educational Research Association, Boston, 1990).

6. Committee on Preschool and Parental Education, "The Family as an Educational Agency," in *Preschool and Parental Education*, Twenty-eighth Yearbook of the National Society for the Study of Education, Part 1, edited by Guy M. Whipple (Bloomington, IL: Public School Publishing Company, 1929), p. 71. Emphasis added.

7. Joyce Epstein, "Toward an Integrated Theory of School and Family Connections: Teacher Practices and Parent Involvement," in *Social Intervention: Potential and Constraints*, edited by Klaus Hurrelmann, Franz-Xaver Kaufmann, and Friedrich Lösel (New York and Berlin: de Gruyter, 1987). For a different perspective, see Barbara Goodson, Janet Swartz, and Mary Ann Millsap, *Working with Families: Promising Programs to Help Parents Support Young Children's Learning*, Final Report to the U.S. Department of Education (Cambridge, MA: Abt Associates, 1991).

8. Committee on Preschool and Parental Education, "History of the Movement in Preschool and Parental Education," in *Preschool and Parental Education*, Twenty-eighth Yearbook of the National Society for the Study of Education, Part 1, edited by Guy M. Whipple (Bloomington, IL: Public School Publishing Co., 1929), pp. 7-43.

9. Joyce Epstein, "School and Family Partnerships," in *Encyclopedia of Educational Research*, 6th edition, edited by Marvin C. Alkin (New York: Macmillan, 1992), pp. 1139-1152.

10. Ronald Gallimore, Joan W. Boggs, and Cathie E. Jordan, *Culture, Behavior and Education: A Study of Hawaiian-Americans* (Beverly Hills, CA: Sage, 1974); Evelyn Jacob and Cathie E. Jordan, eds., "Explaining the School Performance of Minority Students," *Anthropology and Education Quarterly* 18, no. 4 (1987): 259-367; George Spindler and Louise Spindler, *The Interpretive Ethnography of Education: At Home and Abroad* (Hillsdale, NJ: Erlbaum, 1987); Henry Trueba, "Culturally Based Explanations of Minority Students' Academic Achievement," *Anthropology and Education Quarterly* 19 (1988): 270-287.

11. See Molefi Kete Asante, "Afrocentric Curriculum," *Educational Leadership* 49, no. 4 (1991/1992): 28-31.

12. See, for example, Kathryn Au and Jana M. Mason, "Social Organizational Factors in Learning to Read: The Balance of Rights Hypothesis," *Reading Research Quarterly* 17 (1981-82): 115-152.

13. Shirley B. Heath, *Ways with Words: Language, Life, and Work in Communities and Classrooms* (Cambridge, Eng.: Cambridge University Press, 1983).

14. Luis C. Moll and J. Greenberg, "Creating Zones of Possibilities: Combining Social Contexts for Instruction," in *Vygotsky and Education*, edited by Luis C. Moll (Cambridge, Eng.: Cambridge University Press, 1990).

15. S. Jim Campos and H. Robert Keatinge, "The Carpintería Language Minority Student Experience: From Theory, to Practice, to Success," in *Minority Education: From Shame to Struggle*, edited by Tove Skutnabb-Kangas and Jim Cummins (Clevedon, Eng.: Multilingual Matters, 1988).

16. Concha Delgado-Gaitán, "Involving Parents in School: A Process of Empowerment," *American Journal of Education* 100 (1991): 20-46. Delgado-Gaitán provides additional information about the parental involvement component of the program. In addition, I know from having visited the program in 1986 that the teacher was highly successful in forging very productive home-school links. For vacations she developed calendars the children took home. Each day contained a suggested learning

activity for children and parents to work on together. Her classroom program provided children with a wide range of active and highly motivating learning opportunities.

17. Claude Goldenberg and Ronald Gallimore, "Local Knowledge, Research Knowledge, and Educational Change: A Case Study of First-grade Spanish Reading Improvement," *Educational Researcher* 20, no. 8 (1991): 2-14.

18. Thomas Carter and Michael Chatfield, "Effective Bilingual Schools: Implications for Policy and Practice," *American Journal of Education* 95 (1986): 200-232.

19. Tamara Lucas, Rosemary Henze, and Rubén Donato, "Promoting the Success of Latino Language-minority Students: An Exploratory Study of Six High Schools," *Harvard Educational Review* 60, no. 3 (1990): 315-340.

20. Ibid., p. 325.

21. Ibid., p. 334.

22. David Stevenson and David Baker, "The Family-School Relation and the Child's School Performance," *Child Development* 58 (1987): 1348-1357. For a different view, see Sanford Dornbush, Phillip Ritter, P. Herbert Leiderman, Donald Roberts, and Michael J. Fraleigh, "The Relation of Parenting to Adolescent School Performance," *Child Development* 58 (1987): 1244-1257.

23. See, for example, Epstein, "School and Family Partnerships"; M. Elizabeth Graue, Thomas Weinstein, and Herbert J. Walberg, "School-based Home Instruction and Learning: A Quantitative Synthesis," *Journal of Educational Research* 76 (1983): 351-360; R. A. Paschal, Thomas Weinstein, and Herbert J. Walberg, "The Effects of Homework on Learning: A Quantitative Synthesis," *Journal of Educational Research* 78, no. 2 (1984): 97-104.

24. Claude Goldenberg and Ronald Gallimore, "Teaching California's Diverse Student Population: The Common Ground between Educational and Cultural Research," *California Public Schools Forum* 3 (Autumn 1989): 41-56. See also, Herbert J. Walberg, "Synthesis of Research on Teaching," in *Handbook of Research on Teaching*, 3rd ed., edited by Merlin C. Wittrock (New York: Macmillan, 1986), pp. 214-229, for a discussion of the applicability of general findings to specific groups or categories of students. "Most research syntheses yield results that are fairly robust in sign and magnitude across . . . categories of students" (p. 217). Walberg argues that it is scientifically and educationally sound to apply general, robust findings across a wide range of students and populations rather than to assume that procedures must be tailor-made to various individual groups.

25. Carmen Delgado-Contreras and A. Reynaldo Contreras, "Mexican-American Parent Involvement: A Case Study of the First Stage of School Participation" (Paper presented at the Annual Meeting of the American Educational Research Association, Chicago, 1990); Concha Delgado-Gaitán, *Literacy for Empowerment: The Role of Parents in Their Children's Education* (New York: Falmer, 1990); Claude Goldenberg, "Low-income Hispanic Parents' Contributions to Their First-grade Children's Word Recognition Skills," *Anthropology and Education Quarterly* 18 (1987): 149-179; Henry Trueba and Concha Delgado-Gaitán, *Crossing Cultural Borders: Education for Immigrant Families in America* (London: Falmer Press, 1991).

26. Goldenberg, "Low-income Hispanic Parents' Contributions to Their First-grade Children's Word Recognition Skills," pp. 173, 174.

27. Concha Delgado-Gaitán, "Sociocultural Change through Literacy: Toward the Empowerment of Families," in *Literacy across Languages and Cultures*, edited by Bernardo Ferdman, Rose Marie Weber, and Arnulfo Ramírez (New York: State University of New York Press, forthcoming).

28. Trueba and Delgado-Gaitán, *Crossing Cultural Borders*.

29. Robert A. Levine, "Human Parental Care: Universal Goals, Cultural Strategies, Individual Behavior," in *Parental Behavior in Diverse Human Societies, New Directions for Child Development*, no. 40, edited by Robert A. Levine, Patricia M. Miller, and Mary Maxwell West (San Francisco: Jossey-Bass, 1988), pp. 3-11.

30. Delgado-Gaitán, *Literacy for Empowerment*; Goldenberg, "Low-income Hispanic Parents' Contributions to Their First-grade Children's Word Recognition Skills."

31. Unpublished interview, August 3, 1986.

32. Unpublished interview, August 14, 1986.

33. Goldenberg, "Low-income Hispanic Parents' Contributions to Their First-grade Children's Word Recognition Skills."

34. Moll and Greenberg, "Creating Zones of Possibilities."

35. Luis Moll, Cathy Amanti, Deborah Neff, and Norma González, "Funds of Knowledge for Teaching: Using a Qualitative Approach to Connect Homes and Classrooms," *Theory into Practice* 31, no. 2 (1992): 132-141.

36. Ibid., p. 132.

37. Ibid., p. 138.

38. Alma F. Ada, "The Pájaro Valley Experience: Working with Spanish-speaking Parents to Develop Children's Reading and Writing Skills through the Use of Children's Literature," in *Minority Education: From Shame to Struggle*, edited by Tove Skutnabb-Kangas and Jim Cummins (Clevedon, Eng.: Multilingual Matters, 1988), pp. 223-238; Delgado-Gaitán, "Sociocultural Change through Literacy."

39. Ronald W. Henderson and Angela B. García, "The Effects of Parent Training Program on the Question-asking Behavior of Mexican-American Children," *American Educational Research Journal* 10 (1973): 193-201.

40. D. Toomey, "An Examination of Some U.K., U.S.A., and Australian Studies of Parents and Children's Literacy Development: Lessons for School Practice," Unpublished manuscript, Center for the Study of Community, Education, and Social Change, La Trobe University, Australia, n.d.); Keith J. Topping, *Parents as Educators: Training Parents to Teach Their Children* (Cambridge, MA: Brookline Books, 1986).

41. Goodson, Swartz, and Millsap, *Working with Families*.

42. Vivian Gadsden, "Parent-Child Learning Project (PCLP): An Intergenerational Literacy Program Connecting School, Parents, and Children in Learning" (Paper presented at a conference on New Directions in Child and Family Research: Shaping Head Start in the Nineties, Arlington, VA., June, 1991).

43. Goodson et al., *Working with Families*; Pablo Pérez, "Addressing the Needs of Hispanic Parents through a Multifaceted Program" (Paper presented at the Annual Meeting of the American Educational Research Association, Chicago, 1991).

44. Hess and Holloway, "Family and School as Educational Institutions," p. 193.

45. My thanks to Joyce Epstein for helping to clarify this point for me.

46. Bruce C. Davis, "A Successful Parent Involvement Program," *Educational Leadership* 47, no. 2 (1989): 21-23.

47. Graue et al., "School-based Home Instruction and Learning"; Paschal et al., "The Effects of Homework on Learning"; Harris Cooper, *Homework* (New York: Longman, 1989).

48. Ron Brandt, "On Parents and Schools: A Conversation with Joyce Epstein," *Educational Leadership* 47, no. 2 (1989): 24-27.

49. Goodson et al., *Working with Families*.

50. Wayne B. Jennings, "How To Organize Successful Parent Advisory Committees," *Educational Leadership* 47, no. 2 (1989): 42-45.

51. Au and Mason, "Social Organizational Factors in Learning to Read."

52. Epstein, "School and Family Partnerships"; Moles, "Disadvantaged Parents' Participation in Their Children's Education."

53. Graue et al., "School-based Home Instruction and Learning"; Moles, "Disadvantaged Parents' Participation in Their Children's Education"; Paschal et al., "The Effects of Homework on Learning"; Walberg, "Families as Partners in Educational Productivity"; Bloom, "The Effect of the Home Environment on Children's School Achievement."

54. Delgado-Contreras and Contreras, "Mexican-American Parent Involvement"; Delgado-Gaitán, *Literacy for Empowerment*; Moles, "Who Wants Parent Involvement?" idem, "Disadvantaged Parents' Participation in Their Children's Education."

55. Annette Lareau, *Home Advantage: Social Class and Parental Intervention in Elementary Education* (London: Falmer Press, 1989); Delgado-Gaitán, "Involving Parents in School"; Trueba, "Culturally Based Explanations of Minority Students' Academic Achievement."

56. Moles, "Disadvantaged Parents' Participation in Their Children's Education."

57. Ibid.

58. J. David Ramírez, Sandra D. Yuen, and Dena R. Ramey, *Longitudinal Study of Structured English Immersion Strategy, Early-exit, and Late-exit Transitional Bilingual Education Programs for Language Minority Children*, Final Report, Executive Summary (San Mateo, CA: Aguirre International, 1991).

59. Unpublished data, 1987, 1991.

60. A. Millican, "Lennox Schools Give Parents Lessons to Use at Home," Los Angeles *Times*, South Bay edition, 14 June 1991.

61. L. Edgar and A. Sosa, "The Parent Meeting: Involving Parents in Their Children's Education" (Workshop presented at Torrance Area Reading Council Miniconference, Torrance, CA, February, 1990), and personal communication.

62. Unpublished data.

63. Kenji Hakuta, *Mirror of Language: The Debate on Bilingualism* (New York: Basic Books, 1986).

64. Richard Rodríguez, *Hunger of Memory: The Education of Richard Rodríguez* (Toronto: Bantam, 1982).

65. David Dolson, "The Effects of Spanish Home Language Use on the Scholastic Performance of Hispanic Pupils," *Journal of Multilingual and Multicultural Development* 6 (1985): 135-155; Lourdes Díaz Soto, "Families as Learning Environments" (Paper presented at the Annual Meeting of the American Educational Research Association, Chicago, 1991).

66. Hispanic Policy Development Project, *"Make Something Happen": Hispanics and Urban High School Reform*, vol. 1 (New York: Hispanic Policy Development Project, 1984), p. 38.

67. Hakuta, *Mirror of Language*.

68. Thomas J. Shuell, "Cognitive Conceptions of Learning," *Review of Educational Research* 56 (1986): 411-436.

69. California State Department of Education, *English-Language Arts Framework for California Public Schools* (Sacramento, CA: California State Department of Education, 1987); Ralph T. Putnam, Magdalene Lampert, and Penelope L. Peterson, "Alternative Perspectives on Knowing Mathematics in Elementary Schools," *Review of Research in Education*, vol. 16 (Washington, DC: American Educational Research Association, 1990), pp. 57-150; Lauren Resnick, "Constructing Knowledge in School," in *Development and Learning: Conflict or Congruence?* edited by Lynn S. Liben (Hillsdale, NJ: Erlbaum, 1987).

70. Peggy Daisey and Ann Murray, "Parents and Teachers: A Comparison of Perceptions and Attitudes toward Literacy Growth" (Paper presented at New Directions in Child and Family Research: Shaping Head Start in the Nineties, Arlington, VA, 1991); Lisa D. Delpit, "Skills and Other Dilemmas of a Progressive Black Educator," *Harvard Educational Review* 56 (1986): 379-385; Claude Goldenberg, "Methods, Early Literacy, and Home-School Compatibilities: A Response to Sledge et al.," *Anthropology and Education Quarterly* 19 (1988): 425-432; Deborah Stipek, Sharon Milburn, Darlene Galluzzo, and Denise Daniels, "Parents' Beliefs about Appropriate Education for Young Children," *Journal of Applied Developmental Psychology*, in press.

71. Claude Goldenberg, Leslie Reese, and Ronald Gallimore, "Effects of School Literacy Materials on Latino Children's Home Experiences and Early Reading Achievement," *American Journal of Education* 100 (1992): 497-536.

72. Claude Goldenberg, "Evaluation of a Balanced Approach to Literacy Instruction for Spanish-speaking Kindergartners" (Paper presented at the Annual Meeting of the American Educational Research Association, Boston, 1990).

73. Goldenberg, "Methods, Early Literacy, and Home-School Compatibilities."

74. Goldenberg et al., "Effects of School Literacy Materials on Latino Children's Home Experiences and Early Reading Achievement."

75. Delgado-Gaitán, "Sociocultural Change through Literacy."

Glossary

ACTFL. American Council on the Teaching of Foreign Languages.

BILINGUAL EDUCATION ACT. Title VII of the Elementary and Secondary Education Act.

BILINGUAL IMMERSION EDUCATION. Programs combining most significant features of bilingual education for language minority students and immersion education for language majority students.

CIVIL RIGHTS ACT (1964). Prohibits discrimination on grounds of race, color, or national origin in programs receiving federal funds.

DUAL LANGUAGE PROGRAMS. Programs using two languages (the child's home language and the second language) in instruction.

EARLY EXIT PROGRAMS. Programs with full initial access to the curriculum in the students' native language with early transition to English by grade 3.

ENGLISH ONLY MOVEMENT. A movement to prohibit use of languages other than English in local, state, and federal governments.

ENRICHMENT BILINGUAL EDUCATION. Bilingual instruction provided to monolingual students as an academic enhancement.

EQUAL EDUCATION OPPORTUNITIES ACT (1974). Prohibits denial of equal education opportunity through "failure of an educational agency to take appropriate action to overcome language barriers that impede required participation of its students in its instructional program."

ESEA. Elementary and Secondary Education Act.

ESL (ENGLISH AS A SECOND LANGUAGE). Instruction in English for language minority students.

L1. Student's first language.

L2. Student's second language.

LANGUAGE ASSESSMENT BATTERY. Includes tests to measure oral and written proficiency in Spanish and English.

LANGUAGE ASSESSMENT SCALES. Scales used to rate students on oral and written proficiency in Spanish and English.

LATE EXIT PROGRAMS. Programs providing full access to the curriculum in the student's native language with gradual increase in English; native language instruction sustained throughout elementary school.

251

LEP (LIMITED ENGLISH PROFICIENT). Limited proficiency in English skills; LEP is a label applied officially by the U.S. government to language minority students.

LM OR LMS (LANGUAGE MINORITY STUDENTS). Students coming from homes where English is not the predominant language of communication between parents and children.

MAINTENANCE PROGRAMS. Programs stressing preservation of students' home language and culture, with gradual easing into English as the language of instruction.

MONOLINGUALISM. The capacity to use only one language.

NABE. National Association for Bilingual Education.

NELS. Home speakers of non-English languages.

OCR. Office of Civil Rights.

ONE-WAY BILINGUAL EDUCATION. Speakers of one language are placed in a bilingual classroom where they learn the first language while they develop the second.

SHELTERED ESL PROGRAM. Programs for language minority students where English is the language of instruction. Content-area teachers, usually at the secondary level, pursue ESL goals by mediating understanding for the students.

STRUCTURED ENGLISH IMMERSION. Programs where almost all instruction is in English, with a minimum component of special services for language minority students that is usually available for no more than two or three years.

TESOL. Teachers of English to Speakers of Other Languages.

TRANSITIONAL BILINGUAL EDUCATION PROGRAMS. Programs emphasizing relatively rapid transition from an instructional program with native language support (accompanied by English language development) to an all-English instructional program.

TWO-WAY BILINGUAL EDUCATION. Speakers of both languages are together in a bilingual classroom to learn each others' language and work academically in both languages.

U.S. ENGLISH. An organization in support of the English Only movement.

ZONE OF PROXIMAL DEVELOPMENT. The gap between what a student can accomplish independently and what he or she can accomplish with adult help. According to Vygotsky, instruction should be targeted at that area.

Name Index

Abi-Nader, Jeannette, 63
Ada, Alma F., 235, 248
Alatis, James E., 62, 193
Alatis, Penelope, 193
Aliotti, Nicholas C., 34
Alkin, Marvin C., 246
Allen, Patrick, 222
Altman, Howard, 193
Alvarez, María, 170
Amanti, Cathy, 223, 234, 248
Ambert, Alba, 170, 196
Ammon, Mary, 85, 195
Ammon, Paul, 85, 195
Anderson, Richard B., 86, 182, 196
Andersson, Theodore, 36, 39, 59, 61, 62, 63, 83, 86
Andrade, R., 223
Apple, Michael, 59, 62, 64
Arias, M. Beatriz, 1
Armbruster, Bonnie, 182, 196
Asante, Molefi Kete, 246
Astuto, Terry A., 61
Au, Kathryn H., 34, 194, 246, 249
August, Diane, 11, 32, 193

Bach, E., 86
Bain, B., 34
Bain, Josie G., 30
Baker, David, 247
Baker, Keith A., 32, 42, 58, 60, 63, 83, 84
Banks, Cherry A. McGee, 63
Banks, James A., 63
Barnes, Robert E., 13, 32
Barnett-Mizrahi, Carol, 31, 34, 168, 169, 197
Baron, Dennis, 59, 61, 62
Barona, Andrés, 33
Barrera, Rosalinde, 180, 196
Bascia, Nina, 141, 142
Beard, Timothy, 142
Beebe, Leslie, 52, 63
Beebe, Von Nieda, 62
Bell, Terrel H., 2, 14, 32
Benevides, Alfredo, 194
Ben-Zeev, Sandra, 34
Bennett, Barbara, 191, 198
Bennett, Carl A., 86
Bennett, William, 2, 14, 66

Benton, Richard A., 30
Berliner, David C., 33, 194
Berman, Paul, 95, 111, 222
Bernstein, Richard, 62, 63
Betances, Samuel, 4, 24, 30
Bethel, Thomas, 61, 62
Biber, Douglas, 111, 210, 223
Biddle, B. J., 84
Billings, David K., 63
Blair, Robert, 178, 195
Bloom, Benjamin, 225, 245, 249
Bloomfield, Leonard, 86
Boggs, Joan W., 246
Boruch, Robert F., 76, 85, 86
Boyer, Ernest L., 142
Boyer, Mildred, 36, 39, 59, 61, 62, 63, 83, 86
Brandt, Ron, 248
Bransford, John, 223
Bricker, Kathryn, 46
Brinton, Donna, 110, 111
Brooks, Nelson, 193
Brown, H. D., 85
Burt, Marina K., 62
Bush, George, 146

Calfee, Robert, 195
Campbell, Donald T., 76, 85, 86
Campbell, Ernest Q., 60
Campos, S. Jim, 229, 230, 246
Canales, JoAnn, 168, 169
Carini, Patricia, 155, 169
Carpenter, Thomas P., 61, 63
Carrasco, Robert L., 169, 170, 194
Carroll, David, 169
Carter, Thomas P., 31, 222, 230, 247
Casanova, Ursula, 1
Castañeda, Lilian Vega, 141
Castellanos, Diego, 31
Cazden, Courtney B., 30, 35, 169, 170, 224
Cerva, Thomas R., 86
Cervantes, Carolina, 182, 196
Chambers, Jay, 111, 222
Chamot, Anna, 197
Chang, Hedy N., 142
Chapa, Jorge, 222
Chatfield, Michael, 230, 247
Chaudron, Craig, 71, 85

253

Chelemer, Carole, 61
Cheng, Maisy, 33
Chipman, Susan, 20, 33
Chittenden, Edward, 146, 168
Chomsky, Noam, 86
Clark, David L., 61
Clark, Ellen Riojas, 190, 193, 194, 198
Clarke, Mark A., 142
Clune, William H., 61
Cochran-Smith, Marilyn, 176, 194
Cohen, Andrew, 85
Cohen, David K., 60, 142
Cohen, Elizabeth, 197
Cole, Michael, 169, 205, 223
Coleman, James S., 60, 63
Coles, Gary J., 63, 84
Collier, Virginia P., 82, 110
Commins, Nancy L., 223
Conant, James, 174, 194
Contreras, A. Reynaldo, 247, 249
Cooper, Harris, 248
Corbett, H. Dickson, 141
Corcoran, Thomas B., 131, 142, 143
Cordasco, Francesco, 59, 61
Coughran, Consuelo, 193, 197
Crandall, JoAnn, 197
Crawford, James, 31, 32, 33, 59, 60, 61,
    62, 83, 111, 222
Crymes, R. H., 85
Cuellar, José, 223
Cummins, Jim, 19, 25, 26, 29, 30, 33, 34,
    83, 112, 132, 143, 168; 203, 214, 222,
    223, 224, 246, 248
Cziko, Gary, 82, 86, 87

D'Anglejan, A., 33
Daisey, Peggy, 250
Damico, Jack S., 170
Daniels, Denise, 250
Danoff, Malcolm N., 63, 84
Davis, Bruce C., 237, 248
DeAvila, Edward, 19, 33, 169, 197
DeKanter, Adriana A., 32, 42, 58, 60, 63,
    83, 84
Delgado-Contreras, Carmen, 247, 249
Delgado-Gaitán, Concha, 35, 185, 198,
    235, 244, 246, 247, 248, 249, 250
Delpit, Lisa D., 250
DeVillar, Robert A., 112
Dewey, John, 155
Díaz, Raphael M., 19, 22, 23, 30, 33, 34
Díaz, Stephen, 27, 33, 35, 169, 170, 194,
    203, 223
Dickerson, A., 86
Dodge, Bernie, 224

Dolson, David P., 110, 249
Donato, Rubén, 141, 142, 143, 230, 247
Dornbush, Sanford, 247
Douglas, William, 48
Drudy, Patricia, 170
Drum, Priscilla, 195
Dulay, Heidi, 62
Duncan, Sharon, 19, 33, 169
Dunkin, M. J., 84
Duran, Richard P., 169
Dutcher, Nadine, 112
Dworin, J., 223
Dyson, Anne H., 112

Edelsky, Carol, 19, 33, 160, 170, 183,
    196
Edgar, L., 249
Enright, D. Scott, 112
Epstein, Joyce, 226, 227, 229, 239, 246,
    247, 248, 249
Epstein, Noel, 60, 61, 62, 83
Erickson, Frederick, 35, 142
Erlebacher, A. E., 86
Escobedo, Theresa, 196

Fairchild, Halford H., 86, 87, 111, 197
Faltis, Christian J., 84, 111, 112, 171,
    179, 193, 194, 195, 196
Farrar, Eleanor, 142
Feinberg, Stephen E., 85, 87
Ferdman, Bernardo M., 30, 34, 35, 63,
    247
Ferguson, Charles A., 31
Fillmore, Charles J., 86, 112
Fillmore, Lily Wong, see Wong Fillmore,
    Lily
Firestone, William A., 141
Fishman, Joshua A., 5, 30, 31, 34, 36, 59,
    61, 110, 169
Fitzgibbon, Thomas, 168
Flaxman, Erwin, 143
Flores, Bárbara M., 155, 160, 170, 178,
    181, 183, 195, 196, 223
Fordham, Signithia, 63
Foster, Charles, 62
Fraleigh, Michael J., 247
Franke, David, 224
Freeman, David, 169, 178, 193, 195
Freeman, Yvonne, 169, 178, 182, 195,
    196
Friedlander, Monica, 142
Fullan, Michael G., 142

Gadsden, Vivian, 248
Gaies, S. J., 71, 85

Gallego, Margaret, 205, 207
Gallimore, Ronald, 112, 195, 197, 230, 246, 247, 250
Galluzzo, Darlene, 250
Gándara, Patricia, 111, 222
García, Angela B., 235, 248
García, Carlos, 142
García, Erminda, 195
García, Eugene E., 11, 32, 33, 193, 194, 196
García, Ofelia, 30
Gardner, Howard, 155, 169
Gardner, Marta Ann, 185, 186, 187, 190, 197, 198
Garza, S. Ana, 194
Gass, Susan, 197
Genishi, Celia, 112
Giglioli, P. P., 35
Giles, Howard, 52, 63
Gillmore, G., 86
Glaser, Robert, 20, 33
Glazer, Nathan, 45, 61, 62
Gold, Gerald, 62
Goldenberg, Claude, 180, 181, 195, 196, 225, 230, 247, 248, 250
Golubchick, L., 169
Gómez, Mary, 194
González, Josué M., 8, 31
González, Norma, 223, 234, 248
González, Sharon, 195
Goodlad, John I., 115, 127, 141, 142, 174, 194
Goodson, Barbara, 246, 248
Gordon, Edward, 33
Gowan, John C., 34
Graue, M. Elizabeth, 247, 248, 249
Greenberg, Hinda F., 168
Greenberg, James, 35, 112, 170, 223, 234, 246, 248
Grosjean, Francois, 51, 63
Grosse, Christine Uber, 178, 179, 195
Grouws, Douglas, 60
Guerra, Juan, 222
Guntermann, Gail, 194
Guthrie, Grace, 194

Hakuta, Kenji, 19, 20, 22, 23, 29, 33, 34, 35, 59, 60, 79, 82, 83, 86, 87, 220, 224, 249
Handscombe, Jean, 142, 197
Hargett, Gary, 169
Harley, Birget, 222
Harms, R. T., 86
Hartfield, Beverly, 62
Hayakawa, S. I., 12
Hayes-Bautista, David E., 222

Heath, Shirley Brice, 7, 26, 31, 34, 35, 86, 188, 197, 201, 202, 222, 246
Hellmuth, John, 86
Henderson, Ronald W., 235, 248
Henze, Rosemary, 141, 142, 143, 230, 247
Herman, Joan L., 30
Hernández, Carmen, 191
Hess, Robert D., 237, 245, 248
Hiebert, James, 61
Hiller, Richard, 168
Hobson, Carol J., 60
Holloway, Susan H, 237, 245, 248
Hornberger, Nancy H., 59, 60
Hoskins, Julie, 197
Huddy, Leonie, 32
Hudelson, Sarah, 160, 170, 181, 183, 194, 195, 196, 197
Hughes, Robert, 62
Hunter, Sue, 170
Hurrelmann, Klaus, 246
Hymes, Dell, 5, 30, 31, 35, 224

Ianco-Worrall, Anita D., 34
Imhoff, Gary, 31, 32, 60
Inger, Morton, 143
Intili, JoAnn, 197

Jacob, Evelyn, 246
Jacobson, Rodolfo, 84, 111, 177, 195
Janikas, Kristen, 224
Jefferson, Thomas, 6
Jennings, Wayne B., 248
John-Steiner, Vera, 169
John, Vera P., 30, 35, 224
Johnson, Donna, 196
Johnson, Marietta, 155
Johnson, Susan M., 141
Jordan, Cathie E., 246
Joyce, Bruce, 191, 198

Kaczmerek, Kitty, 195
Kagan, Sharon L., 110
Kane, Diane, 170
Karplus, Robert, 197
Katz, Anne, 127, 141
Kaufmann, Franz-Xaver, 246
Keatinge, H. Robert, 229, 230, 246
Keller, Gary D., 61
Kempler, Daniel, 112
Kennedy, Graeme, 200, 203, 222
Kessler, Carolyn, 19, 33, 112
Kilpatrick, William, 155
Kim, Yungho, 141
King, Catherine, 205
Kjolseth, Rolf, 3, 30

Knapp, Michael S., 61
Knop, C., 85
Kopp, Quentin, 47
Kozol, Jonathan, 60
Krashen, Stephen, 111, 170, 184, 197, 210, 223
Kreidler, Carol, 194
Kuhn, Thomas S., 60

La Fontaine, Hernán, 169
Labov, William, 26, 35, 86
Lado, Robert, 86
Lakatos, Imre, 60
Lambert, Wallace E., 21, 22, 23, 24, 25, 30, 33, 34
Lampert, Magdalene, 249
Lareau, Annette, 249
Larter, Sylvia, 33
Legarreta, Dorothy, see Legarreta-Marcaída
Legarreta-Marcaída, Dorothy, 71, 85, 111, 195, 222
Leibowitz, Arnold H., 6, 31, 32, 61
Leiderman, P. Herbert, 247
Lessow-Hurley, Judith, 224
Levine, Robert A., 248
Liben, Lynn S., 249
Liedtke, W. W., 34
Lightfoot, Theodora, 3, 36
Lightfoot, Sara Lawrence, 142
Lindblom, Charles E., 60
Lindholm, Kathryn J., 87, 110
Liston, Daniel, 194
Little, Judith Warren, 198
Long, Michael H., 84, 85, 184, 197
Lösel, Friedrich, 246
Lucs, Tamara, 113, 127, 141, 142, 143, 230, 231, 247
Lumsdaine, Arthur A., 86
Lyons, James J., 31, 60, 62

Macías, José, 185, 198
Macías, Reynaldo, 193
Mackey, William F., 62, 71, 76, 85, 86
Madden, Carolyn, 197
Madrid, Arturo, 60
Mahlois, Marc, 194
Malavé, Lillian, 195
Maldonado-Colón, Elba, 145, 168
Mall, Cindy, 182, 196
Martinez, Robert, 169
Mason, Jana M., 246, 248
Mason, Joseph, 34
Matute-Bianchi, Maria Eugene, 28, 35, 53, 63, 157, 167, 170
McDowell, Gary, 62

McGroarty, Mary, 60, 112, 193
McLaughlin, Barry, 83, 85, 111, 195, 222
McLaughlin, Donald H., 63, 84
McLaughlin, Milbrey W., 141, 142
McNamee, Gillian, 205
McPartland, James, 60
Means, Barbara, 61, 63
Medina, Marcelo, 61
Mehan, Hugh, 27, 33, 35, 169, 170, 188
Meier, Deborah, 155
Mendoza-Friedman, Minerva, 168
Mercado, Carmen I., 144, 155, 167, 169, 170, 181, 182, 196
Merino, Bárbara, 70, 84, 171, 177, 179, 186, 187, 188, 193, 194, 195, 197, 198, 245
Meyer, Michael M., 85, 87
Milburn, Sharon, 250
Milk, Robert D., 88, 179, 190, 195, 198
Miller, Patricia M., 248
Millican, A., 249
Millsap, Mary Ann, 246, 248
Milne, Ann M., 13, 32
Minicucci, Catherine, 111, 126, 141, 142, 222
Minnis, Douglas, 187, 188, 198
Mohan, Bernard, 111
Mohatt, Gerald, 35
Moles, Oliver, 240, 246, 249
Moll, Luis C., 27, 28, 29, 33, 35, 112, 163, 169, 170, 194, 203, 210, 222, 223, 234, 235, 246, 248
Montero-Sieburth, Martha, 7, 31
Mood, Alexander M., 60
Mulhauser, Frederick, 60, 62
Murray, Ann, 250

Navarrete, Cecilia, 169
Neff, Deborah, 223, 234, 248
Nelson, Beryl, 111, 222
Nelson, Chris, 169
Nelson, Keith E., 34
Nelson, L. D., 34
Nelson-Barber, Sharon, 194
Nerenz, A., 85
Nicoloupoulo, Agiliki, 223
Novic, Shimshon, 197
Nussbaum, Joseph, 197

O'Malley, J. Michael, 32, 84, 154, 155, 169
Ochs, Elenore, 201, 202, 222
Odden, Alan R., 61
Oest, Dawn, 181, 182, 196
Ogbu, John U., 28, 35, 53, 63, 157, 167, 170

Oller, John W., 168, 169, 222
Olsen, Laurie, 111, 126, 141, 142, 193, 222
Omaggio, A., 85
Ornstein-Galicia, Jacob, 197
Ortiz, Alba A., 145, 168
Ortiz, Flora, 179, 190, 195, 198
Ovando, Carlos J., 110, 197

Padilla, Amado, 83, 86, 87, 111, 197
Padilla, Raymond V., 194, 195
Padilla, Reynaldo V., 60
Paradis, M., 33
Parke, Ross D., 245
Parrish, Tom, 111, 222
Parsons, Talcott, 226
Paschal, R. A., 247, 248, 249
Pasta, David J., 32, 63, 64, 84, 195, 222
Patterson, Janice H., 61
Patterson, Orlando, 46, 47, 50, 62
Paulston, Christina Bratt, 58, 64, 83
Peal, Elizabeth, 21, 22, 23, 33, 34
Pease-Alvarez, Lucinda, 33, 79, 82, 86, 87, 202, 220, 222, 224
Peña, Arturo, 62
Penfield, Joyce, 197
Pérez, Bertha, 181, 196
Pérez, Pablo, 248
Perlmann, Joel, 8, 31, 61
Perrone, Vito, 155, 168, 169
Persky, H., 169
Peterson, LaCelle, 7, 31
Peterson, Penelope L., 249
Philips, Susan V., 35
Picus, Lawrence O., 61
Pierce, Lorraine Valdez, 154, 169
Pifer, Alan, 30
Politzer, Robert, 85, 191, 193, 198
Polyzoi, Eloussa E., 84
Porter, Rosalie, 60, 61, 83
Powell, Arthur G., 142
Pratt, Caroline, 155
Primeau, J. K., 31
Proper, Elizabeth C., 86
Putnam, Ralph T., 249

Quinn, Mary Ellen, 19, 33
Quintanar, Rosalinda, 187, 188, 198
Ramey, Dena R., 32, 63, 64, 84, 142, 195, 222, 240, 245, 249
Ramírez, Arnulfo G., 72, 73, 85, 111, 191, 198, 247
Ramírez, J. David, 32, 58, 63, 65, 67, 69, 70, 73, 79, 80, 81, 82, 84, 85, 87, 111, 142, 195, 222, 225, 240, 241, 245, 249

Ramos, Suzanne, 50
Reagan, Ronald, 2
Reese, Leslie, 250
Resnick, Lauren, 249
Reyes, Maria de la Luz, 199, 222
Reyhner, Jon, 197
Reynolds, Dorothy J., 63, 84
Richard-Amato, Patricia, 178, 195
Richards, Jack, 193, 222
Rigg, Pat, 112
Ritter, Phillip, 247
Rivas, George, 86
Rivera, Charlene, 112, 168
Roberts, Donald, 247
Rodríguez, Richard, 45, 51, 61, 62, 83, 241, 242, 249
Roen, Duane, 196
Rogers, Theodore, 193
Romero, Migdalia, 141, 144, 169
Romero, Tere, 195
Rosaldo, Renato, 223
Rosselle, Christine, 83
Rossman, Gretchen B., 141
Rueda, Robert, 35
Ruiz, Richard, 38, 61

Saavedra, E., 223
Sacken, Donald M., 61
St. Pierre, Robert G., 86
Schieffelin, Bambi B., 201, 202, 222
Schink, Werner O., 222
Schinke-Llano, Linda, 72, 85
Schultz, Jeffrey, 84, 142
Schustack, Miriam, 205
Scribner, Sylvia, 169
Sears, David O., 32
Secada, Walter G., 3, 9, 32, 36, 60, 61, 62, 63, 83, 86
Segal, Judith W., 20, 33
Segura, Robert D., 222
Seidner, Maria S., 60, 61, 62
Seidner, Stanley S., 60, 61, 62
Seliger, Herbert W., 84, 85
Shannon, Sheila M., 222
Shannon-Morla, Crystal, 224
Showers, Beverly, 191, 198
Shuell, Thomas J., 249
Shuy, Roger, 86, 169
Siegel, Pamela, 170
Sizer, Theodore, 141
Skutnabb-Kangas, Tove, 4, 30, 31, 246, 248
Slavin, Robert, 112
Snow, Catherine E., 111
Snow, Marguerite A., 110, 111
Sosa, A., 249

Soto, Lourdes Díaz, 249
Souberman, Ellen, 169
Spanos, George, 197
Spencer, Maury, 86
Spindler, George D., 35, 185, 188, 194, 198, 246
Spindler, Louise, 185, 188, 198, 246
Spradley, James, 198
Stebbins, Linda B., 77, 86
Stein, Coleman B., Jr., 42, 60, 61, 62, 110, 111
Stern, Carolyn, 69, 70, 77, 84, 86
Stevenson, David, 247
Stevenson, Robert B., 141
Stipek, Deborah, 250
Stromquist, Nelly, 72, 73, 85
Sun, Shirley, 61
Sutton, Christine P., 143
Swain, Merrill, 184, 197, 203, 222, 223, 224
Swartz, Janet, 246 , 248

Talbert, Joan E., 141, 142
Tansley, Paula, 112
Taylor, Donald M., 30
Teitelbaum, Herbert, 168
Terrell, Tracy D., 170
Tharp, Roland G., 112, 197
Thonis, Eleanor, 181, 193, 196
Tiedt, Iris, 187, 198
Tiedt, Pamela, 187, 198
Tikunoff, William, 32, 85, 141
Toomey, D., 248
Topping, Keith J., 248
Torrance, E. Paul, 34
Torres-Guzmán, María, 181, 196
Trueba, Henry, 28, 31, 34, 35, 84, 168, 169, 185, 194, 197, 246, 247, 249
Tucker, G. Richard, 33, 34
Twaddell, Kristie, 193

Ulibarri, Daniel, 86
Unamuno, Miguel de, 1

Valadez, Concepción, 33, 84, 86, 87, 111, 197
Valdman, Albert, 62
Valencia, Richard R., 194, 222
Valencia, Sheila, 161, 169, 170
van Hooft, Karen S., 61
Vásquez, Olga A., 35, 199, 205, 222, 224
Vázquez, José A., see Vázquez-Faría
Vázquez-Faría, José A., 85, 169

Velez-Ibanez, Carlos, 35, 112, 170, 223
Veltman, Calvin, 63
Vera, Arthur, 169, 170
Violand-Sanchez, Emma, 143
von Broekhuizen, David, 141
Vygotsky, Lev S., 23, 28, 34, 35, 156, 169, 205, 223

Waggoner, Dorothy, 13, 14, 32
Wagner, Daniel R., 33
Walberg, Herbert J., 247, 249
Waller, Willard, 226
Wang, William S., 112
Ward, Beatrice, 141
Ware, Herbert W., 143
Weber, Max, 226
Weber, Rose Marie, 247
Weinfield, Frederic D., 60
Weinstein, Thomas, 247
Weiser, Lori, 170
Wesche, Marjorie B., 110, 111
West, Mary Maxwell, 248
Whipple, Guy M., 246
White, Paula A., 61
Whitmore, K., 223
Wilde, Judith, 169
Wilkinson, Cheryl Y., 84, 168
Willig, Ann C., 32, 58, 64, 65, 75, 77, 83, 84, 86, 168
Willner, R., 84
Wilson, Bruce L., 131, 142, 143
Wittrock, Merlin C., 33, 84, 111, 195, 247
Wolfgang, A., 30
Wong Fillmore, Lily, 32, 33, 72, 73, 84, 85, 110, 111, 112, 142, 195, 223, 224
Woo, Joseph, 167, 169
Woolard, Kathryn, 43, 61, 62
Worden, Pat, 205
Wright, Guy, 47
Wright, Pamela, 84
Wu, Jing-Jyi, 34

Yarbrough, Ralph, 55
Yorio, C. A., 85
York, Robert L., 60
Yuen, Sandra D., 32, 63, 64, 84, 142, 195, 222, 240, 245, 249

Zamora, Gloria, 99, 111
Zehler, Annette M., 112
Zeichner, Kenneth, 194
Zessoules, Rieneke, 155, 169
Zirkel, Perry, 168
Zubizarreta, Rosalma, 182

Subject Index

Additive bilingualism, 24-25
American Council on the Teaching of Foreign Languages (ACTFL), 173
American Educational Research Association, 19
American Institutes of Research, evaluation of bilingual education programs by, 58
Aspira consent decree, 147, 168n
Assessment of bilingual students: administrative and instructional functions of, 149-52; adverse effects of mandated testing in, 104, 145; alternate forms of, 154-56, 158-64; analysis of students' learning products in, 160-62; conferences with students and caretakers in, 162-64; demands of alternate forms of, on teachers, 164-66; dominance testing in, 149-51; impact of legislation on, 147-48; informal, nontraditional approaches to, 106, 154-55; instruments used in, to determine eligibility for services, 149-51; limitations of language proficiency tests and standardized achievement tests in, 151-52; observations of students in, 159-60; reconceptualization of, as an integral part of instruction, 156-58; testing in two languages as part of, 147; trends in, 152-54; see also Evaluation of bilingual education, Testing, Tests
Assimilationists, views of, on bilingual education, 39-41

Bilingual ballots, elimination of, in San Francisco, 43
Bilingual education in elementary schools: distribution of language use in, 101-4; linkage of, with policy concerns, 108-9; longitudinal study of three program options for, 92; one-way and two-way options in, 91; programs for, in diverse settings, 97-99; questionable use of tests in, 104; rationale and goals for, 99-100; reasons for advocacy of, 89-90; transitional and maintenance programs in, 11, 91; trends in, 104-8; whole language approaches to, 105-8

Bilingual education in secondary schools: contextual factors in effective programs of, 115-16; curricular and instructional practices in, 125-28; family involvement in, 138-39; language use in nine exemplary programs for (table), 127; staff characteristics in effective programs of, 128-38; structural adjustments in, to improve services to LM students, 124-25; types of organizational structures for, 117-25 (figure), 118
Bilingual education in United States: additive and subtractive programs in, 24-25; alleged dangers of, 46-47; changes in federal support for, 42-43; characteristics of, as a field of study, 18-20; decline of, in early 20th century, 7; definition of, by U.S. Office of Education, 91; failure of large-scale efforts to demonstrate effectiveness of, 78; federal policy regarding, 10; history of, 6-12; impact of anti-German feeling on, 9; impact of *Lau vs. Nichols* (1974) on, 9, 10; marginalizing of field of, from mainstream research in education, 19-20; opposition of English Only movement to, 12; pervasiveness of, in 18th and 19th centuries, 6-7; pluralist and assimilationist views on, 38-40; program for, in Dade County (FL), in 1960s, 7-8; pseudo-evaluations of, 66-67; recurring themes in debates on federal funding for, 44; research on, 18-20, 29-30; sociocultural approach to study of, 27-30; state legislation regarding, 11-12; shifting nature of arguments regarding, 40-43; symbols in controversy over, 44-57; three major studies of, 58; variations in programs of, 17-18; see also Bilingual education in elementary schools, Bilingual education in secondary schools
Bilingual Education Act (Title VII of Elementary and Secondary Education Act of 1968): amendments to (1974, 1978, 1984, 1988), 10-11; differing accounts of passage of, 42; funding under, for LM students, 47; grants

under, for programs for LEP students, 114; initial authorization of bilingual education by, 10; shifting debates over amendments to, 40-43

Bilingual Interdisciplinary Computer-Assisted Curricula (BICOMP), 183, 184

Bilingual programs: staff characteristics in effective programs of, 128-38; studies to identify critical variables among, 70-73; wide variation among, 66-67

Bilingual students, *see* Language minority students

Bilingualism: additive vs. subtractive concepts of, 24-25; bivalent views of, in U.S., 3; cognitive and social advantages of, 3-4; economic advantages of, 2; levels of, 21-22; studies of relationship of, to cognitive abilities, 21-22; theoretical explanations of positive influence of, on cognition, 22-23

Center for Applied Linguistics, 173

Children's English and Services Study (CESS), 13-14

Civil Rights Act (1964), Title VI of, 90, 146-47

CODOFIL (bilingual French/English program in Louisiana), 49-50

Cognition: bilingual education as fertile field for study of, 19-20; relationship of bilingualism to, 21-30

"Constructivist" approach, in teaching science and mathematics, 183-84

Cooperative learning, use of, in bilingual education and ESL classes, 106-7

Cross-cultural awareness: levels of, among prospective teachers, 186-87 (figure), 186; models for promoting, in teacher preparation programs, 187-89

Cultural and linguistic diversity: as symbols for cultural pluralists, 49-54; study of, in teacher preparation programs, 184-89

Cultural pluralists, arguments of, in support of bilingual education, 38-39, 41

Distributed Literacy Consortium: "Fifth Dimension" as core activity of, 205-7; goal of research by, 204; participants in collaborative research by, 205

Elementary and Secondary Education Act (1965), 38, 55, 147

English as a Second Language (ESL): advantages of cooperative learning in, 107; "content-based" approach to, 95-97; different understandings of, 88; general definition of, 93; various forms of, 93

English language: proposed amendment regarding establishment of, as official U.S. language, 48-49; role of, in American society, 44-46

English Only movement, 10, 12

Equal Educational Opportunities Act (1974), provision of, regarding overcoming language barriers in schools, 90

Ethnography: use of, in study of language development, 26; use of, in teacher preparation programs, 185, 188

Evaluation of bilingual education: alternative approaches in, to confirm program implementation, 70-73; critique of pseudo-evaluation approaches to, 66-67; documentation of program characteristics in, 68-70; equating treatment and comparison groups in, 74-76; group composition and attrition as factors in, 76-77; methodological problems in, 68-78; proposals for redirection of, 78-82; public policy as a constraint on, 79-80; *see also* Assessment of bilingual students

Finding Out/Discubrimiento (FO/D), 183, 184

Ford Foundation, support of, for dual language instruction in Dade County (FL), 8

Foreign languages: connections of, with politics, 5; state prohibitions on use of, in schools (1917-60), 9

Home-school collaboration: as a factor in studies of effectiveness of bilingual education programs, 229-32; shift in thinking about, since 1929, 226-27; types of school/family partnerships for, 227-29

Home-school connections, in schools serving LM students: effectiveness of strategies for, 236-37; importance of, 225-26, 232-34; innovative programs for, 234-36; obstacles to establishing, 239-42

Immersion programs, in bilingual education: Canadian experience with, 23-24, 91; questionable appropriateness of, for LM students in U.S., 91-92

Immigrants, schools as focal point for socialization of, 8-9

In-service education: components needed in programs of, 191; programs of, for teachers of culturally diverse students, 191-92

Laboratory of Comparative Human Cognition (at University of California—San Diego), 204

La Clase Mágica, 207-19: aims of, 210; children's choice of language use in, 210-13; encouragement of children's use of primary language in, 214-19; lessons learned from, regarding language as a resource for learning, 219-21

Language acquisition, by children: family and community "funds of knowledge" as a resource for, 28-30; impact of typical classroom practices on, 27, 203; influence of context on, 26-28; out-of-school experience in relation to, 26; patterns of child-adult interaction in relation to, 201-2; sociocultural perspectives on, 200-204

Language minority (LM) students: adverse effects of fragmented structure of secondary schools on, 116-17; contextual factors in effective programs for, 115-16; definition of, 88; design and implementation issues in programs for (table), 94-95; difficulties in defining and counting, 12-14; immigration as a factor in increased number of, 15; inadequacy of programs for, 113, 199; numbers of (tables), 15-18; structures of programs for, in secondary schools, 116-25 (figure), 118; variability in instructional contexts for, 156-57

Language use, in bilingual classrooms: issue of, 101-2; research on, 177-78; varieties of, in nine special alternative instructional programs (table), 127

Lau vs. Nichols (1974), 9, 10, 37, 38, 43, 147

Limited English proficient (LEP) students: definition of, in Title VII, 13; disparate estimates of numbers of, 13-14

Linguicism, definition of, 4

Multiculturalism, arguments in support of, 49-54

National Academy of Science, review of Ramirez et al. study by, 79-80

National Association for Bilingual Education (NABE), 41

National Commission on Secondary Schooling for Hispanics, 242

Nationality Act (1906), 7

Native language: effects of instruction in, on second language learning, 25-26; use of, in nine special alternative instructional programs (table), 127

Needs: debates on way of defining, 54-55; link of definition of, to notion of deficiency, 56-58

New York City Board of Education, 147, 168n

New York State Education Department, 168n

New York State Minority Task Force, 52

School/Family partnerships, types of, 227-29

Selective eclectic introspective model (SEIM), use of, in teacher preparation programs, 188-89

Special Alternative Instructional Programs (SAIPs), 115

Subtractive bilingualism, 4, 24-25

Teachers of English to Speakers of Other Languages (TESOL), 41, 173

Teacher education: calls for reforms in, 174; components of programs for, 174; "collaborative resonance" approach to student teaching in, 176

Teacher preparation programs (for second language teachers): impact of, on prospective teachers, 189-91; methods courses in, 178-79; practices of exemplary teachers as a basis for, 175; published guidelines for, 173; research on "effective teaching" in relation to, 175; shifts in emphasis in, 172-73; study of cultural diversity as a component of, 184-89; teaching of reading and literature in, 180-83

Teachers of LM students: demands of alternative forms of student assessment on, 164-66; research on in-service education programs for, 191-92; shortage of, in California (table), 172

Testing: adverse effects of, on LM students, 145, 154; assessment in contrast to, 146; contradictory purposes of, in bilingual education, 144,

147; legislation as impetus for, in bilingual education, 148

Tests: inadequacy of, for dual language testing, 148; limitations of, for assessing LM students, 145

Transitional bilingual education, 41, 91

U.S. English (organization supporting English Only movement), 3, 12

War on Poverty, 42, 55

Whole language approach, use of, in bilingual education, 105, 108

INFORMATION ABOUT MEMBERSHIP IN THE SOCIETY

Membership in the National Society for the Study of Education is open to all who desire to receive its publications.

There are two categories of membership: Regular and Comprehensive. The Regular Membership (annual dues in 1993, $30) entitles the member to receive both volumes of the yearbook. The Comprehensive Membership (annual dues in 1993, $55) entitles the member to receive the two-volume yearbook and the two current volumes in the Series on Contemporary Educational Issues.

Reduced dues (Regular, $25; Comprehensive, $50) are available for retired NSSE members and for full-time graduate students *in their first year of membership*.

Membership in the Society is for the calendar year. Dues are payable on or before January 1 of each year.

New members are required to pay an entrance fee of $1, in addition to annual dues for the year in which they join.

Members of the Society include professors, researchers, graduate students, and administrators in colleges and universities; teachers, supervisors, curriculum specialists, and administrators in elementary and secondary schools; and a considerable number of persons not formally connected with educational institutions.

All members participate in the nomination and election of the six-member Board of Directors, which is responsible for managing the affairs of the Society, including the authorization of volumes to appear in the yearbook series. All members whose dues are paid for the current year are eligible for election to the Board of Directors.

Each year the Society arranges for meetings to be held in conjunction with the annual conferences of one or more of the major national educational organizations. All members are urged to attend these sessions. Members are also encouraged to submit proposals for future yearbooks or for volumes in the series on Contemporary Educational Issues.

Further information about the Society may be secured by writing to the Secretary-Treasurer, NSSE, 5835 Kimbark Avenue, Chicago, IL 60637.

RECENT PUBLICATIONS OF THE NATIONAL
SOCIETY FOR THE STUDY OF EDUCATION

1. The Yearbooks

Ninety-second Yearbook (1993)
  Part 1. *Gender and Education.* Sari Knopp Biklen and Diane Pollard, editors. Cloth.
  Part 2. *Bilingual Education: Politics, Practice, and Research.* M. Beatriz Arias and Úrsula Casanova, editors. Cloth.

Ninety-first Yearbook (1992)
  Part 1. *The Changing Contexts of Teaching.* Ann Lieberman, editor. Cloth.
  Part 2. *The Arts, Education, and Aesthetic Knowing.* Bennett Reimer and Ralph A. Smith, editors. Cloth.

Ninetieth Yearbook (1991)
  Part 1. *The Care and Education of America's Young Children: Obstacles and Opportunities.* Sharon L. Kagan, editor. Cloth.
  Part 2. *Evaluation and Education: At Quarter Century.* Milbrey W. McLaughlin and D. C. Phillips, editors. Paper.

Eighty-ninth Yearbook (1990)
  Part 1. *Textbooks and Schooling in the United States.* David L. Elliott and Arthur Woodward, editors. Cloth.
  Part 2. *Educational Leadership and Changing Contexts of Families, Communities, and Schools.* Brad Mitchell and Luvern L. Cunningham, editors. Paper.

Eighty-eighth Yearbook (1989)
  Part 1. *From Socrates to Software: The Teacher as Text and the Text as Teacher.* Philip W. Jackson and Sophie Haroutunian-Gordon, editors. Cloth.
  Part 2. *Schooling and Disability.* Douglas Biklen, Dianne Ferguson, and Alison Ford, editors. Cloth.

Eighty-seventh Yearbook (1988)
  Part 1. *Critical Issues in Curriculum.* Laurel N. Tanner, editor. Cloth.
  Part 2. *Cultural Literacy and the Idea of General Education.* Ian Westbury and Alan C. Purves, editors. Cloth.

Eighty-sixth Yearbook (1987)
  Part 1. *The Ecology of School Renewal.* John I. Goodlad, editor. Paper.
  Part 2. *Society as Educator in an Age of Transition.* Kenneth D. Benne and Steven Tozer, editors. Cloth.

Eighty-fifth Yearbook (1986)

Part 1. *Microcomputers and Education.* Jack A. Culbertson and Luvern L. Cunningham, editors. Cloth.

Part 2. *The Teaching of Writing.* Anthony R. Petrosky and David Bartholomae, editors. Paper.

Eighty-fourth Yearbook (1985)

Part 1. *Education in School and Nonschool Settings.* Mario D. Fantini and Robert Sinclair, editors. Cloth.

Part 2. *Learning and Teaching the Ways of Knowing.* Elliot Eisner, editor. Paper.

Eighty-third Yearbook (1984)

Part 1. *Becoming Readers in a Complex Society.* Alan C. Purves and Olive S. Niles, editors. Cloth.

Part 2. *The Humanities in Precollegiate Education.* Benjamin Ladner, editor. Paper.

Eighty-second Yearbook (1983)

Part 1. *Individual Differences and the Common Curriculum.* Gary D Fenstermacher and John I. Goodlad, editors. Paper.

Eighty-first Yearbook (1982)

Part 1. *Policy Making in Education.* Ann Lieberman and Milbrey W. McLaughlin, editors. Cloth.

Part 2. *Education and Work.* Harry F. Silberman, editor. Cloth.

Eightieth Yearbook (1981)

Part 1. *Philosophy and Education.* Jonas P. Soltis, editor. Cloth.

Part 2. *The Social Studies.* Howard D. Mehlinger and O. L. Davis, Jr., editors. Cloth.

Seventy-ninth Yearbook (1980)

Part 1. *Toward Adolescence: The Middle School Years.* Mauritz Johnson, editor. Paper.

Seventy-eighth Yearbook (1979)

Part 1. *The Gifted and the Talented: Their Education and Development.* A. Harry Passow, editor. Paper.

Part 2. *Classroom Management.* Daniel L. Duke, editor. Paper.

Seventy-seventh Yearbook (1978)

Part 1. *The Courts and Education.* Clifford B. Hooker, editor. Cloth.

Seventy-sixth Yearbook (1977)

Part 1. *The Teaching of English.* James R. Squire, editor. Cloth.

The above titles in the Society's Yearbook series may be ordered from the University of Chicago Press, Book Order Department, 11030 Langley Ave., Chicago, IL 60628. For a list of earlier titles in the yearbook series still available, write to the Secretary, NSSE, 5835 Kimbark Ave., Chicago, IL 60637.

2. The Series on Contemporary Educational Issues

The following volumes in the Society's Series on Contemporary Educational Issues may be ordered from the McCutchan Publishing Corporation, P.O. Box 774, Berkeley, CA 94702-0774.

Academic Work and Educational Excellence: Raising Student Productivity (1986). Edited by Tommy M. Tomlinson and Herbert J. Walberg.

Adapting Instruction to Student Differences (1985). Edited by Margaret C. Wang and Herbert J. Walberg.

Aspects of Reading Education (1978). Edited by Susanna Pflaum-Connor.

Choice in Education (1990). Edited by William Lowe Boyd and Herbert J. Walberg.

Colleges of Education: Perspectives on Their Future (1985). Edited by Charles W. Case and William A. Matthes.

Contributing to Educational Change: Perspectives on Research and Practice (1988). Edited by Philip W. Jackson.

Early Childhood Education: Issues and Insights (1977). Edited by Bernard Spodek and Herbert J. Walberg.

Educational Environments and Effects: Evaluation, Policy, and Productivity (1979). Edited by Herbert J. Walberg.

Educational Leadership and School Culture (1993). Edited by Marshall Sashkin and Herbert J. Walberg.

Effective School Leadership: Policy and Prospects (1987). Edited by John J. Lane and Herbert J. Walberg.

Effective Teaching: Current Research (1991). Edited by Hersholt C. Waxman and Herbert J. Walberg.

From Youth to Constructive Adult Life: The Role of the Public School (1978). Edited by Ralph W. Tyler.

Improving Educational Standards and Productivity: The Research Basis for Policy (1982). Edited by Herbert J. Walberg.

Moral Development and Character Education (1989). Edited by Larry P. Nucci.

Motivating Students to Learn: Overcoming Barriers to High Achievement (1993). Edited by Tommy M. Tomlinson.

Psychology and Education: The State of the Union (1981). Edited by Frank H. Farley and Neal J. Gordon.

Reaching Marginal Students: A Prime Concern for School Renewal (1987). Edited by Robert L. Sinclair and Ward Ghory.

Research on Teaching: Concepts, Findings, and Implications (1979). Edited by Penelope L. Peterson and Herbert J. Walberg.

Restructuring the Schools: Problems and Prospects (1992). Edited by John J. Lane and Edgar G. Epps.

Selected Issues in Mathematics Education (1981). Edited by Mary M. Lindquist.

School Boards: Changing Local Control (1992). Edited by Patricia F. First and Herbert J. Walberg.